Education of Children with Special Needs

Education of Children with Special Needs

Editor

M.L. Dhawan

ISHA BOOKS
DELHI-110 033

Education of Children with Special Needs

ISBN: 9788182051720

Printed in 2011 in India by
Isha Books
B-69, New Gupta Colony
Near DDA Market
Delhi-110009

Printed at: G. Print Process, Delhi

PREFACE

Millions of people have some type of physical, mental, or emotional condition that significantly limits their ability to function successfully in our society. Until recently the most commonly used term to refer to people with such conditions was handicapped. Now, however, the preferred word is disabled. The widely recognised disability categories are: autism, deaf-blindness, emotional disturbance, hearing impairments, mental retardation, multiple disabilities, orthopedic impairments, other health impairments, specific learning disabilities, speech or language impairments, traumatic brain injury, and visual impairments.

Students with disabilities show a wide range of differences. The educational needs of students in one disability category is varied from that the other. Yet labelling such students by category is necessary to provide the financial resources needed for special programs and related services. Labelling, however, may minimize a student's individuality and strengths, and may contribute to faulty teacher expectations about a student's capabilities within the classroom.

Within each category of special education, the extent to which the disability interferes with normal functioning varies widely depending upon the individual and environmental conditions. A student with a slight deficit can often compensate enough to avoid any significant educational or social difficulty. However, as the severity of a student's disability increases, so does the need for changes in that student's educational program.

The needs of disabled students may also vary from person to person, so that it is essential that teachers should have special skills and approaches to deal with each category.

The system of special education programs and services for these students are complicated and difficult to understand. Educators are responsible for integrating these students into regular classrooms while meeting their individual needs and adhering to the myriad legislative, procedural, and judicial requirements that protect the rights of all children with disabilities. This book is written to make this complex educational system more understandable and workable for the people who help children with disabilities. It is a simple, useful, and concise reference that summarizes the many facets of special education. The book is intended primarily for teachers, but it should also be of value to school counsellors, psychologists, related services specialists, administrators, and parents.

Editor

CONTENTS

1

Concept and Meaning of Special Education

Special education refers to the teaching of learning-disabled students in ways outside of the norm. This is done by giving students more individual attention than they would normally receive. As such, special education programs are typically more expensive per capita than their counterparts. Nowadays, it is common for special education training to be a requirement to become a certified teacher.

SPECIAL EDUCATIONAL NEEDS

The term 'special educational needs' has a legal definition. Children with special educational needs all have learning difficulties or disabilities that make it harder for them to learn or access education than most children of the same age. These children may need extra or different help from that given to other children of the same age. The law says that children do not have learning difficulties just because their first language is not English. Of course some of these children may have learning difficulties as well.

Children with special educational needs may need extra help because of a range of needs, such as in thinking and understanding, physical or sensory difficulties, emotional and behavioural difficulties, or difficulties with speech and language or how they relate to and behave with other people. Many children will have special educational needs of some kind at some time during their education. Schools and other organisations can help most children overcome their difficulties quickly and easily. But a few children will need extra help for some or all of their time in school. So special educational needs could mean that a child has difficulties with:

- All of the work in school
- Reading, writing, number work or understanding information
- Expressing themselves or understanding what others are saying
- Making friends or relating to adults
- Behaving properly in school
- Organising themselves
- Some kind of sensory or physical needs which may affect them in school.

Help for children with special educational needs will usually be in the child's ordinary, mainstream early education setting or school, sometimes with the help of outside specialists. The Government has set out in the Early Learning Goals of the foundation stage of education for children from 3 to 5 years what most children should be able to do by the end of school reception year. The National Curriculum for children from 5 to 16 years also sets out what most children will learn at each stage of their education. Of course children make progress at different rates and have different ways in which they learn best. Teachers are expected to take account of this by looking carefully at how they organise their lessons, the classroom, the books and materials they give to each child and the way they teach.

So all teachers will consider a number of options and choose the most appropriate ways to help each child learn from a range of activities. This is often described as 'differentiating the curriculum'. Children making slower progress or having particular difficulties in one area may be given extra help or different lessons to help them succeed. The National Literacy and Numeracy Strategies also provide for children to learn to read and write and understand numbers and mathematics in different ways and at different speeds, including special 'catch-up' work and other kinds of support. So you should not assume, just because your child is making slower progress than you expected or the teachers are providing different support, help or activities in class, that your child has special educational needs.

A child's early years are a very important time for their physical, emotional, intellectual and social development. When the health visitor or doctor makes a routine check, they might suggest that there could be a problem. But if parents have any worries of your their own, they should seek advice straightaway. If a child is not yet at school or not yet going to an early education setting, parents can talk to their doctor or health visitor who will be able to offer advice about the next steps to take. When parents work together with their child's teachers it often helps sort out worries and problems. The closer parents work with their child's teachers, the more successful any help for a child can be. If parents think their child has severe difficulties but the early years setting or school disagree they can contact their LEA's special educational needs section and ask for their child to be assessed.

Parents know their child better than anyone.

Parents might like to ask whether:

— The school thinks their child has difficulties

— The school thinks their child has special educational needs

— Their child is able to work at the same level as other children of a similar age

— Their child is already getting some extra help

— They can help their child.

Other organisations parents can get help from are:

— The parent partnership service in the local authority

— Child health services

— Social services

— Local voluntary organisations, mainly charities.

Across the globe, in most societies the children with disabilities have traditionally been segregated for education and it is believed that only specialists would be able to impart education to them. Of late this is being questioned worldwide. There is research evidence to confirm that these children can get meaningful education in mainstream schools. Their presence would also enhance the educational capability of the school and benefit non-disabled children in developing a positive attitude towards the making of a cohesive society/ A sizeable chunk of children in India, disabled or non-disabled, are still out of school and another big number is not able to complete the required minimum number of years.

India, however, has its own strengths and challenges. Absence of a policy on the pattern of Special Educational needs (SEN) gives an opportunity to schools and teachers to design their pedagogy and curriculum that could be inclusive and respond to all children. India's children and the school system are facing challenges on two fronts. At structure level multi-track school systems are developing making the inclusion agenda complicated; private/public schools for rich and upper middle class, government schools for others and non-formal centres for the disadvantaged. Lack of resources and arguments on 'good' and 'effective school' are put forward. But the question of equity, rights, social justice, and ultimate aim of building an inclusive and cohesive society cannot be wished away.

The vital question that arises here is : Do the special children enrolled in "good' and 'effective schools' feel involved, included and participating in the curriculum and learning environment? There is a dire need to reorient the existing education system so that it does not become an instrument for differentiation by separating children according to social class and above all according to their abilities or disabilities. It is time for us, all the normal people to realize that the special children are not to be shunned or frowned upon. Like us they to are human beings capable of loving and bring loved in turn, like us they to are sensitive sentimental and posses their own set of emotions. They too dare to dream and indulge in fantasy.

Though we may not be aware of it, most mentally / physically challenged children have some latent qualities, talents or special abilities It therefore becomes our sacred duty to harness these hidden potentials and help our less fortunate brethren to live healthy, happy ands normal lives.

Of the 500 million disabled people in the world, at least 100 million are believed to be Indians, of which about 12.59 million are children of school-going age. According to the Rehabilitation Council of India's (RCI's) report on Manpower Development, estimated on the basis of census arrived by the The National Sample Survey Organisation (NASSO, a government research body) estimates much higher, about 35 million, as the legal definition, of 'disability' under the Act does not cover all disabilities such as those with cerebral palsy, learning disabilities, muscular dystrophy, epilepsy and multi-disabilities. To take care of the special needs of these children, there are estimated to be about 1200 'special' schools with an enrollment of nearly 55,000, 90% schools concentrated in urban cities. Limited educational opportunities exist for those outside the main categories.

With the planned expenditure on education amounting to just 6% of the GDP, the share of special education in this is almost negligible. Though education finds a pride of place in the Indian constitution, where the Directive Principles (guidelines for future governments) in Article 45 mention the state's role in providing free elementary education to all children within a decade (from 1950) — fifty years on, this objective has remained a pie in the sky, though there have been considerable gains in others areas, such as increased enrollment for kindergarten to postgraduate studies . Even with the 73rd and 74th Amendments of the Constitution (1992, to do with the proclamation of Panchayati Raj) and the devolution of education from the Central government to local bodies in towns and villages, where there is a ready base for community participation, the educational cover to the disabled remains little more than one per cent!

Although education in India is primarily the responsibility of the state governments, In 1976, the 42nd Constitutional Amendment placed it in the Concurrent List of responsibilities that the central and the respective state governments should together discharge. The first National Policy on Education was pronounced in 1968, followed by second in 1986 that spoke about the universalisation of primary education and removal of disparities and creating equal educational opportunities for all marganalised sections — women, scheduled castes, the minorities, the disabled and the educationally backward communities — this dream is yet to be realised.

Though there has existed a National Advisory Council for the Education of the Disabled under the Ministry of Human Resource Development (HRD) since 1955, it was not until 1986 that the Indian government announced a National Policy of Education (NPE), recommending 'Integrated' education in the mainstream school system for children with mild to moderate disabilities and the establishment of special schools for those with severe disabilities.

Later, the Programme of Action, 1992 drafted by the HRD ministry laid clear stress on the inclusion of the educational needs of the disabled while planning the universalisation of elementary education. This was to be achieved through a variety of institutions: special schools (the HRD ministry provided 90 per cent assistance for their establishment), integrated schools and community polytechnics, besides creating opportunities for the disabled in the mainstream schools.

This policy is currently being pursued under the World Bank supported District Primary Education Programme (Outlay US $ 9 million, 1995-96). The National Open Schools and the Indira Gandhi National Open University has now made it possible for disabled children to seek higher education through distance learning modes also. Both these institutions are apex autonomous bodies for running various courses through the distance learning mode and video conferencing to the remotest parts of the country, especially for the marginalised and the socially and economically disadvantaged section of the student community. A recent, welcome shift in the Education policy, as elsewhere in the developed world, has been towards 'Inclusive' learning — a cohort setting where the strength of able and disabled children is proportionate to their presence in the general population, though it still remains a utopian dream.

In fact, a historical analysis shows that India had adopted principles of inclusion much before the west did. Researchers reconstructing the history of education in India have recorded that the country had a sustainable system of education till early 19th century, that got systematically eroded by the Missionary system over the next fifty years under the British rule. During the pre-British era, while there was diversity, there was hardly any disparity of standards in education.

There was one school for all. Even today, small rural schools provide such integrated education, little realising that they are following a system newly discovered in the West as 'inclusive education,' after the 70s acknowledgement of

Wolfensberger's Normalisation Principle, according to which we need to change the environment to suit the child and not the environment to suit the child. 'Disparity on the vertical plane had more to do with class distinction, while diversity on a horizontal plane arose out of the needs of a particular community,' she wrote.

The UNESCO report entitled 'Learning: The Treasure Within' by Jacques Delores, former president European Commission has also paid rich tributes to such ancient practices in India. The segregational concept of special education was introduced by the Christian missionaries during the last two decades of 19th century with the establishment of the first school for the Deaf in Mumbai in 1883 and the first school for the blind at Amritsar in 1887. At that time, there seemed to have been an unspoken conviction that children with disabilities cannot be educated alongside others.

The trend continued until early sixties when international agencies reverted back to programmes of integrated education for visually impaired children, though these programmes were mainly launched in urban communities. Education of mentally retarded children began in late thirties, while that for children with learning difficulties and autism is still in initial phases of development. Government's appreciation of the needs to integrate disabled children finally came in 1974 when the Union Ministry of Social Justice and Empowerment (SJE) launched the centrally sponsored scheme of Integrated Education of Disabled Children (IEDC).

It was at the time of the Independence that the country began to contemplate development of services for the blind, deaf, the orthopedically handicapped and the mentally retarded. The Persons with Disabilities (Equal Opportunities, Protection of Rights and Full Participation) Act, 1995 also took under its ambit leprosy cured children, children with cerebral palsy and mentally ill. Chapter V of the Disability Act provides that appropriate government agencies shall provide access to free education to every child with a disability until he or she attains the age of 18 years. A landmark piece of legislation, the Act also provides for 3% reservation of seats in government and government-aided educational institutes for disabled children and 'special incentives' for public and private enterprises with 3% of their manpower drawn fro the disability sector (Clause41), though what these incentives would be, was not made clear.

Section 26 to 31 of the Disability lays exclusive thrust on creating inclusive learning environment in schools. Amendments to the Rehabilitation Council of India (RCI) Act, 1992 —— that deals with the training of the rehabilitation professionals and the maintenance of a Central Rehabilitation Register — is presently being contemplated and it is possible that other categories like learning disabilities, aphasia, Attention Deficit Hyperactive Disorder and emotional disturbances may also get included in the Amended RCI Act.

Although education is placed on the concurrent list, a great bulk of educational institutions in India is located in the states, coming within the administrative control of local governments. Schools are mainly of three kinds:

— *Municipal*: fully-financed by the government and severely lacking in even the basic infrastructure, ill-staffed and poorly maintained.

— *Partially aided private*: These are secondary schools, mostly owned and run by Private trusts. But, due to their part dependence on government grants, conditions are somewhat better, though there is lot of political interference in the administrative matters.

— *Wholly private*: Run entirely on the tuition fee and donations fro parents. Working conditions here are definitely better.

The appellate advisory body to the government for primary and secondary education is the National Centre for Educational Research and Training (NCERT), while for higher education it is the University Grants Commission (UGC). Though all educational institutes (primary, secondary and higher) come under the jurisdiction of the Human Resource Development (HRD) ministry, for some inexplicable reason, education for the disabled falls under the control of the Ministry for Social Justice and Empowerment, accounting for the persistence with the 'charity' model (guided by motives of philanthropy, rather than what is good for the child) that often determines the policy framework for this sector.

While the UNESCO Consultation on Special Education recognised in 1988 that the responsibility for special education was that of the whole education system, there being no need for a dual system, special schools continue to exist and flourish in India as a consequence of this charity model, while integrated education is primarily the responsibility of the Department of education, under the HRD ministry. The logic is that special schools are a necessary evil for severely challenged children.

Confusion continues to reign over the exact number of disabled in India. Different surveys and different yardsticks have yielded different results. To illustrate, the National Sample Survey (an apex government body) conducted in 1991 estimated the blind population to be four million, while an earlier 1989 study by a renowned researcher Dr Madan Mohan (now accepted by the Ministry of Health as more authentic) estimates it to be 12 million.

Similarly, a study of six districts of Kerala conducted by the state government claimed that 10% of the school going children had learning difficulties, while a similar study by a voluntary action group in, Bangalore, Seva, pegged it to 6%. However, according to the RCI's 1996 report on Manpower Development (commissioned by the Social Justice and Empowerment ministry), the break-up of the population of disabled children in the age group of 5-14 is as follows: hearing impairment (3.24 million), speech impairment (1.96 million), visual impairment (4.01 million), mental retardation (9 million), cerebral palsy (3 million).

Statistics on mental illness are not available. It is now fairly well accepted that about 10% of our school going population, approximately 300 million, have special education needs. According to one estimate, in a class of approximately 40 children, at least one or two are bound to have some mental handicap and would be in need of special education inputs (S.S Varma, former secretary of welfare, government of India). The current education coverage of this huge disability sector is just one per cent. In other words, in a period of 115 years, because of inappropriate strategies and perhaps inadequate awareness, progress has been halting and grudgingly slow.

In somewhat pejorative terms the Programme of Action mentions: 'Approximately 1.4 million disabled children are in the 0-4 years age group requiring identification, assessment, early stimulation and preparation for education. The National Commission on Teachers, a Delhi-based voluntary teachers group recently reported that not more than 5% of the blind and deaf children and perhaps, 0,05% of the mentally retarded are estimated to be in about 800-1000' special schools which for the most part, are located in metropolitan centers. Rural areas, where about 80% of these children are located, remain practically unserved. There was public uproar at a recent attempt to exempt disabled as a separate category from the ongoing census exercise but the bid got aborted in the face of stiff opposition from disabled rights activists.

LEGAL PROTECTION FOR DISABLED CHILDREN

Equality, dignity. autonomy and liberty are the founding principles on which international human rights law is premised. These values have sufficiently influenced the fundamental law of democratic polity and are reflected in the respective constitutions of most states, including that of India.

Equality

The Constitution of India guarantees equality before law and equal protection of law for all its citizens (Article 14). It further prohibits discrimination on the grounds of ?religion, race, caste, sex, place of birth or any of them (Articles 15 and 16). To ensure equality of outcome, Articie 16(3 and 4) of the Constitution encourages the state "to frame any law, make provision for the reservation of appointments or posts in favour of any backward class of citizens which, in the opinion of the state, is not adequately represented in the services"

State Obligations

The last quarter of the 19th century India witnessed a growing political awareness and need for decreasing the harshness of colonial rules. This period was the birth of some historic social reform movements to get rid of some unhealthy social traditions. The period marked by political turbulence and social reforms generated some repulse of efforts aimed at improving the lives of disabled people. The 1880s became witness to the launching of educational services in their germinal forms for the deaf and blind. These modest beginnings of modern educational and rehabilitational services reveal three distinct characteristics. First of all, they were initiated and sustained till Indian Independence in 1947 by social charity.

The growth was very sluggish and sporadic. Finally, they lacked, quite understandably, professional approaches. The Preamble, the Directive Principles of State Policy and the Fundamental Rights enshrined in the Constitution of India, envisage a positive role for the state towards its disadvantaged citizens. Article 41 enjoins, 'The state shall, within the limits of its economic capacity and development make effective provision for securing the right to work, to education and to public assistance in cases of unemployment, old age, sickness and disablement'. Despite such a progressive Constitution and judiciary the approach to disability has been motivated by charity.

Indian society views disability as an individual issue and treats it within the means available to a family. At the same time, with a large section of the Indian population living below the poverty line, families in crisis have historically used the services of philanthropic and charitable institutions. Similarly, the governments of independent India have relied heavily on charitable NGOs to secure basic rights such as education, work, shelter, health and nutrition for persons with disabilities. As a consequence, the entire process of development has surpassed people with disabilities.

A distinct self-advocacy movement of people with disabilities gained momentum during the 1970s towards a sustained campaign demanding protection and recognition of their human rights. To this end, enactment of comprehensive legislation having a rights-based approach with special emphasis on social and economic rights was advocated. Though the government recognised the need for such legislation as early as 1980, such a law was enacted only in 1995. The delay could be attributed to the fact that in distributing legislative power between New Delhi and the state governments, the Indian Constitution kept the disability issue in the state list. The Parliament of India gained competence to legislate on disability issues only with the signing of the Proclamation of Equality and Full Participation of People with Disabilities in the Asian and Pacific region. Article 249 of the Constitution empowers Parliament to legislate on any subject falling in any of the state list in order to fulfil its international obligations.

THE PERSONS WITH DISABILITIES ACT 1995

The Act stipulates to set up a Central Coordination Committee and a Central Executive Committee at the national level. The former is a comparatively larger body while the later is smaller in its size and will translate the decisions of the Central Coordination Committee into actions among other functions. The Act further provides setting up State Coordination and State Executive Committee for different states of the country. The

Act further stipulates the appointments of a Chief Commissioner at the National Level and Commissioners for persons with disabilities in each state, who will ensure the implementation of its provisions. The Act makes it clear that it is in addition to all other existing laws and executive orders meant to serve different groups of persons with disabilities. It is a comprehensive Act and therefore the author plans to deal only with its provisions on education and employment in some depth.

Educational Provisions

Clause 26 (A) of the Act stipulates that the Government and appropriate local authorities shall "ensure that every child with a disability has access to free education in an appropriate environment till he attains the age of 18". It is certainly a laudable provision and will go a long way in promoting the educational facilities for them. The Act talks of different modes of the service delivery to attain this goal. Moreover, it stipulates provisions of aids and appliances as well as researches in this sector. However, it does not set any deadline to achieve the goal of universalization of education for children with disabilities. Consequently, the goal set out in the Act gets defeated to a large extent.

Economic Rehabilitation

Chapter six of the Disabled Persons Act 1995 stipulates the identification of posts which can be reserved for persons with disabilities in various government departments and public sector undertakings. (The public sector undertakings are semi-government facilities). It further stipulates to reserve not less than three percent vacancies for them. (The Government has clarified that the reservation provision applies to all group A, B, C and D categories of employees.). The three percent reservations existed before the enactment of this Act through an executive order but it applied to group C and D posts in government sector and public sector at that time. It further stipulates to motivate the employers in public and private sectors to ensure to have five percent of their work force from people with disabilities and this Act wants the government to achieve this goal by giving certain incentives within the "limits of their economic capacity and development".

Affirmative Action

The Act makes some provisions for preferential allotment of land to the disabled for the following purposes.

1. House
2. Setting up business
3. Setting up special schools and
4. Establishment of research centres, etc.

The Act goes on to stipulate non-discrimination with the disabled persons by taking the following measures.

1. Adapting rail compartments, buses, vessels and air-crafts in such a way to permit easy access to disabled persons.
2. Adapting toilets in rail compartments, vessels, air-crafts and waiting rooms.
3. Installing auditory signals at red lights in the public roads for the visually handicapped
4. Engraving on the surface of the zebra crossing for the visually handicapped.

The First Central Act

The Rehabilitation Council of India Act, 1992 happened to be the First Central Act for the disabled in India. The Act became operational with effect from July 31st 1993, a good beginning indeed. The Act aims at improving and regulating the training programmes for various categories of professionals in different sectors of disability. The Council is required to maintain a register of professionals among other activities It has already taken some steps to improve the training standards of professional though it has a long and arduous road ahead to traverse before claiming success.

THE NATIONAL HANDICAPPED FINANCE AND DEVELOPMENT CORPORATION ACT

The Government of India enacted National Handicapped Finance and Development Corpotation. The Corporation has been launched in October 1997. It aims at extending soft loans to the handicapped persons for launching small ventures for self-employment. It is difficult to comment about its role due to its very brief existence.

TRUST ACT 1999

As certain groups among the disabled are more vulnerable than others, an enactment for the protection of such persons, their property and well-being was felt necessary. The enactment of the National Trust for Welfare of Persons with Autism, Cerebral Palsy, Mental Retardation and Multiple Disabilities Act 1999 (Trust Act), aims to fulfil a common demand of families that seek state provision for their severely disabled wards. The specific objectives of the Trust Act are:

— To enable and empower persons with disabilities to live as independently and as fully as possible within and close to the community to which they belong;

— To promote measures for the care and protection of persons with disabilities in the event of the death of their parent or guardian; and

— To extend support to registered organisations to provide need-based services during the period of crisis in the families of disabled persons covered under the Trust Act.

The Trust Act mandates the creation of a Local Level Committee (LLC) comprising a District Magistrate along with one representative from a registered organisation and one person with a disability. The LLC is vested with the authority to decide upon applications for legal guardianship. The Trust Act also lays down the duties of the guardian. The overall supervision of this Act is vested with a national trust board appointed through a democratic process by registered organisations of parents and others providing services to this segment of the disabled population. The government has contributed Rs. 1 billion to the trust fund and the interest earned is used to support the mandated activities.

MENTAL HEALTH ACT 1987

The subject of health falls under the concurrent list in the Indian Constitution, empowering both the centre and states to introduce measures, including the authority to legislate. The Mental Health Act 1987 is civil rights legislation with a focus on regulating standards in mental health institutions. There are serious questions over the effectiveness of this Act in ensuring protection to persons, property and management of persons covered.

REHABILITATION COUNCIL OF INDIA ACT 1986

The Rehabilitation Council of India (RCI) was set up by the government of India in 1986 initially as a society to regulate and standardise training policies and programmes in the rehabilitation of persons with disabilities. The need for minimum standards was felt urgent as the majority of persons engaged in education, vocational training and counselling of persons with disabilities were not professionally qualified. In addition, poor academic and training standards adversely affect the chance of disabled persons in the world of work.

Therefore, an Act of Parliament in 1993 elevated the status of the Council to a statutory body with the aims of:

— Standardising training courses for professionals dealing with people with disabilities;

— Prescribing minimum standards of education and training of various categories of professionals dealing with people with disabilities;

— Regulating these standards in all training institutions uniformly throughout the country;

— Promoting research in rehabilitation and special education;

— Maintaining a Central Rehabilitation Register for registration of professionals.

The RCI regulates training standards for 16 categories of rehabilitation workers. The Council is proactively promoting training and research initiatives utilising the experience of specialised as well as mainstream academic institutions.

NATIONAL POLICY ON EDUCATION (NPE) AND SPECIAL EDUCATION

The National Policy on Education (NPE), 1986 and the Programme of Action (1992) gives us the basic policy framework for education, emphasizes correcting the existing inequalities. It stresses on reducing dropout rates, improving learning achievements and expanding access to students who have not had an easy opportunity to be a part of the mainstream system. The NPE, 1986 envisaged the following measures for integrating the physically and mentally handicapped with the general community as equal partners, to prepare them for normal growth and to enable them to face life with courage and confidence. The following measures will be taken in this regard:

— Wherever it is feasible, the education of children with motor handicaps and other mild handicaps will be common with that of others.

— Special schools with hostels will be provided, as far as possible at district headquarters, for the severely handicapped children.

— Aarrangements will be made to give vocational training to the disabled.

— Teachers' training programmes will be reoriented, in particular for teachers of primary classes, to deal with the special difficulties of the handicapped children; and

— Voluntary effort for the education of the disabled, will be encouraged in every possible manner.

The Centrally Sponsored Scheme of Integrated Education for the Disabled Children, was introduced in the year 1974 by then Department of Social Welfare with a view to provide educational opportunities for the children with disabilities in common schools, to facilitate their retention in the school system and integrating children with disabilities studying in special schools after they have acquired the communication and the daily living skills at the functional level. In subsequent years the scheme transferred to the then Department of Education in 1982 and was revised in 1992 to include the Non governmental organizations as one of the implementing agencies in addition to the governmental agencies.

The Scheme is presently being implemented in 27 States and 4 UTs through over 41,875 schools benefiting more than 1,33,000 children with disabilities (till the year 2003). Efforts are being made for convergence of different schemes such as the Sarva Shiksha Abhiyan.

RATIONALE OF THE INCLUSIVE EDUCATION SCHEME (IES)

The IES has evolved out of the following major concerns and experiences:

— Many learners with disabilities, however, are still denied any form of education. There are others who are enrolled in schools but are deprived of appropriate education along with their age mates in regular schools. The IEDC scheme has not made significant impact on the enrolment and retention of children with disabilities.

— The 93rd Amendment of the Constitution of India has made education a fundamental human right for children in the 6-14 years age group and all children need to be brought under the fold of education.

— The centrally sponsored scheme of sarva shiksha abhiyan has set time bound targets for achievement of UEE by 2010. This is only possible if the needs of children with disabilities are fully addressed in the mainstream education and all children get the opportunity to go to their neighbourhood schools.

— Realizing the need to provide access to good education to all, the Salamanca Statement and Framework for Action on Special Needs Education (1994) was adopted by the world conference on special needs education: Access and Quality. The Statement endorses the need for fundamental policy shifts required to promote the approach to inclusive education, namely enabling schools to serve all children, particularly those with special educational needs by implementing practical and strategic changes.

— The Government of India has enacted the legislation Persons with Disabilities (Equal Opportunities and Full Participation) Act, 1995 (PWD Act) to achieve amongst other things, the goal of providing access to free education in an appropriate environment to all learners with disabilities till s/he attains the age of eighteen years. The Act endeavours to promote the integration of learners with disabilities in the normal schools. Thus, the right to education for learners with disabilities is enshrined in the PWD Act.

— The National Curriculum Framework for School Education (NCERT, 2000) has recommended inclusive schools for learners with special educational needs by making appropriate modifications in the content, presentation and transaction strategies, preparing teachers and developing learning friendly evaluation procedures.

— Research has shown that Inclusive education results in improved social development and academic outcomes for all learners. It leads to development of social skills and better social interactions because learners are exposed to real environment in which they have to interact with other learners each one having unique characteristics, interests and abilities. The non-disabled peers adopt positive attitudes and actions towards learners with disabilities as a result of studying together in an inclusive classroom. Thus, inclusive education leads to an inclusive society that takes account of the needs of learners with disabilities right from early school years.

— There has been a considerable shift in the understanding of disability. The conceptualization of disability today is radically different from interpretations that existed 30 years ago or when the earlier scheme was framed. Currently disability is conceptualized as a social issue and examines disability in the socio-ecological context. The old conceptualization was medical in nature and talked about pathology, and characterized disability as a deficit within the individual.

— The scheme of Inclusive education is therefore envisaged to provide access to out of school learners with disabilities and to improve enrolment, retention and achievement of these students in the mainstream education. The scheme will also address the needs of learners with disabilities making use of the social model of disability.

INCLUSIVE EDUCATION SCHEME

Inclusive education means all learners, young people - with or without disabilities being able to learn together in ordinary pre-school provisions, schools and community educational setting with appropriate network of support services. In inclusive education the needs of all learners are addressed so that good education can be provided to all. However, since the learners with disabilities form one of the largest group that is still out of the fold of general education, the target group, therefore, on which this scheme will focus would be learners with disabilities. The term 'learners with disabilities' will cover visual impairments

(Blind and Low Vision), speech and hearing impairments, locomotor disabilities, neuromusculoskeltal neurodevelopmental disorders including cerebral Palsy, Autism, mental retardation multiple disability and learning disabilities.

Difference between Integration and Inclusion

Inclusive education is different from integration. In integration learners with disabilities are placed in a regular school without making any changes in the school to accommodate and support the diverse needs. Inclusive education, by comparisons seeks to adapt systems and structures to meet the needs of all learners. Moving from integration to inclusion requires changes/ adaptations at various levels including to the curriculum, attitudes, values, language etc. These adaptations are made by fully involving the learners in the process. Integration was based on a conceptual model that was medical in nature that viewed disability only as a pathology requiring medical care. On the other hand Inclusion is based on a social model of disability that views disability as a socially created problem and management of problem requires social action in the form of environmental modifications necessary for the full participation of persons with disabilities in every sphere of life.

FEATURES OF THE IES

Target Group

IES is a Centrally Sponsored Scheme. It would cover learners with significant deviation or loss in body functions or structures in the age group 0-18 years complying with the provisions of PWD Act, 1995. It will cover the following groups of learners.

- Visual impairments (Blind and Low Vision)/ Impairments in the function of seeing.
- Hearing impairments/ hearing and vestibular functions.

— Locomotor disabilities (movement related functions), neuromusculoskeltal/neurodevelopmental disorders like autism, cerebral palsy, mental retardation and multiple disabilities.

— Speech Impairments/ voice and speech functions

— Learning disability

Under this scheme the Central Government will assist the State and Union Territories in its implementation on the basis of criteria laid down. The provisions would be provided to those suffering from not less than forty per cent of any disability as certified by the committee specially appointed for this purpose at the state level/ district level/block level/cluster level/village level. Financial assistance for all the items covered in the scheme will be on 100 per cent basis. Assistance for programmes would depend on fulfilling the conditions laid down in the scheme.

Implementing Agencies

The Scheme will be implemented through the State governments / UT administrations/ Autonomous organizations/ Voluntary agencies having experience in the field of education and through convergence with government supported programmes. The procedure for grant to the implementing agency is laid down in the later part of the scheme.

Aims and Objective

The Centrally Sponsored IES aims to set out the commitment of Education of Learners with disabilities to the principles of inclusive education. By incorporating the 'social model of disability' the scheme will aim to create an environment that respects and values diversities and attempt to increase access enrolment, retention and achievement of learners with disabilities in general education/regular schools.

Scope

IES is based on the assumption that schools should accommodate all children regardless of their physical, intellectual, social, emotional, linguistic or other conditions. Inclusive education under this scheme will focus upon meeting the special educational needs of learners with disabilities in the mainstream of schooling till senior secondary level. The benefits derived from the scheme would be conditional to the recommendation of the assessment team.

The scope of the Scheme will involve: -

— Early Childhood education including early identification, assessment and stimulations of the very young child with disability. Interventions for children aged up to 6 years would in the form of pre-school training of learners with disabilities for promoting physical, intellectual and social development and school readiness.

— Raising awareness for promoting the understanding of the concept of inclusion and positive attitudes among children, among teachers among administrators and community members towards persons with disabilities.

— Assistance in making school buildings, school activities and events fully accessible to learners with disabilities.

— Adapting curricula that provides differentiate learning experiences to match the needs of all learners including learners with disabilities. Additional assistance and support to learners requiring it within the context of regular curriculum and not a different curriculum would be within the scope of this scheme.

— Appropriate preparation of educational personnel for developing capacity to meet the needs of all learners with disabilities in inclusive schools and to provide leadership in this area. This will include teachers (both special and general), local educational administrators, head teachers etc..

— Building partnerships with key partners in the development of inclusive education and mobilizing community support for the same.

— Allocating or pooling in resources for provision of resource rooms, instructional materials, transport facilities, scholarships, uniforms, assistive devices, support staff etc.

— Monitoring the progress towards inclusive education.

— Coordinating the efforts of educational authorities and those responsible for social work, employment and health.

— Girls with disabilities will remain a special focus and efforts would be made under the scheme to help girls with disabilities to gain access to school, information and guidance for developing their potentialities.

Early Childhood Education

The success of inclusive education depends considerably upon early identification, assessment and stimulation of the young child with disabilities. Recognizing the principle of inclusion, support for pre-school training for learners with disabilities would be available under this scheme for instructional materials and training of staff. (Anganwadi, Balwadis Workers, teachers etc.). Whenever possible, convergence with the schemes of Integrated Child Development (ICD) and Early Childhood Centres of education (ECCE) would be made for this purpose. Awareness programmes for the family members can be organized in conjunction with community services like health etc. Help from the voluntary sector already involved in carrying out early childhood care can be sought for this purpose. Identification of the needs of the child at this level will help in planning intervention programmes.

Attitude Change

Realizing the importance of community acceptance of the rights of the persons with disabilities, the scheme will support programmes to develop positive community attitudes towards learners with disabilities, and to enhance respect for them. These programmes should include educating the media, teachers, peers and community leaders about the changing views regarding the disabled, the importance of inclusive education, the use of proper language for describing the learners with disabilities (not using derogatory labels) and the significance of promoting positive models or success stories. The role of media in this is very powerful. The media can be used to inform the community regarding the new approaches in education particularly about the education of learners with disabilities.

Access

It is important to make schools accessible to learners with disabilities specially the orthopaedically disabled by removing the architectural barriers and adapting the toilets wherever necessary. In addition there are a host of other activities and events that have to be made accessible to the learners with disabilities. These will include access to

— The full curriculum, in appropriate ways

— Information in Braille, on tape, sign language, simple and straightforward language.

— Transport allowance to and from school.

— Escort allowance for children with severe orthopaedic impairments and neurodevelopmental disorders like cerebral palsy, autism mental retardation and multiple disabilities and, girls with disabilities.

The funds under the scheme will make provisions for providing access only in case there are no other provisions for this under other schemes operative at that level. However, the purchase and development of instructional materials and construction of resource room would be covered under the scheme.

Curriculum Support

All learners with disabilities included under the general education system may not require adaptations in the teaching learning process and evaluation procedures. However there may be some who require some adaptations. The Scheme will support for curriculum adaptations required to address the needs of learners with disabilities. The State implementing agency can take the support of special teachers, SCERTs, DIETs, special schools/ centres, non-governmental organizations, State boards or any other community institutions available at the local level for this purpose. The scheme will cover the expenses incurred on organizing the mobilization of such support as certified by the school principal/ educational administrators. The scheme will also support workshops for adaptations in the curricular content and development of supplementary material, self learning material for teachers and students at various levels of school education.

The provision for organizing a workshop/ meeting has also been made under the SSA. Learners with disabilities may require some adaptations in the evaluation procedures according to their special needs. The existing evaluation procedures can be reviewed at the State level and modified accordingly. Also use of appropriate technology in gaining access to the school curriculum is an important part of this scheme. The assessment team can be given the responsibility to decide the type of specific assistive devices required to meet the needs of learners with disabilities studying in inclusive schools.

Training

The scheme will provide for the programme of training with regard to inclusive education to special teachers, general teachers and educational administrators only under the condition that the same kind of training is not being provided under other schemes/ programmes. The knowledge and skills required by the general teachers are mainly those of good teaching and include assessing special needs, adapting curriculum content, utilizing assistive technology, individualizing teaching procedures to suit a large range of abilities etc. All teachers at pre-service and in service level need to have skills of building partnerships with the parents , specialists etc. This training will be imparted through the District Institute of Education and Training or Non Governmental Organizations having knowledge and experience in the area of Inclusive education. In- service training should, wherever possible developed at the school level with the help of trainers and self instructional materials.

In case of special teachers , training will enable them to work in different settings, develop partnerships and play a key role in inclusion of learners with disabilities.

Assessment

Recognizing the importance of early identification and assessment of special needs of learners with disabilities, the scheme will make arrangements for identifying, reviewing and the recommending the support required for short and long term objectives. In making such assessments, the State Government will tap the available local resources like the non governmental organizations, special schools, primary health centres, Village Education Committees, District Rehabilitation Centres etc. The assessment team will be appointed by the coordinator who will also be responsible monitoring the progress of the child as per the IEPs. The assessment team may comprise of some of the members given below.

- Specialists like speech therapist, audiologist, occupational therapist, physiotherapist
- Doctor (eye specialist, orthopaedic surgeon,, ENT specialist)
- Psychologist
- Social workers

However, the nature of the team and the members representing it would be decided by the coordinator keeping the special needs of the learners in mind:

While planning provision for the learner with disability, it would be ensured that the learner, his/her parents, teachers are fully involved in the process

The Assessment should result in individualized education plans (IEPs) for learners with disabilities. These IEPs should be reviewed regularly (every 6 months) and must involve the child, parents, teachers and specialists. The IEPs will help to make the teacher aware of the individual needs of the learner and also give information regarding the appropriate environment for his/her placement (special school, general school, special class etc.).

Partnerships

It is a well established fact that inclusive education revolves around building effective partnerships in which the partners work together to achieve some common goals. Cooperative and supportive partnerships among school administrators, teachers, parents and community would be an important aspect of any decision making under this scheme. The development of parents' associations, neighbourhood associations and partnerships with community members like the elderly and the disabled can also promoted for the following activities:

— Designing and implementation of the programmes

— Supplementing in-school activities

Partnerships under this scheme, would not only be encouraged with the parents of learners with disabilities, parents of learners without disabilities, but also with governmental organizations handling other programmes for learners with disabilities like the National Institutes, Teacher Education Institutions, Welfare departments, health departments other departments under education and Universities etc. and the voluntary sector.

Convergence with programmes like the Sarva Shiksha Abhiyan, ICDS, ADIP, ALIMCO and other programmes at the Central and State level would be sought whenever possible. Linkages with the different organizations will help in creating convergence of resources and funds for addressing the needs of learners with disabilities. Coordination committees at various levels i.e. State, District, Block and Cluster level will help the implementation of inclusive education in a big way.

Resource Room

Resource support to ordinary schools could be mobilized by the special schools and voluntary organizations. These can be used as resource centers for ordinary schools whenever possible. In case resource from such external resource agencies is not available, a resource room can be created at the school level, cluster level or block level.

Other Support Staff

Regular schools with an inclusive orientation must have a provision of support services to meet the needs of all children in the school. Support could be provided by teacher education institutions, special schools and the voluntary sector working in the area. Support can also be mobilized through convergence with the other schemes or programmes being implemented in the States and having a component of education of learners with disabilities. External support from resource personnel from various agencies such as educational psychologists, speech and occupational therapists, physiotherapists, mobility instructors etc. have to coordinated at the local level. The expenses incurred on mobilizing such support in the form of TA/DA and consultancy fee can be covered under the scheme. Support can also be made available at the cluster level and needs of learners with disabilities in a cluster of schools can be addressed.

Procedure

Administrative Cell

An administrative cell will be required to be set up under the State Education Department for coordination and implementation purposes. The best place for setting up the cell would preferably be the SCERTs /SIERTs/SIEs etc. The Cell will comprise of a Joint Director/Deputy Director (in the scale of pay applicable in the State Government), a coordinator who may be a psychologist in the scale applicable to a university lecturer, a Special Educator in the pay scale applicable to a university lecturer the State Government/UT, a stenographer, a lower division clerk and a peon in the pay scales applicable in the State/UT. The administrative cell will be responsible for the implementation of the scheme. Some of the major functions undertaken by the cell would include

— Finalization and onward transmission of proposals

— Selecting the assessment team

— Organizing and coordinating the various activities under the scheme including awareness programmes, training, workshops for curricular adaptations and modification in the examination procedures, selection of special teachers, organizing resource support etc.

— Ensuring convergence whenever possible

— Developing linkages with relevant departments

— Monitoring the progress

Procedures for Grants to State Governments/ UT administrations

Developing proposals for securing Grants

The State Governments/ UT Administrations should formulate their programmes/plans, make assessment of their financial requirements and submit detailed proposals for the next financial year to the Ministry of Human Resource Development (Department of Education, Government of India) by the end of December every year. The proposals should be accompanied by utilization certificates for grants if released in the previous year indicating, inter alias, detailed information regarding areas covered, the number of learners with disabilities covered school-wise, teachers' training programmes conducted etc. The proposal should specify clearly whether for the purpose of various allowances to the learners with disabilities the State Government rates have been taken or in their absence the rates given in this scheme have been adopted.

The proposals will be examined in the Ministry and 50 per cent of the approved grant for the year will be released as the first installment. The remaining 50 per cent of the grant will be sanctioned as soon as the State/UT administration reports utilization of at least 75 per cent of the grant sanctioned earlier. The request for the release of the second installment should be accompanied by an implementation report and a detailed statement of expenditure.

Procedures for Grants to Voluntary Organizations

The State Government/UT Administration should give its views as soon as possible but not exceeding 3 months regarding the organizations' eligibility, suitability, and relevance of the proposal and the capacity of the agency to implement it. Comments should be sent by the State Government even if the proposal is not recommended giving reasons therefore. In case the State Government fails to forward the proposals within 3 months, the voluntary organization would be at liberty to approach the Ministry on its own. In order to be eligible for financial assistance under this scheme the voluntary organizations, public trusts and non-profit making companies should

— have proper constitution of articles of association;

— have a properly constituted managing body with its powers and duties clearly defined in the constitution;

— be in a position to secure the involvement, on voluntary basis, of knowledgeable persons for furtherance of their programmes;

— not discriminate against any person or group of person on ground of sex, religion, caste or creed;

— not be run for the profit of any individual or a body of individuals;

— not directly function for the furtherance of the interests of any political party; and

— not in any manner that incite communal disharmony.

— Should be in existence for minimum of 3 years.

If any agency is already receiving or expecting to receive grant from some other official source for a project for which application is made under this scheme, assistance under this scheme will be made after taking into consideration the grant received, or likely to be received from such other official source. It should also be ensured that an agency already in receipt of a grant from any other official source, Central or a State, should not transfer any part of that liability to a grant to be sanctioned under this scheme. The proposals of the voluntary organizations with the recommendation of the State. Government/ UT Administration should be sent to the Ministry of Human Resource Development (Department of Education), Government of India by the end of December every year for the following financial year.

The proposals will be examined in the Ministry and 50 per cent of the approved grant for a year will be released as the first installment and the remaining 50 per cent after the agency reports utilization of at least 75 per cent of the grant sanctioned earlier. The request for release of the second installment should be accompanied by a progress report and statement of expenditure. The grant will be remitted to the agency directly by Demand Draft/ Cheque drawn in its favour by the Ministry of Human Resource Development, Department of Education.

Conditions of Grant to Voluntary Organizations

1) The Grant-receiving agency will be required to execute a bond on a prescribed form. The bond should be supplied by two sureties if the agency is not a legal entity.

2) An agency in receipt of financial assistance shall be open to inspection by an officer of the Union Ministry of Human Resource Development or the State Education Department.

3) The accounts of the project shall be maintained properly and separately and submitted as and when required. They should be open to check by an officer deputed for monitoring purposes by the Government of India or the State Government. They shall also be open to a thorough-check by the Comptroller and Auditor General of India at his discretion.

4) The audited accounts together with the utilization certificate in the prescribed form duly countersigned by the Chartered Accountant are required to be furnished within six months in respect of a preceding year or after expiry of the duration for which grant is approved.

5) The agency shall maintain a record of all assets acquired wholly or partially out of government grant and maintain a register of such assets in the prescribed proformas. Such assets shall not be disposed of, encumbered or utilized for the purposes other than those for which the grant was given, without prior sanction of the Government of India. Should the agency cease to exist at any time, such properties shall revert to the Government of India.

6) When the State Government/ Government of India has reasons to believe that the sanctioned money is not being utilized for the approved purpose the payment of grant may be stopped and the earlier grant recovered.

7) The institution must exercise reasonable economy in the working of the approved project.

8) The grantee agency shall furnish to the Ministry of Human Resource Development reports as may be prescribed.

9) The decision of the Secretary to the Government of India in the Ministry of Human Resource Development, Department of Education on the question whether there has been breach of violation of any of the terms and conditions mentioned in the sanctioned letter shall be final and binding on the grantee.

Regulations for Relaxation of Rules

State Governments/ UT Administrations/ other implementing agencies should also frame regulations for relaxation of rules relating to admissions, minimum or maximum age limit for admissions, promotions, examination procedures, etc. for improving access of the learners with disabilities to education. Provisions for admission of older learners with disabilities than the normal eligibility (up to 8-9 years instead of 6 years with upper limit till 18 years) is essential

Appointment of Special Teachers

Special education teacher belonging to specific area of disability can be appointed in the school or as itinerant special teacher depending on the student pupil ratio. The teacher-pupil ratio for special education teachers envisaged under this scheme is 1:5. This ratio will be the same for all regular classes as well as for preparatory pre-school classes. In accordance with this ratio the requisite number of special teachers may be appointed in schools (or for a cluster of schools) for learners requiring special teacher support on permanent or contractual basis. The same teachers will provide counselling to the parents, help in identifying the needs of learners with disabilities, participate in the assessment team, assist the general teachers in developing IEPs, help in training programmes and in other ways whenever necessary.

Financial parameters and unit costs

S.No.	Item	Provisions
1	Actual expenses on books and Stationary	Up to Rs.600/- annum/Learner
2	Actual expenses on Uniform at Primary Level.	Up to Rs.800/- annum/Learner.
	Actual expense on Uniform above the Primary Level.	Up to Rs.1000/- annum/Learner.
3	Transport allowance (only in case the child does not reside in the school premises)	Up to Rs. 300/-month/Learner
4	Reader allowance for reading to learners with Visual Impairments.	Up to Rs. 150/- month. /Learner
5	Assessment	Up to Rs. 250/learner
6	Escort allowance for severely disabled with lower extremity disability and for girls with disabilities and children with mental retardation (in case they have no family or community member to escort them).	Up to Rs. 600/- month/Learner.
7	Actual cost of assistive devices including equipment and educational aids	Maximum upto Rs. 3000/- learner for a period specified in the IEP or by the assessment team.
8	Attendant in school for learners with severe orthopaedic impairment at the ratio of 1:5 learners.	Standard Scale of pay as prescribed for class IV employees in the State/ UT concerned.

9	Boarding and lodging charges *[1] for learners with disabilities residing in the hostel of the school where they are studying.	Upto Rs. 800/- month/Learner.
10	Assistance of helper/Ayah for learners with severely orthopaedic impairments residing in school hostel.	A special pay of Rs. 250/- month to any employee of the hostel willing to extend such help in addition to his/her duties.
11	Purchase/Development of instructional materials.	Up to Rs. 500/annum/learner
12	Appointment of Special education teachers (both for school and pre-school level) covering all disabilities except Orthopaedic impairments	Same scale of pay as available to the teachers of the corresponding category in the State/UTs.
13	Training of Special teachers	Through refresher programmes run by the National Institutes and Rehabilitation Council of India or under other programmes of the States.
14	Training of General Teachers RIEs and Voluntary Organizations.	Through SCERTs, DIETs, SSA programme,
15	Orientation of educational administrators, heads of the institutions for 3 days.	Up to Rs.10,000/- annum
16	Resource room[2]	
	Construction of resource room	Up to Rs.1,00,000/-
	Equipment for resource room	Up to Rs.50,000/-

17	Grant for improving access by removing architectural barriers, curriculum support	As per requirement/school
18	Awareness programmes for developing positive attitudes involving print material, video tapes, audio cassettes etc.)	Up toRs.30,000/- annum.
19	Monitoring	As per requirement.
20	Grant for Scholarship (only when it is not being taken for the same purpose from any other source)	As per requirement.

Qualifications

Special teachers so appointed should posses the following qualifications:

— Academic Qualifications as prevalent in the State and Uts.

— Degree/Diploma in special education recognized by RCI

— Teachers with Qualifications in single disability area will be encouraged to specialize in other disability area to take care of wide range of diversities in a general school.

Scale of Pay:

The same scales of pay as available to the teachers of the corresponding category in that State/UT will be given to special teachers. The State Education Department may recruit such teacher for this purpose following the normal recruitment procedures.

The progress under the scheme will be carefully monitored by collecting statistics and evaluating practices annually. This data can be carried out by the State governments/ UT administrations that may identify their key partners for monitoring the progress in schools under this scheme. The report of such evaluations can be made available to the MHRD. However the States can revise the monitoring format to suit their specific needs. The monitoring arrangements should include both qualitative and quantitative data. Collaborations with SCERTs, DIETs State and District resource groups and other district, block, cluster level resources can be developed for this purpose. In all these endeavours girls will remain a specific focus.

2

EDUCATION OF CHILDREN WITH VISUAL IMPAIRMENT

DEFINITION OF BLINDNESS

Blindness can be defined physiologically as the condition of lacking sight. The definition as it applies to people thus legally classified is, however, more complex. The term "blindness" also applies to partial visual impairment: In North America and most of Europe, legal blindness is defined as vision of 20/200 (6/60) or less in the better eye with correction. People with normal acuity who nonetheless have a visual field of less than 20 degrees - the norm being 180 degrees - are also classified as being legally blind.

The World Health Organization (WHO) defines legal blindness as vision of 20/400 (3/60) or less in the better eye with correction. They also accept people with a visual field of less than 10 degrees under that heading. Approximately ten percent of those classified as being legally blind are actually sightless. The rest have some vision, from light perception alone to relatively good acuity.

Causes of blindness

Diseases of the eye: The most common causes of blindness in the world today are cataracts (43% in 1997, according to

WHO), Glaucoma (15%), Trachoma (11%), and Vitamin A deficiency found in children under 5 (6%). People in developing countries are significantly more likely to experience visual impairment as a consequence of treatable or preventable conditions, than are their counterparts in the developed world. Moreover, while vision impairment is most common in people over age 60 across all regions, children in poorer communities are more likely to be affected by a blinding condition than are their more affluent peers. The most common causes of adult visual impairment in North America and Western Europe include age-related Macular degeneration and Diabetic retinopathy.

Conditions and disorders: Another kind of visual impairment, cortical blindness, is the result of brain injury affecting a vital area of the visual system called the occipital lobe. People with cortical blindness can, despite having perfectly normal eyes and optic nerves, still be legally or totally blind. Other conditions, such as Optic Nerve Hypoplasia and Optic Nerve Atrophy, cause visual impairment by affecting those nerve bundles that send visual signals from the eyes to the brain for interpretation. Still other forms of blindness are causes by failures of the retina, such as Retinitis pigmentosa and Macular degeneration.

ALTERNATIVE TECHNIQUES AND TOOLS

Many blind and visually impaired people use a wide range of alternative techniques and specialized tools to accomplish tasks traditionally done using sight.

Techniques

- Folding bills of different denominations in different ways
- Labeling and tagging clothing and other personal items
- Placing different types of food at different positions on a dinner plate

Tools

Tools used to help the blind include:

White Canes: A number of visually impaired people travel independently using this mobility device, typically coloured white with a red tip. This tool is used to extend the user's range of touch sensation, often being 'swept' back and forth across the intended path of travel to detect obstacles. The colour of the cane is intended to promote visibility of the device to sighted people, alerting them to the presence of a blind or impaired user. In many countries, it is not permitted for sighted persons to use white canes. Additionally, some countries mandate that the right-of-way be given to users of white canes or guide dogs, and to blind persons in general.

Magnification: Magnifying glasses, non-prescription "reading glasses", full page fresnel lenses, and 'large text' format books and magazines can make reading more readily-available to those with lessened visual acuity. Modern browsers provide the ability to increase the size of text on web pages, through browser controls, or through user-controlled style sheets, providing the same effect as large-print books, or magnification devices.

Technologies

Clever adaptation of existing technologies as well as new technologies can aid the blind or visually impaired:

- *Braille and Moon type:* Visually impaired people can 'read' written material using a system of embossed print.
- *Talking Thermometers*: Used by visually impaired people, along with enlarged or marked oven dials, when they are cooking. Some blind people also use talking watches, talking clocks, talking scales, talking calculators, talking compasses and other talking equipment.
- *Closed-Circuit Televisions:* Electronic devices that enlarge and contrast many textual items

Web Accessibility Techniques

Persons with visual impairment may use text-based or aural browsers, such as Jaws and Window-Eyes to read content on the internet and worldwide web, as well as other computer programs, particularly word processing programs such as Microsoft Word. Henter-Joyce, the original makers of Jaws, and the makers of many other technology products for blind people have consolidated themselves into one company, Freedom Scientific. Window-Eyes is made by the GWMicro corporation. Legislation has been proposed to make public web space *accessible* in the same way that public buildings are required, in some countries, to be accessible to wheelchairs, walkers, etc. To make web pages more accessible to the visually impaired, the Worldwide Web Consortium recommends the following techniques:

- The use of alt attributes to describe the content or function of visuals, such as animations and images.
- Use of client-side map element and text for image maps.
- Captions and transcripts for audio and descriptions for video content
- Hypertext links that make sense when read out of context, rather than "click here" or similar wording.
- Headings, lists, and consistent page structure to make navigation easier.
- Use css for layout and style, do not use tables for layout or non-tabular data.
- Summarize graphs and charts or use the longdesc attribute
- Provide alternative content for scripts, plug-ins and applets, in case active features are not accessible, or are unsupported by the users browser. This might require an extra text paragraph, an alternate text page, or in some cases an entire alternate, and accessible website.

— Use of the noframes element, and meaningful titles on framed pages, limit the use of frames if possible.

— For tables try to organise data so that it reads sensibly in linear form, always summarise tables.

Guide dogs

A very small number of visually impaired people employ the services of guide dogs, sometimes improperly called, "seeing-eye dogs". These companions are especially trained to lead blind individuals around obstacles on the ground and overhead. Though highly intelligent, guide dogs neither interpret streets signs nor determine when the team ought to cross a street. Visually impaired people who employ these animals must, then, already be competent travellers.

Social attitudes towards blindness

Historically, blind and visually impaired people have either been treated as if their lack of sight were an outward manifestation of some internal lack of reason, or as if they possessed extra-sensory abilities. Stories such as *The Cricket on the Hearth* (Dickens) provided yet another view of blindness, wherein those affected by it were ignorant of their surroundings and easily deceived. The authors of modern educational materials, as well as those treating blindness in literature, have worked to paint a truer picture of blind people as three-dimensional individuals with a range of abilities, talents, and even character flaws. Certain individuals are gifted, and others licentious, but nothing definitive can be said of the blind as a class but that they cannot see well.

LOW VISION

Low vision is a term that denotes a level of vision that is 20/70 or worse and cannot be fully corrected with conventional glasses. Low vision is not the same as blindness. Unlike a person who is blind, a person with low vision has some useful sight. However, low vision usually interferes with the performance of daily activities, such as reading or driving. A person with low vision may not recognize images at a distance or be able to differentiate colours of similar tones. Although low vision can occur at any stage in life, it primarily affects the elderly.

However, low vision is not a natural part of aging. Although most people experience some physiological changes with age (presbyopia), these changes usually do not lead to low vision. Most people develop low vision because of eye diseases. Common causes of low vision, particularly with older adults, include macular degeneration, glaucoma, and diabetic retinopathy. When vision impairment is recognized early, treatment can be more effective, enabling people to maintain as much independence as possible.

You are legally blind when the best corrected central acuity is less than 20/200 (perfect visual acuity is 20/20) in your better eye, or your side vision is narrowed to 20 degrees or less in your better eye. People who are legally blind may still have some useful vision, just like people who have low vision. If you are legally blind, you may qualify for certain government benefits. It is estimated that approximately 17% of people over the age of 65 are either blind or have low vision.

Low Vision Exams

To determine the extent of your useful vision, you will need to have your eyes examined. The examination for low vision differs from typical eye examination. During a low vision examination, your doctor may administer the following tests:

— Refraction (to assess your vision and determine the prescription for your glasses, if glasses may be of any use)

— Visual field (to assess your peripheral vision)

— Ocular motility (to assess how well your eyes move)

Because low vision examinations may involve a variety of tests, they are often more time consuming than the standard examination. For instance, refraction may be done through a telescope or trial lens so you can judge which lens is best.

Symptoms

— Difficulty recognizing objects at a distance (street signs or bus signs)

— Difficulty differentiating colours (particularly in the green-blue-violet range)

— Difficulty seeing well up close (reading or cooking)

The symptoms described above may not necessarily mean that you have low vision. However, if you experience one or more of these symptoms, contact your eye doctor for a complete exam. Your eye doctor can tell the difference between normal changes which are common with age and changes caused by eye disease.

Treatment

The Kellogg Eye Centre Low Vision and Visual Rehabilitative Services Clinic embraces a multi-disciplinary approach to the treatment of low vision. Ophthalmologists, optometrists and occupational therapists make up the team of health care professionals who will work with you starting with your vision examination, and continuing to work with you to identify treatment options, which include:

— Optical devices that will help you adapt, such as magnifiers, telephones or closed-circuit televisions.

— Techniques that will help you utilize your remaining vision.

— Environmental modifications to maximize your remaining vision.

— Adaptive non-optical devices, such as large-print cookbooks and talking watches.

Occupational therapy programs may last as long as several months or be as brief as one session. Occupational therapy treatment is available at Kellogg. Sessions include an evaluation of your environment and suggestions for modifying your home to enable you to become more independent and to improve safety.

Low Vision Aids

Many types of assistive devices are available to assist people with low vision. These items include special glasses and other magnification devices, and large print reading materials, shown above. Other communication aids include computer software and various other technological devices. These items include special glasses and other magnification devices, and large print reading materials, shown above. Other communication aids include computer software and various other technological devices.

IDENTIFICATION AND ASSESSMENT

School districts should co-operate with Ministry of Health personnel to ensure all students participate in a vision screening program for the identification and prevention of visual impairments. Schools should also request a vision and hearing screening whenever they suspect a student is experiencing difficulties or is having trouble learning. The school district should develop and implement referral procedures to ensure that every visually impaired student is identified, and receives an appropriate educational program.

In order to plan the educational program the teacher of the visually impaired should conduct a functional vision assessment to identify the educational implications of the student's vision loss. In the case of students with a severe visual impairment, a qualified orientation and mobility instructor should also assess the students' skills in orientation and mobility.

EDUCATIONAL PLANNING FOR CHILDREN WITH VISUAL IMPAIRMENT

A component essential to the establishment of an effective system of delivery of services to students with visual impairment is the availability of qualified, experienced teachers who have regular classroom experience and in addition are competent to adapt materials, teach Braille, use visual aids and technological devices and plan, develop, deliver, and monitor all aspects of schooling affected by visual impairment. With appropriate support services, many students can follow the curriculum with adaptation of learning resources or instructional methods. When necessary, however, the curriculum should be modified to reflect individual needs. The student's educational requirements and any special measures that are to be taken in order to help meet those requirements should be documented in a formal Individual Education Plan.

When an IEP is developed, the following needs should be considered:

— orientation and mobility skills;

— visual skills;

— specialized skills in reading (e.g., Braille, taped books, enhanced print, CCTV);

— specialized skills in mathematics (e.g., abacus, Nemeth Code);

— access to technology (e.g., Braille 'n Speak, tape recorders, computers);

— daily living skills;

— social skills;

— vocational planning and skill development;

— study skills and note-taking strategies; and

— concept development.

Orientation and mobility (O&M) is an essential component of the curriculum for students with severe visual impairments. It provides students with the skills necessary to know where they are in the school or community, where they want to go and how to get there in a safe and efficient manner with as much independence as possible. Orientation and mobility training should not be restricted to the school environment but should include other environments in which the student is required to function at different times of the day. At the secondary level, school districts may develop and approve orientation and mobility programs or Brailling programs for visually impaired students as locally developed or independent study courses for credit toward graduation.

Most students with visual impairment require specialized equipment (e.g., Braillers, closed-circuit televisions, cassette recorders, optical aids) and adapted learning resources (e.g., Braille texts, enlarged print books, tapes). These tend to be very bulky. Schools should ensure there is adequate, accessible storage available to the student. A working or instructional area for instruction in specific skill development by the itinerant or resource teacher should also be provided. This instructional area should be conducive to effective instruction (i.e., in compliance with health and safety codes, quiet, adequately lit, ventilated and free from distractions).

PERSONNEL TEACHER OF THE VISUALLY IMPAIRED

Where supplemental funding is requested by districts for students with visual impairments, teachers must have appropriate qualifications. A qualified teacher of the visually impaired as one with:

— a valid B.C. Teaching Certificate, and

— a Master's degree or diploma in the education of the visually impaired.

Where a district is unable to employ a teacher of the visually impaired, this requirement may be met by providing regular services through sharing arrangements with other districts or through a fee-for-service arrangement with qualified specialist teachers of the visually impaired.

Orientation and mobility instructor

To ensure that students have access to appropriate orientation and mobility services, school districts should obtain services from qualified orientation and mobility instructors.

Teacher assistants

If the support of a teacher assistant is warranted the teacher of the visually impaired should consult with the classroom teacher to assist him or her in developing, directing, and monitoring the assistant's activities. Teacher assistants should have sufficient training and understanding of visual impairments for the duties they are assigned, and be able to demonstrate an understanding of the social, emotional and educational implications of vision loss.

CURRICULUM FOR VISUALLY IMPAIRED CHILDREN

Structure of Curriculum

The curriculum designed for ordinary children is generally appropriate for visually impaired children. However, some adaptations to the learning materials and the teaching approaches have to be made so that the learning needs of visually impaired children can be met. The curriculum should be balanced with due consideration given to the children's intellectual, personal, emotional and social developments. To teach visually impaired children, the teacher should adopt a consistent, realistic and flexible approach in curriculum planning and implementation.

Curriculum for Totally Blind and Severe Low Vision Children

Chinese Language

Following are some suggestions geared to the needs of the pupil:

(1) *Learning Cantonese Braille*

Chinese Language is a basic subject in the school curriculum. Instead of learning Chinese characters, totally blind and severe low vision children are taught to read and write Cantonese Braille as their medium of learning.

Cantonese Braille is formed by three braille cells: an initial particle, a final particle, and sometimes a tone mark. The children should be encouraged to learn Cantonese Braille as early as possible. First, a Cantonese tone training programme is given to help the children develop their basic reading skills, then they are taught to read and write Cantonese Braille in association with words which they come across in textbooks.

(2) *Other Ways to Help Learning Children Language*

Textbooks and supplementary learning materials can be transcribed into braille. Various language activities such as story-telling, singing, role-play, etc. can be used to reinforce the children's language skills and to improve their understanding of the language.

Great emphasis should be put on the explanation of synonyms and the homophones. In introducing new vocabulary and language items, more explanation or experience sharing is required as visually impaired children have little actual experience. The teacher should also introduce the knowledge of the radicals of Chinese characters to the children. They may also learn to sign their names.

In composition, it is advisable to provide the children with more organized activities such as visits, picnics, debates, radio plays, drama and interviews so that these concrete experiences can help to enrich the content of their composition. For picture-guided composition, verbal clues and descriptions of pictures in braille are also of great help.

Putonghua

Following are some suggestions geared to the needs of the pupil:

(1) *Learning Putonghua braille*

Putonghua is also offered as a subject in special schools for visually impaired children to enable the children to speak and understand the language. The children learn Putonghua by the aural-oral approach. They also learn the written Putonghua braille, which involves distinguishing between the initial particles, the final particles and the tone marks, based on the Chinese romanised transcription system.

(2) *Good Language Models*

The teacher should give good language models. By using various learning activities, such as phonetic games, passage reading, sentence making, dialogue practice, report writing, discussions and audio recording, the children's interest can be stimulated. Emphasis should be placed not only on speaking but also on reading and writing in Putonghua braille.

English Language

English is widely used as a medium of instruction in secondary schools. As some visually impaired children are capable of receiving senior secondary education in ordinary schools, English will be a medium of learning to them and will also be a prerequisite for their future studies. Following are some suggestions geared to the needs of the pupil:

(1) *Adaptations To Textbooks*

To help the children learn English, the teacher has to make adaptations to textbooks, where required, to suit braille-users, e.g. using written descriptions instead of picture cues; using Chinese illustrations where necessary; transcribing reading materials into braille, etc. In addition, teaching aids such as real objects, tactile diagrams, talking cards, cassette tapes, etc. may also be used.

(2) *Learning English Braille*

English Braille is a medium of learning to totally blind and severe low vision children. It represents the letters of the alphabet, part of the word signs, contractions, short-form words and whole words.

At the junior primary level, the children start to learn single-cell word signs, simple dual-cell word signs, contractions, abbreviations and punctuation marks which are generally encountered in textbooks. At the upper primary level, the children learn more complicated two-cell contractions, abbreviations and punctuation marks. At the secondary level, they will have acquired the skills of reading and writing Braille.

Mathematics

Mathematics is an important subject in the curriculum Following are some suggestions geared to the needs of the pupil:

(1) *First-hand Experience*

In learning Mathematics, totally blind and severe low vision children need first-hand experience because they lack visual stimulation related to the development of mathematical concepts such as size, shape, colour, etc. The teacher needs to adapt the learning materials and give examples appropriate to the children's levels of understanding. The mathematical language and terms used should be consistent.

To teach mathematical concepts, the teacher needs to train the children's tactile skills by using teaching aids such as toys, counting apparatus, embossed pictures and diagrams, etc. Learning materials which provide the children with opportunities to touch and count are necessary to help them acquire mathematical concepts. Learning activities used in Mathematics lessons should be closely related to the children's daily life experiences.

(2) *Use of Special Aids*

Mathematics Braille should be introduced for mathematical computation. To provide for practice in the skills of computation, plastic cubes of braille numerals can be a useful tool for basic number work in junior primary classes. When calculation becomes too long or too complicated, calculation frames such as Taylor Board and abacuses can be used in senior primary classes. The children can also be taught to use talking calculators, which simplify operation involving complicated calculations.

In teaching Geometry, statistics and graphs, embossed diagrams should be used. The teacher should ensure that embossed diagrams have been simplified without compromising accuracy.

General Studies, EPA and History

These subjects help to improve the children's understanding of the Hong Kong community and historical events. In primary schools, General Studies is offered and in secondary schools EPA and History are taught. Following are some suggestions geared to the needs of the pupil:

(1) *Suitable Adaptation To Map:* To teach these subjects, learning materials have to be prepared in braille copies and embossed braille maps or pictures should be used. The teacher should simplify the important items depicted from original maps or use separate maps to show different items.

(2) *Use Real Objects or Models*: Teacher should use models or real objects to reinforce the children's learning.

(3) *Arrange Activities:* Activities such as visits to satellite towns, exhibitions and museums, quiz and model-making would help to promote the children's interest, enrich their experience and arouse their social awareness. The teacher should also make use of community resources such as large posters available from Government departments or other agencies to teach related topics.

Biology

Biology helps the children to understand the growth and development of the human body and makes them better aware of the natural environment. Following are some suggestions geared to the needs of the pupil:

(1) *Use of Senses of Hearing, Touch and Smell*: By using their senses of hearing, touch and smell, the children's curiosity in the natural environment can be stimulated.

(2) *Use of Suitable Teaching Aids*: Real objects, living things, models and diagrams can be used to develop the children's power of observation and understanding of concepts.

(3) *Arrange Activities:* Active participation in visits, excursions, rambles and data-collection not only helps to stimulate the children's interest to learn, but also develops in them an enquiring mind and a positive attitude towards nature. However, special safety precautions have to be taken in practical work and outdoor visits.

Computer Literacy

When using the computer, visually impaired children have problems in perceiving visual displays on the screen and the text of a hard copy in ink-print. They may also have difficulties in keying data into the computer. To help the children cope with these problems, adaptations to the syllabus for Computer Literacy is necessary. Additional time is required to teach the keyboard skills and operations of special adaptive devices in order to get access to computers.

Basically a greater part of the syllabus for Computer Literacy for ordinary schools can be followed. However, some areas in the curriculum may have to be modified to strengthen practical skills in the use of the computer and special adaptive devices with emphasis on the following areas:

(1) Training in keyboard skills with manual typewriters before computer operation: Typing is introduced here as a means to master basic keyboard skills with certain degree of accuracy rather than speed. Besides basic keyboard skills, correction of typing errors and simple formatting should be emphasized.

(2) Training in the operation of computer access devices:; The training is most important in that it gives visually impaired children access to the computer. The children have to acquire the following skills in order to operate the computer: screen review skills in braille or in visual enlargement, printing skills with a braille printer and the use of optical character recognition techniques for transformation. Since they have different degrees of vision, the children have to be trained to use one, or more, of the following special adaptive devices before they can manipulate the different processes of a computer system:

(a) Screen enlargement devices or software for low vision children - e.g. VISTA, ZOOMTEXT, LUNA and MAGIC etc.

(b) Voice synthesizers for totally blind and severe low vision children - e.g. DECTALK, ECHO GP, ARTIC VISION, SYNPHONIX, KEYNOTE GOLD etc.

(c) Braille displays of computers for totally blind and severe low vision children - e.g. ALVA, BRAILLEX, NAVIGATOR, and POWERBRAILLE etc..

(3) Learning of programming skills with tactile graphics: The biggest drawback in computer access technology for totally blind and severe low vision children lies in their difficulties in gaining access to the graphics displayed on the computer screen. The current practice is to transform indirectly video graphics to tactile graphics on a braille printer with appropriate computer graphic programmes. Since programming with LOGO language involves quite a lot of graphics with reference to spatial relationship and orientation, which are abstract to visually impaired children, this part of the curriculum should be cut short and should only be briefly introduced. Basic programming skills with other computer languages like BASIC are preferable to LOGO for totally blind and severe low vision children.

(4) Exposure to a variety of computer applications: To help visually impaired children integrate into society, it is essential to expose them to some commonly used computer applications such as word processing, spreadsheet, database management, Internet browsing & Email communications, desktop publishing and digital music compositions and productions etc.

(5) Emphasis on the learning of word-processing: This can be taken as a rehabilitation aid for written communication with sighted people and is also necessary for the children's studies. Although it is easier for Braille users to use specially designed word processing programs, they should also be familiar with other conventional and popular ones. This will facilitate their total integration into society in future.

Music

Through playing musical instruments, singing, listening and creative activities, the children may experience enjoyment and satisfaction in music. A sense of rhythm can also be developed through movements to music, which strengthen the children's body awareness and spatial concept. Following are some suggestions geared to the needs of the pupil:

(1) Listening Activities: To develop aural awareness and musical perception in the children, listening activities such as identifying and comparing environmental and musical sounds, recognizing the tone colour of instruments, differentiating the timbre of the voice, distinguishing rhythm and pitch, etc. can be used.

(2) Use of Braille: It is important to develop the ability to listen with concentration, which may enhance aural memory in music reading. Sight singing and other learning materials can also be transcribed into braille.

(3) Singing demonstrate: The teacher may use his own voice to demonstrate accurate and natural voice production as well as good models of singing.

Art & Craft

Art & Craft is offered in primary schools. The areas of work chosen for the children are mainly print-making, collage, three-dimensional work and art appreciation. Tactile drawing should also be included. Following are some suggestions geared to the needs of the pupil:

(1) Art Appreciation: The teacher should help the children to touch and describe the art work and discuss with them the aspect of art appreciation.

(2) Teach Individual Children: Very often, it is necessary to teach individual children by holding their hands to cut, to fold and to colour.

(3) Use Suitable Tools: The children should not be allowed to use dangerous tools such as cutters and knives. Sometimes the teacher has to use double blunt training scissors to make raised lines or designs for totally blind children to cut or to colour. As for colour designs, the teacher has to give the children more guidance.

Design & Technology

In Design & Technology, the children are taught to appreciate the qualities of different materials and to use these materials for designing. They are also taught the use of hand tools and equipment to make different things. Following are some suggestions geared to the needs of the pupil:

(1) Safety Precautions: For visually impaired children, safety precautions are particularly important and adaptations to hand tools and electrical equipment are required.

(2) Use of Adulteration Tools: Simple jigs can be made by the teacher to assist in specific tasks such as drilling or cutting.

(3) Plan Teaching Tasks: All teaching tasks have to be broken down into steps to give the children a full understanding of the steps of each individual task. Projects should be carefully designed to enable the children to understand all aspects of technical knowledge and skills.

(4) Use of Braille: Measuring devices with Braille readings should also be used.

Physical Education

Physical Education is an indispensable part of the curriculum. Following are some suggestions geared to the needs of the pupil:

(1) A Specific Name to Each Motor Skill: In teaching Physical Education, each motor skill has to be given a specific name so that the children know how to distinguish one from another. Instructions need to be clear and concise.

(2) Use Appropriate Teaching Method and Safety Precautions: Body contact is necessary to help place the children in correct positions in activities such as climbing, swimming, balancing, heaving, vaulting, hopping, skipping, running, rolling, jumping, etc. Sound source devices should be applied in activities such as running, bean bag throwing

and ball games. The teacher should take special safety precautions when conducting Physical Education lessons, outdoor activities, sports and games. Full use must be made of space available so as to minimize the danger of collision during class, group or individual activities.

(3) Keep Apparatus in Proper Places: All apparatus must be kept in proper places. The children should be told where they are in the gymnasium so that they can locate, lift and carry them.

Home Economics

This subject aims at developing in the children a caring attitude towards others; a positive attitude towards health; basic knowledge and skills in fashions and design, cooking, home management, etc. Following are some suggestions geared to the needs of the pupil:

(1) Learning Content: Knowledge of basic food groups, nutritional value, choice and storage of food, balanced diet, good table manners and eating habits, household cleanliness and personal hygiene, dressing and care of personal belongings, etc. should be taught at the initial stage.

Basic knowledge of consumer education is also recommended. The knowledge of consumers' rights and responsibilities and wise shopping will benefit the children greatly in their daily life.

In learning needlework, fashions and design, visually impaired children can do simple stitching and simple household sewing.

(2) Use Suitable Teaching Methods: These basic techniques have to be taught step by step so that the children can practise the correct method confidently.

Great emphasis should be placed on practical work. As totally blind and severe low vision children cannot see demonstrations or work independently, the teacher has to teach them individually and provide them with opportunities to touch the ingredients, raw food, utensils, home appliances, fabric, clothes, etc. Besides touching, the other senses of smell and taste can help them to distinguish whether the food is raw, cooked, tasty, fresh or spoilt.

(3) Use Special Aids: Audible timers with braille marks, talking weighing machines, liquid measurers and thermometers, guards for irons, etc. are the special aids used in Home Economics. In sewing manually, they need a threading tool to assist them in threading needles. To teach stitching, the teacher has to prepare paper patterns as guidelines for the children.

ETV

ETV programmes are available for teaching many subjects in the curriculum. For visually impaired children, ETV can also serve as a good supplement to learning provided the teacher gives detailed explanation of certain screen images or scenes, of which no auditory cues are available.

Communicative and Social Skills Training

Visually impaired children need particularly to learn communicative and social skills. The teacher should provide them with sufficient opportunities for social interaction and exposure to general knowledge and what happens around them both at school and at home. The teacher should help them to develop a pleasant personality, a good body image and a proper way of walking. Visually impaired children should also learn the rules of social courtesy e.g. to initiate and maintain a conversation in a suitable tone and with appropriate facial expressions.

Self-care Skills Training

Since visually impaired children are unable to learn by observation, daily living skills need to be learnt by actual practice. These skills include feeding, dressing, toileting, personal hygiene, cleaning and cooking. These have to be taught right from the lowest class gradually up to senior classes.

Guidance and Counselling

The teacher should maintain effective communication with the children and be consistent in managing their behaviour problems, and in giving appropriate guidance and counselling. He should help them to develop such qualities as self-image, self-esteem, self-confidence, self-awareness, self-discipline, independence, a good personality, a positive learning attitude, good interpersonal relationship, social awareness, etc. The teacher may also work in collaboration with other staff and professionals for effective management of the children's behaviour problems. Career counselling and guidance for school leavers or overage slow learners are necessary to prepare them for vocational training, thus improving their job opportunities, and to help them integrate into society.

Special Training for Totally Blind and Severe Low Vision Children

Tactile and Pre-braille Training

(1) *Tactile Training*: Without vision, the children receive fragmentary information through their sense of touch and form a concept of the 'whole' from the information of the 'parts'. Therefore, tactile training and pre-braille training are very important to visually impaired children. In order to acquire sensory acuity and efficiency, tactile training, manipulative play and art and craft activities are emphasized.

(2) *Pre-Braille Training*: Through pre-braille training, the children learn to be sensitive to the positions of the six cells and to distinguish the difference between dots and lines by using Peg Boards. When they are ready to learn braille numbers, the English alphabet and Chinese braille initial particles, Braille Boards are used for practice. In learning the tone marks of Chinese characters, young children are taught to learn by chanting them to acquire competence.

Another important aspect in training the 'reading fingers' is the skills of scanning and locating text, ranging from the orientation of lines to paragraphs and pages.

(3) *Training in Reading Graphics:* Reading symbolic pictures in raised forms is another specialized area of training since braille textbooks also require the incorporation of graphic illustrations. However, when they are in the form of photos, they are too complicated to be represented in line graphics and thus brief descriptions have to be incorporated.

Orientation and Mobility Training

(1) *Attention to Pupil's General Health Conditions*

Before designing individual orientation and mobility training programmes for visually impaired children, special attention should be paid to their general health conditions, the presence of other physical or sensory impairments and their individual learning difficulties. In order to enhance the children's body image and spatial concept, and to facilitate the integration of sensory and self-protective skills, the elements which address equilibrium, co-ordination, flexibility and agility should be incorporated.

(2) *Training at Junior Primary Level*

Activities organized for visually impaired children at the junior primary level should mainly be carried out in a controlled environment. Emphasis should be placed on the development of awareness and effective utilization of the children's remaining senses such as auditory, tactile, olfactory, kinaesthetic and particularly non-visual cognition. Motivation and positive reinforcement are of paramount importance during this stage of training.

(3) *Training at the Senior Primary Level*

At the senior primary level, which is a crucial period to develop in the children a positive attitude towards the subject, more encouragement has to be given. Emphasis should be put on acquiring skills for non-visual orientation and navigation in a less controlled environment. Training should be conducted outdoors to enhance awareness and utilization of environmental clues and landmarks. This is an appropriate period to develop basic cane skills and to consolidate concepts of sidewalks, blocks, streets and intersections. It is also advisable to take different weather conditions into consideration.

The following activities will enable the children to use the different means of public transport while travelling independently, so that they can integrate into society:

(1) implications of traffic rules and regulations;

(2) auditory analysis of traffic patterns;

(3) development of advanced cane skills;

(4) selection of appropriate means of transport;

(5) use of good judgment under changing conditions;

(6) transfer of acquired skills to new situations;

(7) appropriate interactions with the public.

(4) Training at Secondary Level

At the secondary level, achievement depends on the maturity of the children, their desire and opportunity for independent travelling and the expectations of their parents.

Training in the Use of Rehabilitation Aids

(1) *Optacon*: The Optacon is a portable electronic reading aid which converts the image of a printed letter or a symbol into enlarged vibrating tactile form that visually impaired children can feel with one finger.

Optacon training takes about 50 hours and is divided into 3 stages: the preliminary stage, the basic training stage and the follow-up stage.

(a) At the preliminary stage, the children are trained in the basic skills of handling the machine, learning the printed forms of the capital and small letters, and reading words, phrases and short sentences.

(b) At the basic training stage, the children are trained to read short paragraphs, a full page and later the whole book. Different types of words and formats in the book are also introduced.

(c) At the follow-up stage, the emphasis is on speed reading and reading of practical printed materials e.g. exercises, letters, bank statements and bills. The use of the Optacon allows the children to read directly from the typewriter. The Cathode Ray Tube lens also enables the children to read the computer screen with the Optacon.

(2) *Kurzweil Reading Machine*: The Kurzweil Reading Machine is a machine for totally blind and severe low vision children which reads English ink-print text aloud.

The machine enables the children to expose themselves to learning media other than braille. The teacher should familiarise the children with the English pronunciation produced by the machine, and help them to understand the different functions and the orientation of the keys, to control the machine in reading text and to overcome the difficulties caused by the malfunction of the machine.

(3) VersaBraille: The VersaBraille is a braille word-processor and an electronic data organizer for totally blind and severe low vision children with a braille display and interface ability to computers and printers.

VersaBraille training also emphasizes its communicating function with sighted people. It can help the children to study and do their homework. The teacher should familiarise the children with the orientation of the keys on the control panel by guiding their hands to indicate the actual positions and to distinguish between the 'left' and 'right' movements as well.

CURRICULUM FOR MODERATE LOW VISION CHILDREN

Use of Visual Aids

As moderate low vision children have residual vision only, some visual materials used by the teacher should be enlarged where necessary. For example, in teaching Mathematics, mathematical charts and graphs have to be enlarged or enhanced. In Music, the children should be taught to read music with enlarged notes drawn on the Wyteboard. Pictures or diagrams used in various subjects can be enlarged by projecting them on the wall or screen with slides or transparencies.

Moderate low vision children generally have difficulties in reading and writing print. The use of flash cards in enlarged print can help to promote their visual memory in recognizing Chinese characters and English words in language lessons. These children should be given lots of exercises to familiarize themselves with the order of the strokes of complicated Chinese characters. Similarly, sufficient exercises on the different strokes and curves of English letters are also required. In addition, adequate drills to acquire proficiency in English cursive writing are also important to improve the children's speed of writing.

Use of Optical Aids and Adaptive Equipment

The use of optical aids and adaptive equipment are very important to the children's learning. In watching ETV programmes, the use of distant optical aids can help the children achieve better viewing effect. In learning sewing manually in Home Economics, threading tools are needed to assist the children in threading needles. Sewing magnifiers are also required for sewing. To give the children access to the computer, the teacher should train them to use screen enlargement devices or software so that they can see the visual displays on the screen. For subjects like Art & Craft and Design & Technology, hand tools and electrical equipment have to be adapted to help the children with their practical work.

Special Training for Moderate Low Vision Children

Low Vision Training

(1) Assessment of Children's Visual Ability

Before a vision training programme can be planned, assessment of the children's visual ability should be carried out. Although some children have very limited visual ability, they can use their residual vision so effectively that their functioning appears to be visually oriented. Others having similar visual potential may not be as responsive to visual stimuli. They may behave as if they were unable to see at all. A visual functioning assessment is therefore necessary to determine the present visual functioning level of each child so that individual vision training programmes with suitable visual stimulating materials can be developed to help the children use their limited vision to the full.

(2) Basic Training Programme

The purpose of the basic training programme is to provide the children with appropriate sequence for visual stimulation activities to help them develop their limited visual ability.

These activities should be made interesting and motivating and the amount of visual information provided for the children should not be excessive. Besides, even the slightest effort or improvement made by the children need to be reinforced.

The following are some suggested activities for visual development:

(1) Activities to develop eye muscle control: These activities can facilitate fixation, tracking, focussing and accommodation of eye muscles. As unused and untrained eye muscles become tired quickly, these activities should be carried out for only a very short period of time at the beginning of the training. Then the duration can be increased gradually.

(2) Activities to promote recognition, identification and discrimination of three-dimensional and two-dimensional objects and geometric shapes. These activities can first be introduced by using three-dimensional real objects followed by three-dimensional geometric shapes. Pictures of two-dimensional real objects with black silhouette against a white background and drawings of two-dimensional black solid or outline geometric shapes can then be introduced. As the children show some progress, other colours can be added discriminatingly and more complex pictures or drawings can be used.

(3) Activities to develop visual memory: These activities can be introduced by using geometric shapes to develop patterns. Linear designs and abstract outlines of real objects may be used for further training. Then it may lead to the learning of the English alphabet, Chinese characters and numbers.

(4) Activities to develop eye-hand coordination: Activities such as eye-hand co-ordination and finger dexterity training can develop hand manipulative skills required in the children's daily life.

(5) Activities to develop colour discrimination: Children who are not colour deficient can learn the names of colours and the differences between shades, hues and similar colours through such activities as naming the colours or reproducing colour patterns.

(6) Activities to motivate the use of optical aids: Even young children should be encouraged to use optical aids such as magnifiers and telescopes to help them adjust to classroom learning.

(7) Activities to develop reading and writing skills: Skills of fixation, tracking and focussing should be applied in reading and writing. Speed skill should be developed with the help of interesting activities such as 'Letter Tracking' and 'Search-A-Word'. The teacher should also help individual children to decide the best angle and distance of the reading materials from their eyes.

(8) Activities in computer-assisted learning: Computer activities can reinforce and consolidate visual skills training.

(9) Activities using closed circuit television: These activities provide low vision children who have extremely limited visual acuity or constricted visual fields with opportunities to learn print even if braille is their main medium of learning. It also reinforces visual memory by providing sharp contrast and enlarged print for low vision children who use print as a medium. This is particularly effective in learning complex Chinese characters.

Orientation and Mobility Training

Orientation and mobility training programmes for moderate low vision children should emphasize the development of awareness and functional utilization of their residual vision. Consideration should be given to the effects of illumination and weather conditions as well.

TRAINING OF MILD LOW VISION CHILDREN IN SPECIAL CLASSES OPERATED IN ORDINARY SCHOOLS

Objective

Special classes for mild low vision children operated in ordinary schools aim at providing these children with education in an ordinary school setting.

Teaching Approach

Low vision children in special classes follow the ordinary school curriculum. Since the children have different visual problems and learn at a pace different from that of their peers, individual attention from the teacher is essential. Project work and unit teaching are encouraged. In teaching these children, the teacher should take into account the teaching objectives, the different levels of ability of the children and ways to adapt learning materials to suit individual learning needs. The teaching approach should be flexible enough to meet the different levels of ability of the children in coping with the ordinary school curriculum.

Use of Teaching Aids and Equipment

The teacher should make the best use of projectors and audio aids to enhance the visual efficiency of the children and to alleviate constant eye strain. Colourful pictures, simple charts with bold outlines and word cards with large print should also be used whenever possible. The children should be taught and encouraged to use such tools as telescopes and magnifiers properly. Clear and concise explanations or instructions should be given to help the children learn more effectively, e.g. in the study of specimens and in experiments during science lessons, in learning the formation and structure of Chinese characters, etc.

Emphasis in Teaching

At the beginning of the primary level, emphasis should be put on training the children in visual skills to enhance their visual efficiency, e.g. eye-hand co-ordination training. The teacher should also help the children to develop self-care skills and to observe classroom discipline. At the secondary level, low vision children are offered education in special classes with emphasis on social integration. Preparation should be made while they are in junior secondary classes to facilitate their total integration in senior secondary classes. Therefore the teacher should give the children adequate guidance and counselling and encourage them to take an active part in extra-curricular activities at school.

CURRICULUM GUIDELINES FOR VISUALLY IMPAIRED CHILDREN WITH MENTAL HANDICAP

There are quite a number of visually impaired children in Hong Kong who are also mentally handicapped. These children cannot cope with the curriculum designed for children who are only visually impaired. They need to follow a curriculum basically similar to that designed for mentally handicapped children, but with modifications where required. They need programmes specially designed to prepare them for living and functioning in their homes, the neighbourhood and the community; to equip them with study/work skills and habits for further studies/vocational training; to enable them to achieve as much independence as possible and become contributing members of the community.

Visually impaired children who are also mentally handicapped learn and progress at a slower pace than their peers who are only visually impaired. They are likely to experience difficulties in academic subjects requiring abstract thinking and complex learning strategies. They may have difficulties in language and motor co-ordination. They also need enhancement in developing their personal and social skills. The main subject areas for these children can be grouped as follows:

Academics

(1) Basic skills in functional Mathematics: To enable them to cope with daily life, the children are taught the concepts of size, speed, weight and measurement, and other basic concepts in Mathematics, e.g. 'full', 'empty', 'more', 'less', etc. Concepts of good management of time and proper use of money are also important in enabling the children to lead an independent life.

(2) Basic reading and writing: The children are also taught some basic vocabulary required for survival and social needs, e.g. 'exit', 'toilet', 'male', 'female', 'danger', 'poison', etc. They also learn to read and write their names and addresses. For those who have residual vision and are capable of learning braille, pre-braille training is provided.

Language and Communication

Through speech and language training, the children learn to use speech as a means of communication and to interpret non-verbal and graphic means of communication. The development of language and communication skills help the children to learn concepts more easily and to express themselves more effectively.

Personal and Social Developments

(1) Self-care skills: Self-care skills help the children to attain personal independence. Such skills include the ability to look after one's daily needs, e.g. feeding, taking a bath, attending to one's belongings and observing safety rules.

(2) Growth and sex education:The children are taught their sex differences and the correct attitude towards the opposite sex and members of the family. Training in personal hygiene and household cleanliness is also provided.

(3) Social skills: Learning how to get along with people and how to behave in different situations is very important throughout one's life. The children should know the

different roles they play in school, in their families and in the community. They should be helped to develop a positive attitude towards people.

Motor Development

(1) Perceptual motor training: Perceptual motor training is essential to the children in developing their concentration, discrimination, concept formation and the use of the senses. Relevant exercises are given to make the children aware of their body image, to improve their eye-hand co-ordination and to relate to the environment.

(2) Orientation and mobility training: Individual and group training sessions are carried out in school and in the neighbourhood. All the children have to learn to find their way around the school. This is a very important part of their adjustment to the environment.

(3) Physical training: A variety of activities are provided. The children learn how to co-operate with others in the course of learning different sports and games. Quite a number of social skills can be reinforced in controlled situations.

(4) Rhythm and movement: Mime and role play are interesting to the children when they work through musical activities and rhythmic movement. They can explore what they can do with different parts of their bodies and learn how to co-ordinate their limbs to give better postures.

Aesthetic and Creative Activities

(1) Music: Most visually impaired children with mental handicap are interested in music. They love singing all sorts of songs and listening to various kinds of music. They also enjoy playing musical instruments and performing in percussion groups.

(2) Art & Craft: Through art and craft activities, the children learn to be creative and imaginative. They learn how to

express their feelings with the help of different colours and shapes. They can differentiate the qualities of the materials used, e.g. hard and soft, smooth and rough, light and heavy, etc. These activities help them to concentrate and reinforce their finger dexterity. They also learn to appreciate beauty and to cooperate when working in a group.

Low Vision Training

(1) Basic training: Basic training programmes are provided to help the children develop their limited visual ability. Every programme consists of a sequence of visual stimulation activities for different aspects of visual development such as:

(a) activities to train visual focus;

(b) activities to promote visual recognition and differentiation;

(c) activities to train eye-hand co-ordination;

(d) activities to develop eye muscle control.

The children are also encouraged to use their residual vision in games and activities, e.g. ball games and matching games.

(1) Reading and Writing (Chinese)

(a) Reading: The children are taught to read in the sequence of words, phrases, sentences and paragraphs. They are encouraged to use optical aids in reading. Various activities are also carried out to improve their reading skills.

(b) Writing: The children are taught pre-writing skills through a variety of activities such as:

— colouring pictures with outlines provided;

— joining incomplete lines;

— joining dots;

— drawing a line within parallel lines, e.g. straight lines, zig-zag lines and wavy lines.

They also learn to write in the sequence of words, phrases and sentences.

TEACHING STUDENTS WITH VISION IMPAIRMENTS

The degree of impairment and the student's background and training (like the degree of proficiency in Braille) will affect the usefulness of the various strategies and suggestions. The student with a vision impairment will most likely need assistance in all aspects of science programs. The various strategies given below will work for most vision impaired students--some may not. Accessible description will be necessary for pictures, graphics, displays, or field sites, etc.; the student's identification queries; and differentiation of items where touch will not discriminate; and in orientation and mobility aspects in unfamiliar situations.

Bring to the student's attention science role models with disabilities with a similar disability to that of the student. Point out that this individual achieved by a combination of effort and by asking for help when needed.

— A wide selection of magnifying devices are available that can be used by visually impaired students to assist in reading or working with objects that need to be observed.

— A screen reader, low vision projection screen, or an item like outspoken or a similar system can be used to read a computer screens.

— A screen magnifier may be used to enlarge print on a computer screen.

— General Information Access for Persons with Vision Loss

— Visual material needs to be accompanied by a verbal description. If you are demonstrating how to use a piece of equipment, be sure to describe the equipment and what you are doing to operate it. Read overheads aloud and describe the content of slides. In a conference presentation setting, you will probably want to provide all descriptions yourself. If you are showing a videotape, describe the action. If you distribute videotapes as handouts, any action or an explanatory text that is crucial to understanding the text of the presentation should be narrated.

— If there are multiple speakers (such as a panel), have each speaker introduce himself or herself to the audience so that the speakers' voices are keyed for the audience as to their identity.

— Be certain that your presentation can be clearly heard by everyone in the room and repeat all questions from the audience, prior to answering.

— Handouts should be available in large print, audiotape, computer disk, and/or Braille formats. If this is not possible prior to your presentation, note the various individuals' preferred formats and then make your materials available to them within a short time after your presentation.

Large Print * - People who have some functional vision may be able to see print if it is large enough. Prepare print information on white paper with sharp, black ink. Standard print is generally 10-12 point type. Large print is 16-18 point and up, generally an enlargement setting of 160-175% on a copy machine. In the case of documents that already exist in print form, use a copy machine to enlarge each page onto 11 x 17 paper. Try darker settings on the copy machine to increase contrast without producing streaks. Many computer programs offer a variety of font types and sizes.

Teacher Presentation

— By verbally spelling out a new or technical word, you will be helping the student with a vision impairment, as well as for other students.

— An enlarged activity script, directions, or readings of a detailed lesson can be used for a low vision person and for use in describing tactile 3D models .

— Use an overhead projector to show step-by-step instructions. Mask all the instructions except the one(s) that you want to present.

— Use an opaque projector whenever possible to enlarge a text or manual.

— All coloured objects used for identification related to a lesson, experiment, or other directions should be labelled with a Braille label maker or otherwise tacitly coded for most students with vision impairments.

— Describe, in detail, visual occurrences, visual media, and directions including all pertinent aspects that involve sight.

— Use a sighted narrator or descriptive video (preferably the latter) to describe aspects of videos or laser disks.

— Describe, in detail, all pertinent visual occurrences or chalkboard writing.

— Where needed, have lesson or direction materials Brailled, use an enlarged activity script, or recorded ahead of time, for class handouts.

— Have tactile 3D models, raised line drawings, or thermoforms available to supplement drawings or graphics in a tactile format when needed.

— Whenever possible, use actual objects for three dimensional representations.

— Modify instructions for auditory/tactile presentation.

— Use raised line drawings for temporary tactile presentations.

— Use an overhead projector, chalkboard, graphs, or slides as you would normally, but provide more detailed oral descriptions, possibly supplemented with thermoforms where appropriate.

— Allow student to use a tape recorder for recording classroom presentations or the text.

— Make all handouts and assignments available in an appropriate form: e.g., regular print, large print, Braille, or on a cassette, depending on the students optimal mode of communication.

— Use a monocular or a private eye (electronic miniature television) or similar devices for long range observations of chalk board or demonstration table presentations.

Laboratory

1) Describe and tactually/spatially familiarize the student with the lab and all equipment to be used.

2) Consider alternate activities/exercises that can be utilized with less difficulty for the student, but has the same or similar learning objectives.

3) Use an enlarged activity script, directions, or readings for a low vision student (or taped script for a student who is blind) for use with tactile 3D models.

4) Make all handouts and assignments available in the appropriate form for the student: e.g., regular print, large print, Braille, or tape depending on the students optimal mode of communication.

5) Assistance may be needed for converting certain laboratory materials from a visual to a tactile format.

6) Have the student with a vision impairment do a trial run on the equipment before the activity.

7) Allow more time for the laboratory activities.

8) Always try to keep materials, supplies, and equipment in the same places.

9) Use a microprojector or similar device to help the visually impaired student to examine images from a microscope.

10) Place the student and/or tape recorder an appropriate distance from the activity to permit hearing and/or the recording of results or observations.

11) Use an overhead projector or opaque projector to show step-by-step instructions. Mask all the instructions except the one(s) that you want followed for students with vision impairments.

12) Use Descriptive Video for videos or laser disks. If Descriptive Video is not available, use a sighted narrator to describe movies, videos, laser disks, or slides.

13) Provide means for the acquisition and/or recording of data in an appropriate mode for the student.

14) Use tag shapes for showing relationships (such as distance comparisons) buttons, or other markers on a "layout" board.

15) A Braille label maker will be useful for identifying materials and containers in the laboratory for the vision impaired student with a vision impairment who reads Braille.

16) Make equipment available that the student with a vision impairment can access in interpreting and understanding the results of laboratory exercises (e.g. audible readout voltmeters, calculators, talking thermometers, magnifiers, etc.

17) Use a hot plate for heating instead of Bunsen burner.

18) Label material, supplies, and equipment with regular print, large print, and/or Braille, as appropriate for the vision impaired student.

19) Pair the student with a vision impairment with a sighted student. Then have the non-impaired student describe the activities and outcomes as they are observed.

20) A low vision projection screen can be use to magnify images up to 720X.

21) Use a portable communication board to provides auditory scanning of laboratory materials such as: pictographic symbols, letters, and/or words.

22) When using a computer, the student with a visual disability can use a voice input device or a remote voice system to verbally enter commands.

23) Prior to the enrollment of a student with a visual impairment in class, obtain laboratory equipment that have available ability to produce adaptive outputs such as: a large screen, print materials, or various audio output devices.

24) Various Braille devices can be used to assists vision impaired students when reading.

25) For "reading" the outputs of balances and other instruments, one can use a Braille N' Speak device (Blazie Engineering)

26) Have a lab assistant help you if necessary to make sure that students with visual impairments are being assisted.

Group Interaction and Discussion

— Describe and tactually/spatially familiarize the student to the classroom.

— Place the student and/or recorder an appropriate distance from the activity to permit recording of material.

— Use a tape recorder.

— If the student is partially sighted, be sure he/she is seated where lighting is appropriate.

— Use a note taker who takes notes in the appropriate mode.

Text Reading Systems

— Paid or volunteer readers or writers can assist a student with a visual impairment with texts, materials, and library readings.

— Offer to read, or arrange to have read, written information for a person with a visual impairment, when appropriate.

— Arrange, ahead of time, for audio book acquisition of the text or other reading materials through the Talking Book Service, Recordings for the Blind and Dyslexic, text reading systems, or audio output devices.

— Various Braille devices can be used to assists vision impaired students when reading.

Field Experiences

— Make all handouts, safety information, and assignments available in an appropriate form (e.g., regular print, large print, tactile Braille, or cassette).

— Consider alternate activities/exercises that can be utilized with less difficulty for the student, but has the same or similar learning objectives.

— Use a sighted guide.

— Do detailed description and narration of objects seen in science centers, museums, and/or field activities.

— The use of a laser cane or mowat sensor can be useful in assisting the student in unfamiliar surroundings.

— An enlarged activity script, directions, or readings for descriptions of a field/activity for a low vision person to use with field observations.

— Suggest that the student use a standard tape recorder.

Research

— Review and discuss with the student the steps involved in a research activity. Think about which step(s) may be difficult for the specific functional limitations of the student and jointly devise accommodations for that student.

— Use appropriate lab and field strategies according to the nature of the research.

— Various Braille Devices can be used to assists vision impaired students when reading.

— Suggest that the student use a tape recorder with a sighted person on the various activities.

— Research on Mowatt sensor

Testing

- Make arrangements for tactile examinations, if touch is not normally permitted (say, in a museum) then contact the curator for tactile access to a museum display items or say, in a zoo for access to a plant/animal species and/or collection).
- Place the student being tested close to the activity if tactile examination is necessary.
- Present examinations in a form that will be unbiased to visually impaired students. Ask the student for the approach he/she finds to be most accessible.
- One possible accessible method is to record test questions on tape and have the students record their answers on tape in an area which has minimal disturbance for other students.
- Use an enlarged activity script, directions, or readings to go along with the testing material.
- Allow more time.
- Allow calculators to be used during the test.
- Make use of larger print (e.g. 14 pt; 20 pt sized or as needed).
- Make use of visual magnification (magnifier or magnifying machine), audiocassette, Braille/Braille graphs/Braille device for written responses, large block answer sheet.

3

Education of Children with Hearing Impairment

DEFINITION OF DEAFNESS

The word *deaf* is used and understood in two ways. First, there is the medical, pathological and audiological sense of the word, in which *deafness* describes a disease or impairment. *Deaf*, often capitalized, may also describe a culture and community whose members may or may not be able to hear but for whom the medical condition of deafness is somehow relevant or present to their lives. This split in perspectives causes what can seem to be odd constructions using the word. For example, a person could be said to be deaf but not Deaf. Conversely, one could be Deaf and yet not be deaf. Therefore, it can be important to discern which sense the word is being used by a speaker or writer.

Causes of deafness

There are four major causes of hearing loss.

Genetic

— Deafness can be inherited. Both dominant and recessive genes exist which can cause deafness. If a family has a dominant gene for deafness it will persist across generations because it will be expressed in the offspring even if it is inherited from only one parent. If a family had genetic deafness caused by a recessive gene it will not always manifest as it will have to be passed onto offspring from both parents.

— Dominant and recessive deafness can be syndromic or nonsyndromic. Recent gene mapping has identified dozens of nonsyndromic dominant (DFNA#) and recessive (DFNB#) forms of deafness.

— The most common type of congenital deafness in developed countries is DFNB1, also known as Connexin 26 deafness or GJB2-related deafness.

— The most common dominant syndromic forms of deafness include Stickler syndrome and Waardenburg syndrome.

— The most common recessive syndromic forms of deafness are Pendred syndrome, Large vestibular aqueduct syndrome and Usher syndrome.

Disease or illness

— High fevers can damage the inner ear

— Measles often results in auditory nerve damage

Medications

— Some antibiotics can cause deafness in higher doses.

Physical trauma

— There can be damage either to the ear itself or to the brain centres that process the aural information conveyed by the ears.

— Victims of head injury are especially vulnerable to hearing loss or tinnitus, either temporary or permanent.

— Exposure to very loud noise (90 dB or more, such as jet engines at close range) can cause progressive hearing loss. Exposure to a single event of extremely loud noise (such as explosions) can also cause temporary or permanent hearing loss.

Medical treatments

In addition to hearing aids there exist cochlear implants of increasing complexity and effectiveness. These are most useful in treating the postlingually or late deafened individuals. Some success has been observed in implanting these devices in deaf-born infants and very young children, although the practice is still controversial.

Adaptations to deafness

Many deaf individuals use certain assistive devices in their daily lives. Deaf individuals can communicate by telephone using Telecommunications devices for the deaf (TDD) Some people call the device by its original name of teletypewriter (TTY). This device looks like a typewriter or word processor and transmits typed text over the telephone. Other names in common use are textphone and minicom. In 2004, mobile textphone devices came onto the market for the first time allowing simultaneous two way text communication.

In the U.S., the UK, the Netherlands and many other western countries there are telephone relay services so that a deaf person can communicate with a hearing person via a human translator. Wireless and internet text messaging are beginning to take over the role of the TDD. Other assistive devices include those that use flashing lights to signal events such as a ringing telephone, a doorbell, or a fire alarm.

Historical attitudes toward deafness

For much of time, deaf people were thought to be mentally

retarded. Isolated deaf people rarely, if ever, learned language, which is fundamental to much of human thought. Aristotle believed that the deaf were incapable of learning or thinking. The kind of prejudice based on speech and hearing that Aristotle expressed has influenced attitudes toward deaf people and the teaching methods for and expectations of deaf students for ages.

Education of the deaf

For most of history deaf people were not thought capable of learning and so were not educated at all. The first free school for the deaf in history was set up in France in 1760. France used the signs that the students used to communicate with one another in order to teach to them. In other places, the emphasis was on lipreading and speaking English. The debate between which of these two approaches is the most efficacious to deaf students has gone on for hundreds of years and continues today.

Oralism versus manualism

There are two opposing perspectives on how to teach language to deaf people:

- Manualism holds that deaf students should be taught primarily in sign language.
- Oralism holds that deaf students should be taught primarily (or exclusively) to speak and lip-read.

The rationale behind the latter method is that deaf people will have to interact with hearing people most of the time, so they must learn to communicate as hearing people do. The rationale behind the former method is that sign language is a natural form of communication while lip-reading and speaking are extremely difficult for those who cannot hear. Those who prefer the sign-language method take the approach that spoken language should be used only as an auxiliary language. In practice, deaf people have been observed to learn and communicate much faster and more fluently when taught in sign language than when taught orally.

In the U.S., the sign-language method was primarily used until 1880, when the second International Congress on the Education and Welfare of the Deaf (composed of 163 hearing and 1 deaf individual) voted to use the oral approach to teach deaf students. Part of the reason for the emphasis on oralism was the melting pot ideology, that everyone should share the same culture and speak the same language. Also, because sign language was not recognized as a true language, it seemed deficient as a method of communication. One of the major factors in changing public opinion was William Stokoe's findings, published in 1960, that American Sign Language was a true language.

The findings were not immediately accepted, but they played a major role in shifting the emphasis of teaching back toward manualism. A growing movement in deaf education today is called bi-bi, which stands for bilingualism/biculturalism. This method aims to respect and foster Deaf cultural identity, stress and strengthen sign language competence, while simultaneously teaching and encouraging skills that facillitate functioning in the dominant hearing culture, such as English mastery.

There are two kinds of cause in hearing impairments

— Pre-lingual hearing impairment in which the impairment is congenital, a condition that exists at birth, before the individual has acquired speech and language, thus rendering the disability more severe because the sufferer is unable to communicate from the outset.

— Post-lingual hearing impairment where hearing loss is adventitious and develops due to disease or trauma after the acquisition of speech and language, usually after the age of six.

Post-lingual hearing impairments are far more common than pre-lingual impairments. Typically, hearing loss is gradual, and often detected by family and friends of the people so affected long before the patients themselves will acknowledge the disability. In cases where the causes are environmental, the treatment is to eliminate or reduce these causes first of all, and then to fit patients with a hearing aid, especially if they are elderly. When the loss is due to heredity, total deafness is often the end result. On the one hand, persons suffering from gradual deterioration of their hearing are fortunate in that they have learned to speak. On the other, they often suffer from social isolation, because they can no longer understand their friends, who cannot communicate effectively with them.

Ultimately, unless the affected person becomes skilled in speech-reading (lip-reading), or receives a cochlear implant, he/she will depend on sign language for communication. In some cases, the loss is extremely sudden. Most often, the cause is unknown. Sometimes, it can be traced to specific diseases, such as meningitis, or to ototoxic medications, such as Gentamicin. In both cases, the final degree of loss varies. Some suffer only partial loss, while others become profoundly deaf. In the former case, hearing aids can be used with varying degrees of success, depending on the exact nature of the loss. In the latter, ultimately the affected person will depend on speech-reading and/or sign language for communication.

Partial Loss of Hearing

People who are hard-of-hearing have moderate amounts of hearing loss but not enough to be considered deaf. The phrase hard-of-hearing, normally used as an adjective or adverb, can also be used as a noun, referring to people with hearing impairment as the hard-of-hearing. Hearing impaired persons with partial loss of hearing may find that the quality of their hearing varies from day to day, or from one situation to another. They will also, to a greater or lesser extent depend on both hearing-aids and lip-reading, similarly to more severely disabled people. They may perhaps not always be aware of it, but they do admit to it being important to see the speaker's face in conversation.

Many people with hearing loss have better hearing in the lower frequency ranges (low tones), and cannot hear as well or at all in the higher frequencies. Some people may merely find it difficult to differentiate between words that begin with consonantal sounds such as the fricatives or sibilants s, z. or th, or the plosives d, t, b, or p. They may be unable to hear thin, high-pitched or metallic noises, such as birds chirping or singing, clocks ticking, etc. Often, they are able to hear and understand men's voices better than women's.

Others will find their condition so much worse if circumstances in their immediate environment affect the way they are able to use their hearing-aids, or prevent them from employing their lip-reading skills. A room with a high ceiling and a lot of reverberation will affect the sound of a speaker's voice adversely. The position of the listener, too, sitting at a right angle to the speaker at a long seminar table, thus being able to hear only with one, maybe the ineffectual ear, can make a difference. Difficulties can also arise for the listener trying to lip-read, if the speaker is sitting with his back against the light-source and is in this way obscuring his face.

The speaker's accent; the topic under discussion, possibly with many unfamiliar words; the softness of his voice; possibly his having a speech impediment; a habit of holding a hand in front of his mouth or turning his face away at times: all these tendencies cause problems to the hard-of-hearing, especially when they have to rely on lip-reading. The rustling of papers, and notebook pages being turned are precisely the noises that will be the first thing hearing-aids pick up.

Social Impact of hearing loss

Those who lose their hearing later in life, such as in late adolescence or adulthood, face their own challenges. For example, they must adjust to living with the adaptive devices that make it possible for them to live independently. They must also adapt to using hearing aids and/or learning sign language. Loneliness and depression can arise as a result of isolation (from the inability to communicate with friends and loved ones) and difficulty in accepting their disability. The challenge is made greater by the need for those around them to adapt to the person's hearing loss.

How to communicate with someone who has a hearing loss

- Ask the person what will be most useful for them; this varies from one individual to another.
- Speak normally. Do not shout or over-enunciate. Both of these make it more difficult to understand speech, not less.
- Conversely, do not mumble, cover your mouth, or whisper when speaking. All of these can conceal vital speech-reading cues that hearing impaired people use to decipher what is being said. A "favourite" pet peeve of the hearing impaired is people who speak from another room - How are they to speech-read with a wall between them and the speaker? Additionally, speak while facing the hearing impaired person.
- If asked to repeat yourself, don't. Rephrase instead. By using different words, your friend will be able to use two data sets to understand what you meant. (This is good advice for those with normal hearing, too!) Obviously, if only one word was missed, you can try just repeating that word, or a synonym. This is the area where people vary most: some hearing-impaired people find rephrasing very frustrating, because they have to start over: when a sentence is repeated, they can put together the syllables or words they heard the first time with those in the repetition. When in doubt, ask "Should I repeat that exactly?"

— Emphasize keywords in your phrases. Most hearing-impaired people can piece together keywords (along with the context of the conversation) into a statement that they can understand.

— Reduce background noise by turning off the TV and radio, and closing windows. All of these can provide distractions that cause communication to break down completely. They also impede the perception of whatever auditory cues your friend is able to pick up and use.

— For small children learning to talk, use context to help them decipher what you are saying. (Additionally, some studies indicate that hearing impaired children who are allowed to lead conversation acquire speech much more successfully than those whose parents attempt to guide conversation for them.)

HEARING AID

A hearing aid is a device used to help the hard-of-hearing hear sounds better. In the past, a funnel-like amplification cone, called an "ear trumpet" or "ear horn", was used. Now, however, the most common style is a small electronic device that fits into the wearer's ear. The first variety of this device had a rectangular battery pack connected by a thin wire, intended to be held in a pocket. During the mid- to late 20th century, this type of power storage was replaced by a more inconspicuous sort in models in which small, circular batteries were placed in the inserted unit itself.

EDUCATIONAL PROGRAMMING FOR INDIVIDUALS WITH DEAF-BLINDNESS

Deaf-blindness is a term which indicates that there are deficits in both the auditory and visual senses, creating the need for modification of special educational practices for individuals with either deafness, blindness, or retardation alone. The term is best applied from a functional perspective which goes beyond medical and clinical determination of severity of two major sensory deficits. Historically, we have evidence that individuals with deaf-blindness can be educated successfully. However, until the middle of the 1960's, individuals identified as having deaf-blindness were born with such infrequency that educational programs for them were available only in a few locations. With the rubella epidemic in the 1960's came an increase in the number of children who were diagnosed as having congenital deaf-blindness. This larger population created a need for the development of programs, curricula, methods, materials, and trained personnel to meet the students' educational requirements in locations throughout the world.

Organizations of parents and professionals were formed and governments responded by supporting efforts to produce and distribute special methods and materials for use with students with deaf-blindness. These efforts were largely successful and resulted in appropriate and accessible education for students with deaf-blindness due primarily to rubella. However, the diversity of etiologies within the population of individuals with deaf-blindness is greatly increasing. This diversity creates a wide range of functional abilities within the group of individuals with deaf-blindness. The diversity of etiologies may also contribute to the large number of individuals who are to identified as having deaf-blindness until they are about ten years old. Data indicate that very few of the students reported in the National Census of Individuals with Deaf-blindness are identified while they are pre-school age.

This shift in age of identification as well as functional diversity has surfaced at a time when public awareness of deaf-blindness (particularly within the United States) has diminished. The low awareness level is a result of many factors, including an increase in professional interest in individuals with severe and multiple disabilities, and the common notion that rubella is the only cause of deaf-blindness. Another important factor that emerged in the 1970's and 1980's was the willingness of the federal government to allow funds designated for programs and services for individuals with deaf-blindness to be allocated to other special populations. Individuals with deaf-blindness have unique needs in he areas of communication, mobility, and sensory development that must be addressed. Intervention during the early developmental period is critical for the emotional, social, communication and cognitive development of the child.

Principles of Educational Programming

1. Early identification of sensory deficits is essential to provide optimal opportunities for individuals with deaf-blindness.
2. Communication is the cornerstone of an educational plan for a student who has deaf-blindness.
   a. No one mode of communication is appropriate for all individuals with deaf-blindness. Communication options may include: movement based signals, object cues, natural gestures, signs, tactual symbols, braille, oral and written language and augmentative communication.
   b. A deaf-blind individual's needs, abilities and preferences should determine the primary mode of communication.
   c. Communication with individuals with deaf-blindness is frequently accomplished in a one-to-one relationship.
3. Educational placements for children and youth with deaf-blindness should be selected on the basis of individual abilities and needs rather than predetermined by an educational label or type of service currently available. Age of onset of sensory impairments, amount of auditory and visual impairments, mode of communication, cognition, and existence of additional disabilities are major factors in determining the appropriate educational settings.
4. Teachers who have had specific training in the educational specialty of deaf-blindness are necessary to provide optimal integrated programming for students with dual sensory impairments. Although there is a severe shortage of trained

teachers, a student with deaf-blindness must have access to specially trained individuals who have knowledge of the impact of concomitant sensory deficits on the development of communication, cognition, motor skills and social/emotional well-being. This integrated knowledge produces a better educational environment for a child than a program patched together from recommendations by specialists from related areas.

5. There are a variety of appropriate educational alternatives for children and youth with deaf-blindness:

   a. Regular education classrooms with appropriate support services and technology;

   b. Classrooms for students with visual impairments;

   c. Classrooms for students with hearing impairments;

   d. Classrooms for students with deaf-blindness;

   e. Classrooms for students with severe/profound impairments;

   f. Residential schools for the blind;

   g. Residential schools for the deaf;

   h. Specific programs in residential schools for the deaf and/or blind;

   i. Hospital or medical settings;

   j. In-home services.

6. A functional program that is integrated into the community is essential for individuals with deaf-blindness. That program must include opportunities to develop communication, social, recreational and leisure skills, prevocational/vocational training, transition planning, self-help and domestic skills, and orientation and independence within all environments.

7. Integration of appropriate related and support services is necessary for a successful educational program for a student

with deaf-blindness. Specialists in orientation and mobility, regular physical education, adaptive physical education, speech pathology, physical therapy, occupational therapy, audiology and auditory training, vision services, and psychological services may contribute assessment, direct instruction, or consultation.

Needs for the Future A number of advances in educational deaf-blind individuals in recent years have been made. Many programs must be continued, many need enhancement, and new and innovative programs and services must be encouraged. Professionals, families and consumers should:

a. Monitor governmental funding and regulation.

b. Advocate for quality services for deaf-blind children, youth, and adults on the international, national, and local level.

c. Advocate for increased funding of personnel preparation programs.

d. Organize and participate in conferences, workshops, and training sessions.

e. Provide public awareness and information about deaf-blindness.

f. Advocate for early identification of deaf-blindness.

g. Advocate for efforts to increase the accuracy of the census of individuals with deaf-blindness at both the local and national level. Accurate reporting will result in an improved programming for the educational and vocational needs of individuals.

h. Cooperate with the National Coalition on Deaf-Blindness and the International Association for the Education of the Deaf-Blind and others concerned with individuals with deaf-blindness.

i. Advocate for preservice training in the specialty of deaf-blindness for teachers, counsellors, rehabilitation workers and orientation and mobility specialists.

j. Encourage teacher preparation programs for the visually impaired, hearing impaired, and severe disabilities to add deaf-blindness and alternative communication techniques including movement based communication to their curricula.

k. Actively participate in local, national, and international organizations of professionals, families and consumers.

Position DVI recognizes the uniqueness of each individual with deaf-blindness and supports decisions made by educators and parents which reflect a student's own mode of communication, most appropriate and enabling educational placement, and integration of appropriate related services. DVI upholds the right of an individual with deaf-blindness to have a specially trained teacher. In order to ensure access to needed services, DVI supports expansion of personnel preparation programs and services, and active support and cooperation of other national and international organizations working to increase awareness of, and services to, individuals with deaf-blindness, including infants, children, youth, and adults. DVI also supports the need for monitoring government programs and advocating for adequate funding for all deaf-blind programs and services.

Identification and Assessment

Most children with significant hearing loss will have been identified through an audiological assessment prior to entering the school system. A few children, however, particularly those with less severe hearing loss, may not have been identified prior to school entry. Under the audiological services protocol agreement between the Ministries of Health and Education, all students in the initial school entry year receive a hearing screening. Any student who fails the screening should be referred to the nearest health unit or audiology clinic for a complete hearing assessment. Indeed, any student referred for special education services during his or her school career should be referred for a hearing assessment in order to determine whether an intermittent or chronic hearing loss is the primary cause of any exhibited learning or behavioural problem.

Hearing loss is generally measured in terms of decibel loss using standards agreed on internationally. However, decibel losses do not always correlate with educational implications and are therefore not a sole criterion for determination of need for educational intervention. Any degree of hearing loss has educational implications, so following the identification of a student's hearing loss an assessment to determine the strengths and weaknesses of the student in the areas of language development and communication skills may be required. This assessment, usually administered by a teacher of the deaf and hard of hearing, may include the administration of standardized tests in the areas of ability and achievement, as well as curriculum-based assessment and observation and teacher reports. Program planning decisions and recommendations for placement of the student in a specific program should occur only once a full assessment has been completed.

EDUCATIONAL PLANNING FOR CHILDREN WITH HEARING IMPAIRMENT

The educational program for a student who is deaf or hard of hearing should not be confined to the regular program but should also include specific instruction in:

— language development;

— auditory management;

— speech development;

— speech reading;

— sign language as required; and

— deaf culture when appropriate.

In addition to addressing the direct effects of hearing loss and language development, the IEP should address the social and vocational needs which arise as a result of the hearing loss and which are known to be significant. Most students who are deaf or hard of hearing can and should be educated in their local school district. Typically, programming for students with hearing loss involves one or more of the following services:

— a regular class with direct, frequent support from a qualified itinerant teacher of the deaf and hard of hearing;

— a resource room staffed by a teacher of the deaf and hard of hearing;

— a self-contained class staffed by a teacher of the deaf and hard of hearing who has access to the appropriate support services; and/or

— an individual program for students with hearing loss and additional special needs.

The prevalence of hearing loss is low. Therefore, the provision of a full range of services within a single school district is not always feasible. In such cases, school districts are encouraged to collaborate to provide regional programs that serve the needs of students in several districts. In particular, the social and emotional needs of adolescent students who are deaf or hard of hearing may require more than itinerant services. Where there are a sufficient number of students, local or regional school programs for the deaf and hard of hearing should be developed to launch a flexible and comprehensive program complete with qualified staff and the appropriate support services.

When the needs of a particular deaf or hard of hearing student cannot be met locally or regionally, or where special circumstances prevail, the student may be referred to the Provincial Educational Review Committee for Deaf and Hard of Hearing students for recommendations for programming and/ or determination of eligibility for Provincial Resource Programs designed for students with hearing loss.

PERSONNEL TEACHERS OF THE DEAF AND HARD OF HEARING

Where supplemental funding is requested by districts, teachers must have appropriate qualifications. A qualified teacher of the deaf and hard of hearing as one with: a valid B.C. Teaching Certificate

Where a district is unable to employ a qualified teacher of the deaf and hard of hearing, this requirement may be met by providing services through sharing arrangements with adjacent districts or through a fee-for-service arrangement with qualified specialist teachers of the deaf and hard of hearing.

Teacher assistants

If the support of a teacher assistant is warranted, the teacher of the deaf and hard of hearing should consult with the classroom teacher to assist in developing, directing, and monitoring the assistant's activities. Teacher assistants working with students who are deaf or hard of hearing should have sufficient training and understanding of hearing loss for the duties they are assigned. Teacher assistants should be able to demonstrate: an understanding of the social, emotional and educational implications of hearing loss; and competence in the communication mode of the student(s).

Where the role of the teacher assistant is to facilitate communication between the student and others in the environment the district should ensure the teacher assistant can demonstrate proficiency in the communication mode of the student. In instances where sign communication and/or oral interpretation is required and the individual is not a qualified interpreter, districts are advised to arrange for qualified interpreters to evaluate the communication competency of the teacher assistant.

STRATEGIES FOR TEACHING STUDENTS WITH HEARING IMPAIRMENTS

Over time, the average hearing impaired student shows an ever increasing gap in vocabulary growth, complex sentence comprehension and construction, and in concept formation as compared to students with normal hearing. Hearing impaired students often learn to "feign" comprehension with the end result being that the student does have optimal learning opportunities. Therefore, facilitative strategies for hearing impaired students are primarily concerned with various aspects of communication. Other problems arise because deafness is an invisible disability. It is easy for teachers to "forget about it" and treat the student as not having a disability. It has also been shown that hearing impaired students with good English skills also have good science concept formation.

Deaf: "A hearing impairment which is so severe that a child is impaired in processing linguistic information through hearing, with or without amplification, which adversely affects educational performance."

Hard of Hearing: "A hearing impairment, whether permanent of fluctuating, which adversely affects a child's educational performance but which is not included under the definition of 'deaf'."

Deaf-Blind: "Simultaneous hearing and visual impairments, the combination of which causes such severe communication and other developmental and educational problems that a child cannot be accommodated in special education programs solely for deaf children or blind children."

General Courtesy

— Since facial expressions, gestures, and other body language will help convey your message:

— Get the attention of a student with a hearing impairment before speaking and communicating and always face the student.

— If not facing a student with a hearing impairment, gently touch a student on the shoulder or on the arm to indicate that you want to talk to him/her.

— Do not be alarmed if the student does not understand and you cannot understand him/her. Generally, you will become accustomed to each other in time.

— When communicating, always face the student with a hearing impairment.

— Facial expressions, gestures, and other body language will help convey your message.

— For reinforcement repeat new vocabulary in different contexts.

— Sequence topics so that new material is related to that previously learned.

— The use of visual aids is most helpful since vision is the student's primary means of receiving information.

— Use written announcements (assignments, due dates, exam dates, changes in the class schedule, special event dates, etc.).

— If ambiguities or difficulties arise in the home concerning assignments or lessons, have the parents make a note of these difficulties. Follow-up in written detail.

— Provide an outline in advance of the lesson/activity to give to the student in advance, also list your expectations.

— Write all homework assignments, class instructions, and procedural changes on the chalkboard.

— Use captioned films, videos, and laser disks.

— Use interpreter where needed.

— Avoid seating the student in heavy traffic areas.

— Do not touch or pet a hearing dog. These animals are working animals and it may be hazardous for the hearing impaired student if the dog is distracted.

— Avoid vibrations and excessive noise.

— Make chalkboard notes legible.

— Do not talk while writing on chalkboard.

— Eliminate background noises. Sounds taken for granted and normally ignored by hearing individuals, are amplified by a hearing aid and interfere with the communication of the person who is hard of hearing.

— Establish, with the student, a procedure in case of an emergency. For example, agree that for a fire drill (or fire) the teacher will write on board "Fire drill FIRE—go out backdoor." (Also, if you have a signing student, learn the signs for emergency, fire, go, etc.)

— Get the attention of a person with a hearing impairment before speaking.

— If necessary, use written notes to communicate.

— Supplement audible alarm systems with simple visual alarms such as flashing lights.

— When teaching a student with a hearing impairment, ask where he/she would like to sit, in order to communicate in an optimal manner.

General Strategies

— Bring to the student's attention science role models with disabilities with a similar disability to that of the student. Point out that this individual got ahead by a combination of effort and by asking for help when needed.

— Obtain feedback from your hearing impaired students at every opportunity as an indicator of the student's level of understanding.

— If the student lip-reads:

— Have students sit closer to the lecturer.

— Look directly at the student.

— Speak slowly, naturally, and clearly.

— Slowing down slightly may help.

— Do not exaggerate your lip movements or shout.

— If you have a mustache, keep it well trimmed.

— If the student uses an interpreter:

— Speak directly to the student rather than to the interpreter

— Signing may be distracting at first, but you and the other students will soon become accustomed to the interpreter's presence.

— Give the student and the interpreter outlines of the lecture or written material, in advance, so that they can become familiar with new technical vocabulary.

— Interpreters should not give their opinion of a student's progress as this can violate the student's rights.

— Provide scripts of video and laser media when possible for both the interpreter and the student with a hearing disability (with or without captioning).

— The interpreter is not to answer lesson related questions from the student with a hearing impairment. The student should direct all lesson related questions to the instructor.

— The interpreter should stand closer to the section of the chalkboard that is being used by the instructor, thereby allowing the student to simultaneously see both the signs and the writing on the board.

— When writing materials for hearing impaired students:

  — Break up long sentences.

  — Reduce difficult vocabulary load.

  — Reduce concept density.

  - — When using a pronoun be sure that the antecedent is very clear.
  - — Do not omit words such as: "that" where such words will clarify a sentence connection.
  - — Stay with simple coordinating conjunctions (e.g., but, so, for, and) and avoid less common transitional words (e.g., however, as a consequence, nevertheless, although).
  - — Keep cause-and-effect expressions in a very simple in form.
  - — Keep conditional expressions which influence the meaning of a statement to a minimum (such as; if, when, assuming that, suppose, provided that, etc.).
  - — If there is no other way to avoid using a difficult word, include a brief explanation in parentheses, however keep parenthetical explanations to a minimum.

— If an important basic or technical word is to be taught:

  - — Make meaning and application absolutely clear.
  - — Use context as a memory aid.
  - — For a new term, repeat the word numerous times in a variety of contexts.

— Certain language forms are generally to be AVOIDED:

  - — Passive voice verbs.
  - — Negative forms of verbs and other expressions of negation.
  - — Too many modifying forms, such as prepositional phrases, relative clauses. (If a relative clause must be used, the relative pronoun [who, which, that, where, etc.] should be next to the word to which it refers).
  - — Stylistic embellishments, such as rhetorical inversions.

— Colloquial and idiomatic expressions.

— Cut wordiness while retaining simple English.

— Avoid the use of idioms.

Teacher Presentation

The Americans with Disabilities Act (ADA) requires that materials and information be available in alternate formats whenever possible and reasonable to do so. It is a good idea to assume that there will always be people in your audience who have difficulties seeing your material or hearing your presentation. When you make your presentation accessible to persons with hearing or vision loss, everyone in your audience will benefit. Strategies to Create Information Access for Persons with Hearing Loss

Environment

* Provide the audience with a clear and direct view of your mouth and face.
* Speak from a well-lighted area of the room.
* Reduce background noise by turning off slide projectors or other types of apparatus when not in use.
* Speak clearly and naturally and at your normal pace, unless you are asked to slow down.
* For those with mustaches, trim so the lips show clearly

Interpreters

* Sign language interpreters are certified professionals who use American Sign Language or Signed English to interpret spoken English for people who are deaf or hard of hearing.
* If a sign language interpreter is used, introduce yourself to the interpreter and go over technical and specialized

vocabulary before beginning presentations.

* Interpreters at conference presentations should stand on one side of the platform at the front of the room, even with extra lighting if needed, in order to be clearly seen from anywhere in the audience.

* When replying to a query from a hearing impaired individual using an interpreter, speak to the hearing impaired person, NOT to the interpreter.

Captioning

* Captioning is the on screen text display of spoken words or sounds that are part of a video or film presentation. Captioners are usually trained as stenographers and use special software to add captions to a previously produced video.

* Video or film production services can also include captions as part of your original production.

* If showing a videotape, have it captioned. (Open captions are preferred for this purpose as closed captions can be seen only with the use of a decoder.) If there is a script or transcription already available, this will make the captioner's job easier.

* If captioning is not feasible, arrange for an interpreter to sign the audio portion of the tape. If possible, make the tape available to the interpreter a day, or so, before your presentation.

Auditory materials

* Audiotapes, videotapes, and other auditory materials can be translated into print format to make them accessible to people who are deaf or hard-of-hearing. When transcribing video, be sure to mention any sounds and actions that may occur independent of the spoken text, and indicate

settings or changes of scene as well. To find a transcriber, look in the Yellow Pages under "Transcribing Services."

* If available, use Assistive Learning Devices. These devices consist of a transmitter that sends electronically enhanced sound to receivers worn by individuals who are hard-of-hearing.

* If available, use A Computer-Aided Realtime Translation (CART), which, usually originally trained as a court or stenographer, uses a stenotype machine with a phonetic keyboard and special software.

A computer translates the phonetic symbols into English captions almost instantaneously. Presenters should provide conference organizers with a copy of their presentation or outline and a list of any unusual or technical words that will be used. The CART reporters will add these words to their computer to make translation faster and more accurate. For conference workshops, captions should be output to a large screen located to one side of the presentation area. Lights in this section of the room should be kept low so that the words on the screen can be easily read.

— Avoid standing in front of windows or light sources that may silhouette the instructor and hinder visual cues.

— Begin explanations with concrete examples, working from the concrete to the abstract.

— Present only one source of visual information at a time.

— Erase the chalkboard except for the items being discussed to reduce "visual pollution."

— Engage the attention of the student with a hearing impairment before communicating with the class.

— If possible, face the light source and keep your hands away from your face when speaking.

— Use an FM audio trainer for hard-of-hearing students.

— If a lip reader, refer to General Strategies.

— Use captioned films/videos/laser disks, whenever possible.

— If the student with a hearing impairment does not understand, try repeating. If the student still does not understand, rephrase a thought or use a different word order.

— Repeat the questions other students in the class asked so that students with hearing impairments know what you are refering to.

— Maximize the use of visual media.

— It is crucial that students with hearing impairments have good note takers. It is impossible to simultaneously lip-read and take notes, or to watch/read an interpreter and take notes.

— Carbonless note taking paper can be used. The paid or volunteer note taker needs to take legible notes and then give the student with a hearing impairment the original (or a copy).

— Obtain feedback from your student at every opportunity as an indicator of the student's level of understanding.

— For reinforcement repeat new vocabulary in different contexts.

— Sequence topics so that new material is related to that previously learned.

— The use of visual aids is most helpful since vision is the student's primary means of receiving information.

— Use written announcements (assignments, due dates, exam dates, changes in the class schedule, special event dates, etc.).

— If ambiguities or difficulties arise in the home concerning assignments or lessons, have the parents make a note of these difficulties. Follow-up in written detail.

— Provide an outline in advance of the lesson/activity to give to the student in advance, also list your expectations.

— Write all homework assignments, class instructions, and procedural changes on the chalkboard.

— Use captioned films, videos, and laser disks.

— Use interpreter where needed.

— Avoid seating the student in heavy traffic areas.

— Reduce excessive noise as much as possible to facilitate communication.

Laboratory

— Refer to the section on interpreters and lip reading above in the General Strategies.

— Consider alternate activities/exercises that can be utilized with less difficulty for the student, but has the same or similar learning objectives.

— Avoid seating the student in heavy traffic areas.

— As you demonstrate a procedure or technique, deliberately alternate between speaking (use FM audio trainer for hard-of-hearing) and manipulating the materials. This allows the student who is hearing impaired to look at one thing at a time.

— If the student does not understand, try repeating; if the student still does not understand, rephrase a thought or use a different word order.

— Keep visual pollution on chalkboard to a minimum. Leave on the chalkboard only what you are discussing.

— Write new vocabulary words on the chalk board before a lesson or laboratory.

— Make chalkboard notes legible.

— Do not talk while writing on chalkboard.

— Maximize the use of visual media and demonstrations.

— Repeat new vocabulary in different contexts for reinforcement.

— Assign students with hearing impairments to a laboratory station that allows an unobstructed view of the chalkboard and the instructor and/or interpreter.

— Begin explanations with concrete examples, working from the concrete to the abstract.

— Insure that the student with a hearing impairment receives information about any changes in experimental procedure by writing on the board or paper.

— Label equipment and materials to aid in the learning of new vocabulary items.

— Provide concise, step-by-step directions prior to the laboratory activity and preview it with the student, if possible.

— Provide indicator lights for the on/off status of equipment.

— When a partner is needed, the teacher should assist in finding an understanding lab partner for a student with a hearing impairment.

— Use captioned film/video/laser disk material.

— Obtain feedback from your hearing impaired students at every opportunity as an indicator of the student's level of understanding.

— Use signaling devices to alert the student to a significant sound in the lab.

— Use an overhead projector to show step-by-step instructions.

— Mask all the instructions except the one that you want followed next.

— Write all homework assignments and laboratory procedural changes on the chalkboard.

— Present only one source of visual information at a time.

— Use written announcements (assignments, due dates, exam dates, changes in the class schedule, special event dates, etc.).

— In advance, provide an outline of the activity and give to the student your expectations.

— If non-captioned videos or movies are shown, a dim light is needed so that the student who uses an interpreter can see the interpreter's signing.

Reading

— Provide or adapt reading materials at appropriate reading levels and provide resource material at these same reading levels (see writing section in the general strategies).

— Use highly visual materials (e.g., many figures, pictures, diagrams) in reading assignments.

— Use reading materials that follow the writing guidelines given above in the General Strategies section.

— Writing styles for hearing impaired individuals:

— When writing materials for hearing impaired students:

—Break up long sentences.

—Reduce difficult vocabulary load.

—Reduce concept density.

— When using a pronoun be sure that the antecedent is very clear.

— Do not omit words such as: "that" where such words will clarify a sentence connection.

— Stay with simple coordinating conjunctions (e.g., but, so, for, and) and avoid less common transitional words (e.g., however, as a consequence, nevertheless, although).

- — Keep cause-and-effect expressions in a very simple in form.
- — Keep conditional expressions which influence the meaning of a statement to a minimum).
- — If there is no other way to avoid using a difficult word, include a brief explanation in parentheses, however keep parenthetical explanations to a minimum.

— If an important basic or technical word is to be taught:

- — Make meaning and application absolutely clear.
- — Use context as a memory aid.
- — For a new term, repeat the word numerous times in a variety of contexts.

— Certain language forms are generally to be AVOIDED:

- — Passive voice verbs.
- — Negative forms of verbs and other expressions of negation.
- — Too many modifying forms, such as prepositional phrases, relative clauses. (If a relative clause must be used, the relative pronoun [who, which, that, where, etc.] should be next to the word to which it refers).
- — Stylistic embellishments, such as rhetorical inversions.
- — Colloquial and idiomatic expressions.
- — Cut wordiness while retaining simple English.
- — Avoid the use of idioms.

— Group Interaction and Discussion

- — Be quite clear as to which topic is being discussed.
- — Expect and encourage the student to participate in class by answering questions, giving reports, and volunteering for other verbal activities.

— Clearly identify who is speaking or asking a question (pointing is OK).

— In group or team settings, develop procedures so the student who is hearing impaired can express his/her communication needs to others.

— In group situations or discussions which include a student who is speech reading (lip reading) it is very helpful to have students sit in a horseshoe or circle for better inclusion of students with hearing impairments.

— Repetitions or summaries of the most relevant classroom questions, responses, and discussions are helpful to the student with a hearing impairment.

— Show special awareness. Call the person who has a hearing impairment by name to initiate communication, (or a nod or a hand gesture is acceptable).

— You may need to get the student's attention by tapping him/her gently on the shoulder, arm, or waving your hand or using a similar visual signal.

— A circle is the best seating arrangement for a hearing impaired student. Seat the student with his/her "better" ear towards the class.

Field Experiences

— Adapt as many activities as possible to a visual mode.

— Consider alternate activities/exercises that can be utilized with less difficulty for the student, but has the same or similar learning objectives.

— Whenever possible, allow for direct access to and manipulation of materials.

— Use flash cards for clarity in field exercises.

— Use an Interpreter.

Research

— Review and discuss with the student the steps involved in a research activity. Think about which step(s) may be difficult for the specific functional limitations of the student and jointly devise accommodations for that student.

— Use appropriate lab and field strategies.

Testing

— Refer to the writing section of the general strategies prior to writing test questions.

— After tests or quizzes, give answers by using the overhead projector or give answers in writing.

— Avoid overly complicated language in exam questions and clearly separate items when spacing them on the exam sheet.

— Avoid the use of abbreviations or idioms, except for standard ones.

— Due to difficulty with vocabulary, students may require extra time.

— Interpreters may be asked to interpret a test. Because of the complex language involved, an interpreter can often rephrase a question so that a student is able to better understand the intent of the question.

— Interpreters should not be used as proctors for tests.

— Supplement oral or signed explanations with written material.

— Use short sentences because they are easier and quicker to comprehend than longer sentences.

— Keep the test reading materials at appropriate reading levels.

— Provide small group setting with preferetial seating, auditory amplification, and screens to block out distraction, allowing students to hear more clearly.

4

Education of Children with Mental Retardation

DEFINITION OF MENTAL RETARDATION

Mental retardation (abbreviated as MR), is a term for a person who has limitations in mental functioning and in skills such as communicating, taking care of him or herself, and social skills. A general, defined condition with various symptoms, caused by a lack of development of the brain before birth. These limitations will cause a child to learn and develop more slowly than a typical child. Children who have retardation may take longer to learn to speak, walk, and take care of their personal needs such as dressing or eating. They are likely to have trouble learning in school. They will learn, but it will take them longer. There may be some things they cannot learn.

There are three criteria before a person is considered to have mental retardation, their IQ is below 75, they have significant limits in two or more adaptive behavioural areas, and the condition is present since childhood. Down syndrome, fetal alcohol syndrome and fragile X are the three most common genetic causes of mental retardation. Mental retardation is claimed to not be a disease. Mental retardation is also claimed to not be a type of mental illness, such as depression. There is no cure for mental retardation. However, with appropriate supports most individuals with retardation can learn to do many things.

SIGNS OF MENTAL RETARDATION

There are many signs of mental retardation. For example, retarded children may:

— sit up, crawl, or walk later than other children;

— learn to talk later, or have trouble speaking,

— find it hard to remember things,

— not understand how to pay for things,

— have trouble understanding social rules,

— have trouble seeing the consequences of their actions,

— have trouble solving problems, and/or

— have trouble thinking logically.

About 87 percent of retards will only be a little slower than average in learning new information and skills. When they are children, their limitations may not be obvious. They may not even be diagnosed as having mental retardation until they get to school. As they become adults, many people with retardation can live independently and may not be recognized by others in the community as having a disability. The remaining 13 percent of individuals with mental retardation score below 50 on IQ tests. These people will have more difficulty in school, at home, and in the community. A person with more severe retardation will need more intensive support his or her entire life. Every retarded child is able to learn, develop, and grow. With help, all retarded children can live a satisfying life.

How is Mental Retardation Diagnosed?

Mental retardation is diagnosed by looking at two main things. These are:

— the ability of a person's brain to learn, think, solve problems, and make sense of the world (called IQ or intellectual functioning); and

— whether the person has the skills he or she needs to live independently (called adaptive behaviour, or adaptive functioning).

Intellectual functioning, or IQ, is usually measured by a test called an IQ test. The average score is 100. People scoring below 70 to 75 are thought to have mental retardation. To measure adaptive behaviour, professionals look at what a child can do in comparison to other children of his or her age. Certain skills are important to adaptive behaviour. These are:

— daily living skills, such as getting dressed, going to the bathroom, and feeding one's self;

— communication skills, such as understanding what is said and being able to answer;

— social skills with peers, family members, adults, and others.

To diagnose mental retardation, professionals look at the person's mental abilities (IQ) and his or her adaptive skills.

Ranges of IQ

The following data based on the Wechsler adult IQ test (WAIS) was used in 1958: Today the following ranges are in standard use:

Class	IQ
Profound mental retardation	below 20
Severe mental retardation	20-34
Moderate mental retardation	35-49
Mild mental retardation	50-69
Borderline deficiency	70-79

CAUSES OF MENTAL RETARDATION

Doctors have found many causes of mental retardation. The most common are:

— *Genetic conditions.* Sometimes mental retardation is caused by abnormal genes inherited from parents, errors when genes combine, or other reasons. Examples of genetic conditions include Down syndrome, Fragile X syndrome, and phenylketonuria (PKU).

— *Problems during pregnancy.* Mental retardation can result when the baby does not develop inside the mother properly. For example, there may be a problem with the way the baby's cells divide as it grows. A woman who drinks alcohol or gets an infection like rubella during pregnancy may also have a baby with mental retardation.

— *Problems at birth.* If a baby has problems during labour and birth, such as not getting enough oxygen, he or she may have mental retardation.

— *Health problems.* Diseases like whooping cough, the measles, or meningitis can cause mental retardation. Mental retardation can also be caused by extreme malnutrition (not eating right), not getting enough medical care, or by being exposed to poisons like lead or mercury.

Traditional terms

The three traditional terms denoting varying degrees of mental deficiency long predate psychiatry. They were originally used in English as simple forms of abuse, and this is still the main usage. Their now obsolete use as psychiatric technical definitions is of purely historical interest. There have been some efforts made among mental health professionals to discourage use of these terms.

Idiot stems from Gr. Idiotos - someone who does not participate in politics. The term now indicates the greatest degree of mental deficiency, where the mental age is 2 years or less, and the person cannot guard himself against common physical dangers. The term is gradually being replaced by the term profound mental retardation.

— Imbecility was a type of mental deficiency less extreme than idiocy and not necessarily inherited. It is now usually subdivided into two categories, known as severe mental retardation and moderate mental retardation.

— Moron was defined by the American Association for the Study of the Feeble-Minded in 1910, following work by Henry H. Goddard, as the term for an adult with a mental age between eight and twelve; mild mental retardation is now the more widely-accepted term for this condition. Alternative definitions of these terms based on IQ were also used.

PLANS FOR DEVELOPMENTALLY DISABLED CHILDREN

One of the best approaches to use to modify behaviours for mild to severe mentally disabled children is to use behavioural objectives.

Synopsis

— Behaviour objectives are statements that will describe no more than 3 things about the individual's behaviour.

— State exactly what the behaviour is that is being exhibited.

— Describe how often and how much the behaviour is being exhibited.

— Indicate the specific circumstances for when the behaviour occurs.

Behaviour objectives must be stated very specifically and in observalble and measurable terms, you need to think about how the behaviour will be measured. Writing effective behaviour objectives requires a great deal of practice, be prepared to reflect on your objectives and learn from them. You will soon find out what works and what doesn't.

Starting Out

What is the behaviour? Think about verbs when considering behaviour.

Examples could be: cries, feeds self, runs, sits, swallows, says, lifts, chews, holds, walks etc. These statements are all measurable and easily defined. Let's practice writing a few behaviour objectives using some of the above examples: If we use the word 'feeds self'. We can state that "Student LM will use a spoon without spilling food on 5 attempts to feed. We can use the word 'walks' and state that Student LM will walk to the coatrack at recess time without assistance. Both of these statements are clearly measurable and one can determine if the objective is being met successfully or not.

An important item to remember when stating your objectives is to specify a time limit for when the behaviour is being achieved. Specify the number of repetitions that will be required and state the accuracy level. You can also state the level of performance you are looking for. For example, feed him/herself without spilling food. You may also set the conditions for the pinpointed behaviours. For example: Student LM will eat meals, using a spoon without spilling food on at least 5 attempts at lunch time. Or, Student LM motions for the teacher's attention after a task has been completed when the teacher is NOT busy with another student. Again, notice that these statements are all measurable and observable.

GENTLE TEACHING

Gentle Teaching is a non violent approach for helping people with special needs and sometimes challenging behaviours that focuses on four primary goals of care-giving:

— teaching the person to feel safe with us

— teaching the person to feel engaged with us

— teaching the person to feel unconditionally loved by us

— teaching the person to feel loving towards us

Gentle Teaching is a strategy based on a Psychology of Interdependence that sees all change as being mutual and bringing about a feeling of companionship and community-symbols of justice and non-violence. How often do we hear ourselves and others say, You know...it is not difficult to teach a person to behave like we want him or her to. We just modify their behaviour— reward what we want and punish what we don't want. If it doesn't work in the beginning, we'll just use some more punishment and we will succeed....or more structure, or more restraint, or more ..."

Is it really so easy ?.... It may be so if we are not interested in the emotional well-being of the other, when it doesn't matter if the other is afraid of us and when we are only focused on obedience. In reality we see that this approach doesn't work at all. As soon as we let go of punishment, restraint, or external structure, the challenging behaviour appears again in some form. Also, in many cases the behaviour we want to disappear is just replaced by another difficult one. Some people get the same punishment for many years without any "success"

A sad example of this is a woman who is treated with Electro Aversive Therapy for over 22 years. She received over 1,200,000 electro-shocks and still had self-injures behaviour. But, the central question is not to do away with punishment; rather, it is to define what do we want the person to become. The challenge is to mend shattered hearts, not broken bodies or brains. It is the emotional well-being that is central— feelings of being safe, engaged, loved, and loving. And, these do not come from reward or punishment, but from the teaching of feelings of companionship.

A Psychology of Interdependence

Gentle Teaching is not just another technique to deal with difficult behaviours of people with mental retardation. It is the expression of the Psychology of Interdependence, so it has to do with more than just challenging behaviours. It has to do with how we exist as human beings, how we see our self, how we see our relations with important others etc. . The Psychology of Interdependence is based on the following basic assumptions:

— Each human being is made up of a mind-body-spirit

— Each human being hungers for a feeling of being-with-others and having a feeling of companionship

— Bonded relations are the fundament for developing human basic values into a moral life and into personal life-goals

In our work with people with mental retardation the Psychology of Interdependence helps us create a culture of life for those who need our help. Not just the people with challenging behaviours, but everyone.

Companionship

The central purpose of giving care to anyone is to establish a feeling of companionship. This is literally taught. It is more than being "nice" to someone. It is an emotional prerequisite in all human-beings; having a warm circle of significant others in our life who help us to feel safe, wanted envalued Companionship expresses the feeling of belonging together and to share the important events of life. The word "companionship" comes from the Latin words "com = together" and "pan = bread".

Everyone needs to have companions in life. Without companions you feel lost and isolated. People with mental retardation , and especially those with challenging behaviour, have learned not to trust others or even have learned to be afraid of others. They don't have companions they can trust an have to learn the feeling of companionship from the beginning. People with a mental retardation often don't know what a feeling of companionship is. They are submitted to others who are - at least in their own experience - domineering them and there grows an emotional gap between them in stead of a bonded relation.

These people have to be taught a feeling of companionship. The first step in this process is that care givers and other important others have to find out what the Psychology of Interdependence means for themselves and for their posture towards the other. They can start creating a culture of interdependence, a culture of life, by changing their own behaviour and looking at the other, not as a person with behaviour problems, but as a person who has not yet learned the feeling of companionship.

Basic Values

Everyone has personal objectives in life which are important. Not all objectives are equally important. One may be more important than the other. These objectives are the expressions of Basic Values and together they make a profile of the personal quality of life expectations.

These are the eight basic values

Bodily Integrity	being healthy, being decently clothed, being clean, being well fed, etc
Feeling Safe	wanting to be with others, not being afraid of people with whom you live, not being afraid to go outside, feeling relaxed in interactions with others, etc
Feeling Self-Worth	seeing oneself a good, being recognized as a person, feeling pride, expressing personal gifts and talents

Having a Life Structure	sensing a life-plan, having daily routine, having your own rituals and beliefs
A Sense of Belongingness	having a close circle of friends, loving others and being loved by others, having a home, feeling companionship
Social Participation	being able to have contact with the community, living between others, partaking of community-life
Having meaningful daily activities	enjoying one's daily activities, having activities which fit in your life-plan
Inner Contentment	feeling inner harmony, free from traumatic experiences

Within these basic values there is no fixed hierarchy. Everyone has his own priorities, based on his own life experiences and the culture he lives in. At the start of our life, these basic values are not expressed in more or less concrete objectives and behaviour to achieve our objectives. We develop our life-stile and our objectives while we grow-up be learning from our parents and other important people. The basis for this learning is a feeling of trust and safety with the others and an emotional stability within our self. If we don't feel safe with others, we will not learn from them and we will not develop our personal life-stile. As a result we will be forced to live the life-stile of persons we are depending on and we will be disciplined in many details of our life.

Often people with mental retardation didn't develop their own expressions of the basic values, or they didn't develop "proper" expressions. For example: in order to feel safe you may be aggressive to someone else (attack is the best defence) or in order to create your own structure, you act aggressively in order to provoke a predictable reaction of your care givers. Helping people in need, we have to determine how important the basic values are to him or her and which expressions he/ she has developed to achieve the important basic values. Then we can teach him/her other and perhaps more proper expressions, related to his/her priorities in life

Companionship and the quality of life

Gentle teaching focuses on teaching a person to share the feeling of companionship with others. This feeling has a great impact on the total quality of life and this explains why gentle teaching is so important for many persons who don't feel safe and connected with others. At least six out of the eight basic values are influenced by the feeling of companionship. By the warmth of our touch we teach the person that his body is respected and is seen as his personal temple. Strengthening his feeling of self worth is an essential part of building a relation.

The feeling of companionship fundamentally increases the feeling of safety and the sense of belongingness. Because we value the emotions of the person and we are aware of his existential questions, we improve his inner contentment. Being his companion, we are also a personal guide in his life and we can give him a basic structure by helping whenever he needs our help. The remaining two basic values of quality of life, social participation and having sensemaking daily activities may not be directly influenced by the feeling of companionship, but when a person feels safe and connected to us, we sure can help him participating in the community and social life we can help him developing skills he may need for sensemaking daily activities. Companionship has a tremendous impact on the persons overall quality of life. This explains maybe why gentle teaching is successful in supporting people with special vulnerabilities.

The quality of life profile

Everybody is looking out for a Quality of Life that fits with him. The *quality of life* is the balance between the expression of our basic values and the degree in which we achieve our personal goals and expectations. To find out how we can help a person, who lacks a good QOL, we need to find out on which expressions he is most vulnerable. For example, we all need to feel safe. If a person lacks this essential value, the care giver has to define this as a primary goal and effectuate a plan of support around this. And, this might then take precedence over other values at that moment in time. The QOL-profile is an instrument that might help us making a quick scan of a persons quality of life. On a number of items, which all have to do with quality of life, you make a judgment on how it impacts the QOL of the person who needs your help. You can also add some individual items in order to make the instrument more personal.

IDENTIFICATION AND ASSESSMENT

The process of identification and assessment of students with behaviour disorders or mental illness sometimes begins at the classroom level, although these students are often identified in the community by mental health professionals. To be identified in this category, the behaviours in question should not be transitory but should generalize to different settings and individuals. When teachers first notice a problem, they will consult with the parents and attempt alternate strategies to manage the behaviour or support the student in the classroom. If these prove unsuccessful, the teacher may seek assistance from other school-based services or from the school-based team. The teacher's observations should be incorporated into an identification and assessment process for educational purposes, as should the assessments of other professionals.

The school-based team may access other school or district support services, and/or request additional assessment. It may also be appropriate at this stage to involve the family's physician, child and youth mental health services, or other community agencies in the identification and intervention process. Assessment should:

— analyze the student's functional behaviours in various settings and with different people who regularly are a part of her/his environment (functional behaviour assessment);

— integrate information from the different aspects of a student's life;

— focus on strengths as well as needs;

— rule out or address other conditions which may be precipitating or contributing to the behaviour (e.g., hearing loss, learning disabilities, side-effects of medication);

— clarify the characteristics of the behaviour disorder or mental illness;

— address the possibility of other medical or health impairments;

— contribute to the process of planning and evaluating the student's educational program.

The findings of the assessment should be used to plan support, interventions, and services needed by the student.

EDUCATIONAL PLANNING FOR CHILDREN WITH METAL ILLNESS

In accordance with the process described in these sections, planning is done collaboratively by relevant school and district staff, parents and, when appropriate, relevant professionals, service providers, or agencies and the student. An Individual Education Plan (IEP) must be developed for each student included in these categories. The IEP will describe:

— current behavioural and learning strengths and needs;

— the goals for the student's program referenced to measurable objectives;

— the behavioural strategies used to achieve the goals and measures for tracking student achievement of the goals;

— if applicable, specification of the components of the curriculum that will be adapted and/or modified;

— the resources needed to support the student;

— the names of staff responsible (school, community agencies) for implementing the plan;

— the role of the parents in supporting the plan;

— means of evaluating the efficacy of supports/interventions and a timeline for evaluation;

— decisions regarding where the plan will be implemented; and

— plans for transitions.

In general, these intervention programs should be implemented in the settings in which the behaviours are occurring, rather than through a change in placement. However, integrated approaches should not place the student, his/her peers, or those providing services in an "at risk" position. Some of these students may require more specialized services, including part or full-time placement in specialized learning environments (resource room, teaching and evaluation centre, or programs provided in co-ordination with other agencies) until the student can be assisted to re-enter the regular classroom on a full-time basis and/or successfully enter the world of work.

Students with Serious Mental Illness

For students identified in the funding category of Students Requiring Intensive Behaviour Interventions or Serious Mental Illness, there must be one or more of the following additional services provided:

— direct interventions in the classroom by a specialist teacher or supervised teachers' assistant to promote behavioural change or provide emotional support through implementing the plan outlined in the IEP;

— placement in a program designed to promote behavioural change and implement the IEP; and/or

— ongoing, individually implemented social skills training, and/ or instruction in behavioural and learning strategies.

The above may be complemented/co-ordinated with:

— in-depth therapy, counselling and/or support for the student or family in the community; or

— pharmacological treatment as prescribed and monitored by a physician.

In addition to the requirements for moderate support described above, the following are also required:

— an IEP, which is co-ordinated with intervention/care plans developed by appropriate community service providers or agencies in consultation with the family;

— evidence of a co-ordinated, cross-agency community planning such as integrated case management or 'wrap-around' planning;

— documentation of previous plans and interventions, to demonstrate that the district has exhausted its own resources and capacity to manage within the typical range of special education support/interventions;

— evidence of a planned inter-agency or service provider review process, in a stated time frame, recognizing that many behavioural problems will be ameliorated if the interventions are appropriate.

Evidence of inter-agency or service provider involvement, without intensive and collaborative on-going planning and service co-ordination, is not sufficient in itself to warrant funding in this category. Placement in this special education funding category is not intended to be static from year to year, as it is expected that an intensive and coordinated approach, including in some cases medical intervention, will result in changes. Reviews should be conducted at least two times a year, and more frequently if warranted. Districts may claim students in subsequent years in this category only if they are justified in doing so because of particular circumstances surrounding the intensity of each student's requirement for services and case management, as reflected in the student's IEP.

ROLE OF PERSONNEL TEACHERS

With sufficient training and experience, classroom teachers will be capable of including most students requiring behaviour and mental health supports and providing a program in which they can be successful, provided that support is available when needed. Inservice training opportunities and a collaborative team approach are recommended to support and encourage the development of skills required. Boards should ensure that teachers whose responsibilities are primarily concerned with programming for students with behaviour disorders or mental illness have appropriate training. These teachers should possess general training in the area of special education with additional coursework in the education of students with mental illness or behaviour disorders, motivational techniques, and behaviour management.

The skill set for teachers in these programs should include:

— behavioural observation, analysis, strategies and management;

— consultative and collaborative skills;

— direction/supervision of behavioural intervention programs;

— adaptation of curriculum to meet a wide range of student learning needs; and

— counselling skills.

Child and youth counsellors and teachers' assistants

Child and youth counsellors or teachers' assistants working with students requiring behaviour supports/ interventions should have sufficient skills and training for the duties they are assigned including:

— an understanding of behaviour disorders;

— observational, motivational, and behaviour management skills; and

— communicative and collaborative skills.

It should be noted that teachers' assistants work under the general supervision of a teacher or administrative officer. Inservice training should include opportunities to further develop skills in these and related areas.

Students with Intellectual Disabilities

A student with an intellectual disability will usually be identified before entering the school system. For students with a mild intellectual disability, however, difficulties with adaptive behaviour may not have been previously documented. Adaptive behaviour is the effectiveness or degree to which the individual meets the standards of personal independence and social responsibility. A psychoeducational assessment will be used to determine a student's level of functioning and should be based on a variety of measures of intellectual ability and adaptive behaviour, as well as information from the family and, where available, other service providers. Instruments such as the Vineland Adaptive Behaviour Scales and the Adaptive Behaviour Scale should be used in the assessment of an individual's adaptive behaviour. The most frequently used tests in assessing intellectual ability are the most current revisions of the Stanford-Binet and the Wechsler Intelligence scales.

The formal psychoeducational assessment will determine the student's level of functioning and must include information regarding:

— academic and life skills;

— communication skills;

— sensory disorders;

— social-emotional development; and

— specific aptitudes.

PLANNING AND IMPLEMENTATION

Most students with intellectual disabilities benefit from and may learn best from being with age peers, but generally also require additional intervention. As they proceed through elementary school, their IEPs should specify any modifications or adaptations to programs, use of special materials, and the measures of progress. Parents must be given the opportunity to participate in the planning process, and to the extent that they are able, students should also participate.

The older the student, the greater the need for concrete educational objectives. At the secondary level, a student with an intellectual disability should have the opportunity and option to access a variety of educational and social experiences both within the school and in the community. For many students, continued participation in academic areas, with appropriately adapted programs and support where needed, is both reasonable and desirable. For other students, increasing community integration and work experience/work placement opportunities are most enabling. If a student with a severe to profound intellectual disability has a sensory impairment, physical disability or medical/health needs, support services from a teacher's assistant as well as the expertise of an occupational therapist, a physiotherapist, a speech-language pathologist, or an itinerant specialist may be required.

These other professionals should work with the school-based team so that joint planning can take place and information can be shared. The older the student or the more severe the disability, the greater is the need for functional educational objectives. Since the skills taught should be those that afford many opportunities for practice, and since teaching should be in preparation for adult life in the community, the student will need an increasing degree of educational instruction in community environments.

ROLE OF PERSONNEL TEACHERS

With sufficient training and experience, classroom teachers will be capable of including students with intellectual disabilities and providing programs in which they can be successful, provided that specialized support is available when needed. Inservice training opportunities and a collaborative team approach are recommended to support and encourage the development of the necessary skills and understandings which the classroom teacher may require. Teachers with responsibilities for supporting students with intellectual disabilities should fulfill the qualifications described for Learning Assistance. In addition, they should have advanced coursework in:

— the characteristics and needs of students with intellectual disabilities;

— specialized instructional methodologies and technologies; and adaptation and modification of programs for students with intellectual disabilities; and

— functional life skills and career development.

Recent and ongoing technological advances in adaptive devices related to computer access, environmental controls and augmented communication have greatly enhanced learning opportunities for students with intellectual disabilities. It is expected that specialist staff will stay informed about current developments and introduce new technologies as appropriate and as resources permit.

Teachers' assistants

Teachers' assistants who work in classrooms with students with intellectual disabilities should have sufficient skills and training for the duties they are assigned, including:

— the social, emotional, and educational implications of intellectual disabilities;

— functional life skills and career development; and

— technological support.

It should be noted that teachers' assistants work under the general supervision of a teacher or administrative officer. Inservice training should include opportunities to further develop skills in these and related areas.

DEFINITION OF MENTAL HANDICAP

There are several definitions of the mental handicap, among which that of the International Classification of the Handicaps (C.I.H)., that of the Guide Table and that of the Associations representing the persons mental defectives:

— The International Classification of the Handicaps uses the term of " deficiency of the intelligence " disturbances of the degree of development of the cognitive functions such as the perception, the attention, the memory and the thought as well as their deterioration following a pathological process

— The Guide table uses the term of " mental handicap " distinguished from those of " physical handicap " or from "mental illness": " any loss of substance or change of a function (office) or a psychological, physiological or anatomical structure ".

— UNAPEI: a handicaped person is a separate, at the same moment common and singular person. She is common, because she knows the needs of all, she arranges rights of all and she carries out the duty of all. She is singular, because she is confronted with more difficulties than the other citizens, and who are the consequence of one or several deficiencies. So, the mental handicap is translated by more or less important difficulties of reflection, conceptualization, communication and decisions. These difficulties should be compensated with a human, permanent and evolutionary accompanying, adapted to the state and to the situation of the person.

Differences with the Mental illness

There is very often confusion between mental handicap and mental illness. National union of the Friends and Family of Mental Patients (UNAFAM): " the person mentally ill person suffers from confusions of different previous history which soil his (her) mode of behaviour in a momentary or durable way, and unevenly grave ".

UNAPEI: " the person mentally ill person is marked by a mental disturbance of her faculties (powers) susceptible to be cured or reduced by means of an adapted therapy ".

History of Mental Handicap

— In the conception: diseases genetics, chromosome aberrations, blood incompatibility...

— During the pregnancy: radiation ionisante, viruses, medicines, parasites, alcohol, tobacco...

— In the birth: intellectual suffering of the newborn child, the prematurity...

— After the birth: infectious, viral or metabolic diseases, poisonings, traumatism cranial, accidents of work or the road, drownings, asphyxiations...

Specific needs of the persons mental defectives

The mental handicap leads, as compensation, a " help to the decision " or " helps to choose " or " help to the behaviour of its life " which brings an accompanying or an adapted human support. The coverage of this compensation raises (finds) obligations of the company in conformance with the solidarity. The handicap consists in the limitation of the free exercise of the individual social roles: exercise a profession and a domestic role, form, go and come, choose its place of residence...

For the concerned person, the mental handicap pulls the necessity of having an accompanying and a support adapted to its needs and to its degree of handicap. Various social, medical, educational and school services are conceived to answer the specific needs of the person mental defective: prevention, diagnosis, premature intervention, assistant to the parents and to the families, the education, the education, the vocational training, the residence, the social integration, the leisure activities, the forming, the economy, the legal protection, the information of the public.

It is necessary to remind that, in spite of the lack of room of reception and support and certain attitudes of refusal, the person affected by a mental handicap needs, arranges rights and carries out the duty of every persons. Besides, she knows one or several handicaps (physical and\or sensory coming to add to the mental handicap) which lead(drive) her (it) to need a compensation which it is up to the community to guarantee to her in conformance with the national solidarity.

The National Union of the Associations of Relatives (parents) and Friends of Persons Mental defectives (UNAPEI) is an union of local Associations (APEI), secondary roads (ADAPEI), regional (URAPEI). She (it) was created in 1960. The Associations which she (it) federates welcome, listen, bring supports, solutions and advices. They create and manage 2700 establishments and services specialized in the reception and the accompanying of 180 000 persons mental defectives (children and adults).

THE UNAPEI has for objective to make recognize the dignity of the persons mental defectives. She defends their interests and those of their families. To affect her objectives, she acts with the Government, the parliamentary assemblies, the administrations, the local governments, the social bodies, the European and international institutions.

The International Classification of the Handicaps (deficiencies, incapacities and disadvantages) contains three different and independent classifications, each referring to a specific level of the consequences of the diseases:

— The deficiencies relative to any change of the body or the physical appearance, as well as to an organic or functional abnormality, that she that is the cause;

— The incapacities which reflect the consequences of deficiencies in terms of functional activity of the individual;

— The disadvantages which relate to the damages resulting for the individual of his deficiency or its incapacity.

STRATEGIES FOR TEACHING STUDENTS WITH BEHAVIORAL DISORDERS

Behavioural disorders also known as conduct disorders are one of the most common forms of psycho pathology among children and young adults and is the most frequently cited reason for referral to mental health services. The appearance of behavioural disorders is increasing dramatically in K-12 classrooms. As a result their presence severely constrains the ability of the school systems to educate students effectively. The prevalence of behavioural problems among children and young adults is substantial. Many surveys indicate that behavioural disorders vary among young adults, ranging from 2 and 6% in K-12 students.

This percentage translates into 1.3 to 3.8 million cases of behavioural disorders among the school and pre-college population. Behavioural disorders become apparent when the student displays a repetitive and impact persistent pattern of behaviour that results in the significant disruption in other students. Such disturbances may cause significant impairments in academic, social, and or occupational functioning. Such a behaviour pattern is consistent throughout the individuals life. Among the characteristics of a behavioural disorder among children and adolescents are:

— Initiation of aggressive behaviour and reacting aggressively towards others.

— A display of bullying, threatening, or intimidating behaviour.

— Being physically abusive of others.

— Deliberate destruction of other's property.

— Showing little empathy and concern for the feelings, wishes, and well being of others.

— Showing callous behaviour towards others and lack of feelings of guilt or remorse.

— They may readily inform on their companions and tend to blame others for their own misdeeds.

Bring to the student's attention science role models with disabilities with a similar disability to that of the student. Point out that this individual got ahead by a combination of effort and by asking for help when needed.

— Ask previous teachers about interactive techniques that have previously been effective with the student in the past.

— Expose students with behavioural disorders to other students who demonstrate the appropriate behaviours.

— Direct instruction or target behaviours is often required to help students master them.

— Have preestablished consequences for misbehaviour.

— Administer consequences immediately, then monitor proper behaviour frequently.

— Determine whether the student is on medication, what the schedule is, and what the medication effects may be on his or her in class demeanor with and without medication.

Then adjust teaching strategies accordingly.

- Use time-out sessions to cool off disruptive behaviour and as a break if the student needs one for a disability-related reason.
- In group activities, acknowledge the contributions of the student with a behavioural disorder.
- Devise a contingency plan with the student in which inappropriate forms of response are replaced by appropriate ones.
- Treat the student with the behavioural disorder as an individual who is deserving of respect and consideration.
- When appropriate, seek input from the student about their strengths, weaknesses and goals.
- Enforce classroom rules consistently.
- Make sure the discipline fits the "crime," without harshness.
- Provide encouragement.
- Reward more than you punish, in order to build self-esteem.
- Praise immediately at all good behaviour and performance.
- Change rewards if they are not effective for motivating behavioural change.
- Develop a schedule for applying positive reinforcement in all educational environments.
- Encourage others to be friendly with students who have emotional disorders.
- Monitor the student's self-esteem. Assist in modification, as needed.
- Self-esteem and interpersonal skills are especially essential for all students with emotional disorders.
- Do not expect students with behavioural disorders to have immediate success; work for improvement on a overall basis.

- As a teacher, you should be patient, sensitive, a good listener, fair and consistent in your treatment of students with behavioural disorders.
- Present a sense of high degree of possessiveness in the classroom environment.

Teacher Presentation

After a week, or so, of observation, try to anticipate classroom situations where the student's emotional state will be vulnerable and be prepared to apply the appropriate mitigative strategies.

- By using examples, encourage students to learn science so they can emulate adult behaviours.
- Check on the student's basic capacity to communicate and adjust your communications efforts accordingly.
- Use a wide variety of instructional equipment which can be displayed for the students to look at and handle.
- When an interest in a particular piece has been kindled, the instructor can talk to the student about it and show him or her how to use it.
- Instructions should be simple and very structured.
- Group participation in activities is highly desirable because it makes social contacts possible.
- Monitor the student carefully to ensure that students without disabilities do not dominate the activity or detract in any way from the successful performance of the student with the behavioural disorder.
- Teachers should reward students for good behaviour and withhold reinforcement for inappropriate behaviour.
- Some aggressive students act as they do because of a subconscious desire for attention, and it is possible to modify their behaviour by giving them recognition.

- Have the individual with the behavioural disorder be in charge of an activity which can often reduce the aggressiveness.
- Special efforts should be made to encourage and easily facilitate students with behavioural disorders to interact.
- Show confidence in the students ability and set goals that realistically can be achieved.
- Plan for successful participation in the activities by the students. Success is extremely important to them.
- The environment must be structured but sensitive to the needs of these youth with behavioural disorders.
- Expose students with behavioural disorders to other students who demonstrate the appropriate behaviours.
- Direct instruction or target behaviours is often required to help students master them.
- Consultation with other specialists, including the special education teacher, school psychologist, and others may prove helpful in devising effective strategies.
- Keep an organized classroom learning environment.
- Devise a structured behavioural management program.
- As an educator you serve a model for the students who are behaviorally disturbed. Your actions therefore, must be consistent, mature, and controlled. Behavioural outbursts and/or angry shouting at students inhibit rather than enhance a classroom.
- Provide a carefully structured learning environment with regard to physical features of the room, scheduling, routines, and rules of conduct.
- If unstructured activities must occur, you must clearly distinguish them from structured activities in terms of time, place, and expectations.

- Let your students know the expectations you have, the objectives that have been established for the activity, and the help you will give them in achieving objectives.
- When appropriate, seek input from the students about their strengths, weaknesses and goals.
- Do not expect students with behavioural disorders to have immediate success; work for improvement on a overall basis.
- Be fair and consistent, but temper your consistency with flexibility.
- You should refer the students to visual aids and reading materials that may be used to learn more about the techniques of skill performance.
- Present a sense of positiveness in the learning environment.
- Remain calm, state the infraction of the rule, and avoid debating or arguing with the student with a behavioural disorder.
- Have preestablished consequences for misbehaviour.
- Administer consequences immediately, then monitor proper behaviour frequently.
- Enforce classroom rules consistently.
- Make sure the discipline fits the "crime," without harshness.
- Provide encouragement.
- Reward more than you punish, in order to build self-esteem.
- Praise immediately and all good behaviour and performance.
- Change rewards if they are not effective for motivating behavioural change.
- Find ways to encourage the student.

— Be positive and supportive.

— Develop a schedule for applying positive reinforcement in all educational environments.

— Encourage others to be friendly with students who have emotional disorders.

— Monitor the student's self-esteem. Assist in modification, as needed.

— Self-esteem and interpersonal skills are especially essential for all students with emotional disorders.

Laboratory

Use the appropriate general strategies, given above.

— Consider alternate activities/exercises that can be utilized with less difficulty for the student, but has the same or similar learning objectives.

— If unstructured activities must occur, you must clearly distinguish them from structured activated in terms of time, place, and expectations.

— Be sensitive when making team pairings for activities so that the student with an emotional disorder is supported.

— Use a wide variety of instructional equipment which can be displayed for the students to look at and handle.

— When an interest in a particular piece has been kindled, the instructor can talk to the student about it and show him or her how to use it.

— Activity instructions should be simple but structured.

— Monitor carefully to ensure that the students without disabilities do not dominate the activity or detract in any way from the successful performance of the student with the behavioural disorder.

— If unstructured activities must occur, you must clearly distinguish them from structured activated in terms of time, place, and expectations.

— Special efforts should be made to get students with behavioural disorders to interact in laboratory activities.

— If a student must be denied permission to use the equipment, this should be done on an impersonal basis so the student will not feel hurt or discriminated against.

— Plan for successful participation in the laboratory activities by the students with behavioural disorder. Success is extremely important to them.

— To ensure success consider the special needs and interests of each person; give friendly, patient instruction in the laboratory skills; and continually encourage a wider interest in activities.

— When a student displays a reaction of dislike to the activities this dislike usually stems from fear or lack of experience for the activity or factors inherent within the situation itself.

— Some students with behavioural disorders may go to great lengths to avoid class participation. To feign their disorder is the method most frequently used, in hope of being excused from participation.

— Every effort should be made to arouse the interest of such students in laboratory activities, so they will learn to perform the activities with success and pleasure.

Group Interaction and Discussion

Acknowledge the contributions of the student with an emotional disorder.

— Call for responses and participation commensurate with the student's socialization skills.

— As the student's comfort level rises and when a safe topic is available, encourage the student to be a group spokesperson.

— Along with the student, devise a contingency plan in which inappropriate forms of response are replaced by appropriate ones.

— Gradually increase the challenges in the student's participation in group exercises while providing increased positive reinforcement.

— Help the student to feel as though he or she has something worthwhile to contribute to the discussion.

— Some students may experience considerable strain in social adjustment in a group context. It may be necessary to work gradually toward group activities. One can devise a strategy of progressing from spectatorship to one-to-one instruction and eventually to small group discussion.

— Should monitor carefully io ensure that the nondisabled students do not dominate the discussion or detract in any way from the successful performance of the student with the behavioural disorder.

Reading

— It is necessary to target specific prosocial behaviours for appropriate instruction and assessment to occur such as:

— Taking turns, working with partner, following directions.

— Reading in group or with others.

— Increasing positive relationships by means of awards when they read appropriately.

— Demonstrating appropriate reading

— Instructional strategies involving self-control, self-reinforcement, self-monitoring, self-management, problem solving, cognitive behaviour modification, and metacognitive skills should be focused on teaching students reading skills

Research

— Review and discuss with the student the steps involved in a research activity. Think about which step(s) may be difficult for the specific functional limitations of the student and jointly devise accommodations for that student.

— Use appropriate laboratory and field strategies.

— Depending on the site of the research check the previous two sections.

— Show clear examples of what the students should expect as an outcome of their research.

Field Experiences

Use appropriate general strategies.

— Consider alternate activities/exercises that can be utilized with less difficulty for the student, but has the same or similar learning objectives.

— In field activities acknowledge the contributions and assistance of the student with an emotional disorder.

— Help the student to feel as though he or she has something worthwhile to contribute to the field trip.

— Use a buddy system.

— Gradually increase the challenges in the student's participation in field exercises while providing increased positive reinforcement.

— Group participation in field activities is highly desirable because it enhances social contacts.

— Make the student with the behavioural disorder become one of the field trip leader of an activity which can often reduce their disorder.

— Special efforts should be made to get students with behavioural disorders to interact with other students.

— You should encourage students to practice field skills during their free hours.

— Every effort should be made to arouse the interest of such students in activities, so they will learn to perform the activities with success and pleasure with appropriate behaviours.

Testing

— Be sensitive to the student's reactions to the various aspects of assessment.

— For each student, accumulate in his or her portfolio several examples of work (quizzes, assignments, projects) that demonstrate knowledge of the subject matter or the unit of study.

— Make special arrangements for the student with an emotional disorder according to what their special needs are and that they do not compromise the integrity of the testing situation.

— Stay on top of student progress through informal assessment, don't wait until it's too late to discover that there is a problem.

— Provide private room/smaller group setting/alternative test site (with proctor present); alternatively screens to block out distractions.

STRATEGIES FOR TEACHING STUDENTS WITH INTELLECTUAL IMPAIRMENTS

Most students classified as intellectually impaired are not described by clearly identifiable syndromes, but many times, their impairments have known etiologies. Further, many students are not diagnosed as mentally disabled until well into their preschool or early elementary school years. Early identification of marker characteristics that predispose children to mental impairment allows for environmental intervention to reduce or prevent eventual developmental delay. For some children, the primary factors that produce mental impairment can be found in their environments. For still other children, the interaction of organismically-based influences and environmental variables also result in mental impairment or seriously delayed development. These variables, organismic and environmental, that contribute to mental impairment and delay are termed "risk factors" in development.

Research to identify and to help control (intervene, mitigate, and prevent) risk factors and the adverse outcomes of mental impairment are the aims of this theme. Intellectual impairment means significantly subaverage general intellectual functioning which exists concurrently with deficits in adaptive behavior and manifested during the developmental period that adversely affects a student's educational performance.

According to the above definition, three IQ criteria must be met before an individual should be classified as mentally retarded:

1. subaverage intellectual ability (IQ 70 or lower)
2. problems in adaptive functioning
3. manifested before the age of 18

Mental Impairment is one of the most frequently occurring disabilities that occurs in the inclusive classroom. In the US, some 13.3% of all students in special education are classified as being mentally impaired. For example, in West Virginia, there are 15.4% who are mildly impaired, 4.8% moderately impaired, 0.7% severely impaired, and 0.5% profoundly impaired. Total percent of mentally disabled in West Virginia is 21.4%. In terms of IQ range, four groups are classified (by IQ) as:

— Students who are mildly impaired have an IQ range of 51-70 and are in many ways quite similar to their peers who are not impaired.

— Students who have moderate impairments have an IQ range of 36-50 and are more obviously developmentally delayed. Students who are moderately impaired can learn to take care of their personal needs and perform hands-on vocational tasks.

— Students who are severely impaired have an IQ range of 21-35 and are more dependent on others for basic needs. Students who are severely impaired can learn basic self-care and can contribute partially to self-support usually under supervision.

— Students who are profoundly impaired have an IQ range below 20 and may be largely dependent on others for their care.

Bring to the student's attention science role models with disabilities with a similar disability to that of the student. Point out that this individual got ahead by a combination of effort and by asking for help when needed.

— Preparation for experience in the learning environment best occurs when all students of different backgrounds and abilities learn and socialize together in classrooms and other school settings. In these instances where all have a chance to achieve and receive instruction designed to develop and enhance successful living within the school and general community.

— Keep up-to-date on the student's accomplishments in therapy.

— Never assess a student's capabilities solely on the basis of their IQ or other standardized test scores (especially at the limits of the IQ definition).

— Each student with an impairment needs to be in an age/achievement appropriate learning environment with peers who are not impaired.

— After some time in the learning environment, which includes a mentally impaired student, the teacher, as an observer, should record the behavior that varies from the "norm" and which may indicate the need for referral for counseling and/or psychological intervention including drug therapy, if necessary.

— Develop a protocol for the student to tell you when he/she anticipates a need for assistance.

— When it appears that a student needs help, ask if you can help. Accept a "No Thank You" graciously.

— Encourage classmates to accept the student with a mental impairment.

— Be aware that a student with an impairment may frequently be treated with therapeutic medications that affect performance and speed.

— Acknowledge that high, but realistic, expectations should be maintained to encourage full realization of social and educational potential.

Personal interactions with mentally impaired students:

Speak directly to the student with an impairment as you would any other student.

Involvement with other children: The teacher should, where possible, get to know the non-impaired students, engaging them and providing them a connecting link between these students and the students with impairments. The teacher shouldn't be seen as the person who relates only to the student with an impairment.

Modeling for others: The teacher should be aware that his or her interactions with the impaired student will serve as a model for interactions with students who are impaired. This may be particularly important in assisting others in areas such as communicating with the student with an impairment about behavior that does not appear appropriate in science teaching/learning activities.

Backing off: Often, interactions occur without the involvement of a teacher. At times, in fact, the presence of an adult may inhibit interactions, and it may be necessary to "Back off" and let things happen on their own.

Interactions in the context of school activities: It is important to observe the interactions of the student with others in the learning environment. For instance, what types of interactions occur, and at what times? Some activities are more conducive to getting students together than others. The teacher should note and promote opportunities for interactions, even if that means revising plans for teaching skills to allow for spontaneous interactions and play. Remember that not all interactions are verbal. Cheering together, sitting together and watching an event or doing an activity, or working as a team field or laboratory to build something are all examples of nonverbal/verbal interactions.

Learning strategies, such as mnemonics, provide quite good ways to access information, It can be an essential component in learning for many students with disabilities (a mnemonic is defined as a word, sentence, picture, device, or technique for improving or strengthening memory).

5

Education of Children with Learning Disabilities

Learning disabilities refers to a number of disorders that may affect the acquisition, organization, retention, understanding or use of verbal or nonverbal information. These disorders affect learning in individuals who otherwise demonstrate at least average abilities essential for thinking and/or reasoning. As such, learning disabilities are distinct from global intellectual disabilities. Learning disabilities result from impairments in one or more processes related to perceiving, thinking, remembering or learning. These include, but are not limited to: language processing, phonological processing, visual spatial processing, processing speed, memory and attention, and executive functions (e.g. planning and decision-making).

Learning disabilities range in severity and may interfere with the acquisition and use of one or more of the following:

— Oral language (e.g., listening, speaking, understanding)

— Reading (e.g., decoding, phonetic knowledge, word recognition, comprehension)

— Written language (e.g., spelling and written expression)

— Mathematics (e.g., computation, problem solving)

Learning disabilities may also involve difficulties with organizational skills, social perception, social interaction and perspective taking.

Learning disabilities are life-long. The way in which they are expressed may vary over an individual's lifetime, depending on the interaction between the demands of the environment and the individual's strengths and needs. Learning disabilities are suggested by unexpected academic under-achievement or achievement that is maintained only by unusually high levels of effort and support.

Learning disabilities are due to genetic and/or neurological factors or injury that alters brain function in a manner that affects one or more processes related to learning. These disorders are not due primarily to hearing and/or vision problems, social-economic factors, cultural or linguistic differences, lack of motivation, inadequate or insufficient instruction, although these factors may further complicate the challenges faced by individuals with learning disabilities. Learning disabilities may co-exist with other disorders such as attentional, behavioural or emotional disorders, sensory impairments, or other medical conditions.

IDENTIFICATION AND ASSESSMENT

— Schools and school boards are responsible for assessing students for the purposes of planning instruction and support services and identifying them as students with special needs.

— Students with learning disabilities often experience difficulties in the acquisition of basic academic skills and/ or in school performance and are characterized by unexpected academic under-achievement or achievement that is maintained only by unusually high levels of effort and support. The severity of these academic difficulties is such that students demonstrate:

— persistent difficulties in the acquisition of pre-academic skills such as recognition of letters and numbers in the early primary years; and/or

— persistent difficulties in the acquisition of reading, writing and/or numeracy skills.

— Students with learning disabilities may demonstrate a significant discrepancy between estimated learning potential and academic achievement as measured by norm-referenced achievement instruments in Grades 4-12.

— Students with learning disabilities demonstrate a significant weakness in one or more cognitive processes (e.g., perception, memory, attention, receptive or expressive language abilities, visual-spatial abilities) relative to overall intellectual functioning, as measured by norm-referenced assessment instruments, which directly impact their performance.

Most students included in the Learning Disabilities category cab be identified by the school system through the progressive assessment and systematic documentation process:

— comprehensive assessment of learning needs and use of alternative instructional strategies by classro teacher;

— consultation with the parent and student, with possible screening to investigate whether there is a health basis for the learning difficulty;

— collaboration with school-based personnel to develop additional assessment and intervention strategies;

— referral to the school based team for further assistance in implementing strategies or coordination of support services; and

— possible referral for an extended assessment (psycho-educational assessment) to determine the presence, nature, severity and educational implications of a learning disability and provide additional information for planning.

In some cases, students may have been identified in clinical settings. The assessment is often multidisciplinary, supplementing the psycho-educational assessment with information from a speech-language pathologist or an occupational therapist.

The assessment of a student with a learning disability should integrate information from a number of sources, for example:

— information from the family about health, social-emotional adjustment, developmental history;

— overall intellectual functioning, specific cognitive abilities, socio-emotional status;

— pre-academic or academic skills; and

— learning strengths and weaknesses, and their implications.

Assessment information should contribute to the process of planning and evaluating the student's education program.

EDUCATIONAL PLANNING FOR CHILDREN WITH LEARNING DISABILITIES

Learning disabilities vary considerably in their severity and impact on learning. Students with severe learning disabilities will generally require intensive intervention. Students whose learning disabilities have not been identified and addressed early frequently exhibit secondary emotional and behavioural difficulties. Students may be gifted and learning disabled. Students with learning disabilities require an educational plan that builds on their strengths while remediating or compensating for their disabilities. Research suggests two main approaches for supporting students with learning disabilities:

— intense direct instruction; and

— instruction in learning and compensatory strategies.

This instruction may take place in regular classrooms, but this does not preclude the use of different learning environments such as small group instruction in a resource room, self-contained classes or other specialized settings. The goal of the placement should be to meet the students' educational needs. Some ways to support students with learning disabilities could include, but are not limited to the following:

— direct remedial, corrective, tutorial or skill-building instruction;

— adapted, modified or supplementary curriculum and materials;

— alternate instructional and/or evaluation strategies, including adjudicated provincial examinations;

— use of equipment, including computer and audiovisual technology;

— social skills training;

— instruction and practice of self advocacy skills; and

— learning strategies instruction.

EVALUATION AND REPORTING

Personnel Teachers

With sufficient training and experience, classroom teachers will be capable of including most students with learning disabilities and providing a program in which they can be successful, provided that specialized support is available when needed. Inservice training opportunities and a collaborative team approach are recommended to support and encourage the development of the necessary skills and understandings which the classroom teacher may require. Teachers with responsibilities for supporting students with learning disabilities should fulfill the qualifications described for Learning Assistance teacher. In addition, their qualifications should include advanced coursework in:

— characteristics and needs of students with learning disabilities; and

— specialized instructional and remedial strategies, technologies, materials and curricular adaptations.

As well, they should have training and demonstrated skills in:

— social skills development and behaviour management;

— co-operative planning and collaborative consultation; and

— assessment, classroom management and motivation.

Teachers' assistants

Teachers' assistants working with students with learning disabilities should have sufficient skills and training for the duties they are assigned, including:

— an understanding of learning disabilities;

— collaborative and communication skills;

— strategies for motivating students; and

— behaviour management skills.

It should be noted that teachers' assistants work under the general supervision of a teacher or administrative officer. Inservice training should include opportunities to further develop skills in these and related areas.

ATTENTION DEFICIT DISORDERS

Attention deficit disorders are disorders characterized by serious and persistent difficulties in attention span, impulse control, and hyperactivity. Attention Deficit Disorder (ADD) is a chronic disorder that can begin in infancy and extend through adulthood. It can have a significantly negative effect on an individual's life at home, in school, or in the community. There are two types of attention deficit disorders: undifferentiated Attention Deficit Disorder (ADD) and Attention Deficit

Hyperactivity Disorder (ADHD). In undifferentiated ADD, the primary and most significant characteristic is inattentiveness but hyperactivity is not present. These students still manifest problems with organization and distractibility, even though they may seem quite and passive. These students also tend to be overlooked more easily in the classroom, and may be at a higher risk for academic failure than those with ADHD.

To be diagnosed as having ADHD a student must display, for six months or more, at least eight of the following characteristics prior to the age of seven:

1) fidgets, squirms, or is restless
2) has difficulty remaining seated
3) is easily distracted
4) has difficulty waiting for his/her turn
5) blurts out answers
6) has difficulty following instructions
7) has difficulty sustaining attention
8) shifts from one uncompleted task to another
9) has difficulty playing quietly
10) talks excessively
11) interrupts or is rude to others
12) does not appear to listen
13) often loses things necessary for tasks
14) frequently engages in dangerous actions

CHICAGO, Sept. 30 (AP) - The American Academy of Pediatric Me4dcine has issued its first guidelines for treating attention deficit hyperactivity disorder, suggesting that stimulant drugs may be most effective but that behavioral techniques should also be used. The guidelines appear in the October issue of the medical journal Pediatrics, which will be released Monday. As many as

3.8 million school-age children, most of them boys, are believed to have attention deficit disorders. Symptoms may include a short attention span, impulsive behavior and difficulty sitting still.

The guidelines, which fall in line with those issued in recent years by the National Institute of Mental Health, were created in consultation with child psychiatrists and psychologists. They suggest that the evidence favoring medications like Ritalin is stronger than the evidence about behavioral therapy. Symptoms improve in at least 80 percent of children on stimulants, and medication should be switched if it is not working, the guidelines say. Critics say that many doctors and teachers turn to drugs like Ritalin as an easy fix and that their long-term effects are uncertain. The guidelines say any treatment should begin only after a diagnosis is certain and doctors, parents and teachers have discussed appropriate treatment goals. The guidelines say drugs should be used with behavioral techniques, including time-outs for hitting. They call for rewarding children when they complete tasks, like homework.

General Strategies

Bring to the student's attention science role models with disabilities with a similar disability to that of the student. Point out that this individual got ahead by a combination of effort and by asking for help when needed.

Student monitoring, self management, discipline, and encouragement can be a very important aspect for academic success. Below are the two basic aspects of AD/HD facilitation.

Self-monitoring techniques can be very effective in the school setting. Self-monitoring of attention involves cueing the student so that he/she can determine how well he/she is attending to the task at hand. Cueing is often done by providing an audio tone such as a random beep, timer, or the teacher can give the cue. The student then notes whether he/she was on or off task on a simple recording sheet. Self-monitoring techniques are more likely to be effective when tied to rewards and accuracy checks.

Behavior management techniques must often be used in the learning environment. By examining a student's specific problem behavior, understanding it's antecedents and consequences, teachers can help students with AD/HD to develop behaviors that lead to academic and social successes.

Provide supervision and discipline:

— Monitor proper behavior frequently and immediately direct the student to an appropriate behavior.

— Enforce classroom rules consistently.

— Avoid ridicule and criticism. Remember that students with AD/HD have difficulty staying in control.

Providing Encouragement:

— Reward more than punish.

— Immediately praise any and all good behavior and performance.

— Change rewards if they are not effective in motivating behavioral change.

— Find alternate ways to encourage the AD/HD students.

— Teach the student to reward himself or herself. Encourage positive self-talk (e.g., "You did very well remaining in your seat today. How do you feel about that?"). This encourages the student to think positively about himself or herself.

— Bring to the student's attention science role model who has a disability similar to that of the student with an impairment. Point out that this individual got ahead by a combination of effort and by asking for help when needed.

— Reduce the amount of materials present during activities by having the student put away unnecessary items. Have a special place for tools, materials, and books.

— Reward more than you punish, especially with positive reinforcers.

— Try to be patient with an AD/HD student.

— Seat students with AD/HD in the front near the teacher with their backs to the rest of the class. Be sure to include them as part of the regular class seating.

— Place these students up front with their backs to the rest of the class to keep other students out of view.

— Surround students with AD/HD with good peer models, preferably students whom the AD/HD student views as significant peers.

— Encourage peer tutoring and cooperative/collaborative learning.

— A class that has a low student-teacher ratio will be helpful to a student with AD/HD.

— Avoid all distracting stimuli. Try not to place students with AD/HD near air conditioners, high traffic areas, heaters, doors, windows, etc.

— Avoid transitions, physical relocation, changes in schedule, and disruptions.

— Be creative! Produce a somewhat stimuli-reduced study area with a variety of science activities. Let all students have access to this area.

— Encourage parents to set up appropriate study space at home, with set times and routines established for study. Also, use this home area for parental review of completed homework, and periodic notebook and/or book bag organization.

— Educational, psychological, and/or neurological testing is recommended to determine learning style, cognitive ability, and to rule out any learning disability (LD is common in about 30% of students with AD/HD).

— A private tutor and/or peer tutoring will be helpful to a student with AD/HD.

— Have a pre-established consequences for misbehavior, remain calm, state the infraction of the rule, and avoid debating or arguing with the student.

— Avoid publicly reminding students on medication to "take their medicine."

Teacher Presentation

— Consult with special education personnel to determine specific strengths and weaknesses of each student.

— Maintain eye contact during verbal instructions.

— Make directions clear and concise. Be consistent with all daily instructions.

— When you ask an AD/HD student a question, first say the student's name and then pause for a few seconds as a signal for him/her to pay attention.

— To help with changes in assignments, provide clear and consistent transitions between activities and notify the student with AD/HD a few minutes before changing activities.

— Repeat instructions in a calm, positive manner.

— AD/HD students may need both verbal and visual directions. You can do this by providing the student with a model of what he/she should be doing.

— You can give an AD/HD student confidence by starting each assignment with a few questions or activities you know the student can successfully accomplish.

— Self-monitoring techniques can prove effective in the school setting. Self-monitoring of attention involves cueing the student so that he/she can determine how well he is attending to the task at hand. Cueing is often done by providing an audio tone.

— Behavior management techniques must often be used in the school. By examining a child's specific problem behavior, understanding it's antecedents and consequences, educators can help students with AD/HD develop behaviors that lead to academic and social success.

— Develop an individualized education program. By identifying each student's individual strengths and specific learning needs, you can design a plan for mobilizing those strengths to improve students academic and social performance.

— Gradually reduce the amount of assistance, but keep in mind that these students will need more help for a longer period of time than the student without a disability.

— Require a daily assignment notebook as necessary and make sure each student correctly writes down all assignments. If a student is not capable of this, the teacher should help the student.

— Initial the notebook daily to signify completion of homework assignments. (Parents should also sign.)

— Use the notebook for daily communication with parents.

Laboratory

— Gradually reduce the amount of assistance, but keep in mind that these students will need more help for a longer period of time than the student without a disability.

— Consider alternative activities/exercises that can be utilized with less difficulty for the student, but has the same or similar learning objectives.

— Require a daily assignment notebook as necessary and make sure each student correctly writes down all assignments. If a student is not capable of this, the teacher should help the student.

— AD/HD students may need both verbal and visual directions. You can do this by providing the student with a visual model and a verbal description of what he/she should be doing.

— You can give an AD/HD student confidence by starting each lab assignment with a few questions or activities you know the student can successfully accomplish.

— To help with changes in assignments, provide clear and consistent transitions between activities and notify the student with AD/HD a few minutes before changing activities.

— Make sure all students comprehend the instructions before beginning their tasks (the AD/HD student will probably need extra assistance).

— Simplify complex directions. Avoid multiple commands.

— Repeat instructions in a calm, positive manner.

— Help the students feel comfortable with seeking assistance (most students with AD/HD will not ask for help).

— Assign only one task at a time.

— Modify assignments as needed for the AD/HD student.

— Keep in mind that students with AD/HD are easily frustrated and they need assurance of things that are common in science, e.g., when an experiment does not turn out as expected. Stress, pressure, and fatigue can help reduce their self-control and can lead to poor behavior.

Group Interaction and Discussion

— Help the students feel comfortable in seeking assistance (most students with AD/HD will not ask for help, especially in a group activity).

— Gradually integrate the AD/HD student into the interactive system

Reading

Provide additional reading time.

Use "previewing" strategies by being aware of the following reading problems:

- Reversals when reading (i.e., "was" for "saw", "on" for "no", etc.)
- Reversals when writing (b for d, p for q, etc.)
- Transposition of letters and numbers (12 for 21, etc.)
- Loss of place when reading, line to line and word to word.
- Shorten the amount of required reading.
- Avoid oral reading.
- For all assignments, clearly identify expectations in writing.
- Make required book lists available prior to the first day of class to allow students to begin their reading early or to have texts put on tape.
- Encourage the use of books-on-tape to support students reading assignments.
- Provide students with chapter outlines, or handouts, that highlight key points in their readings.
- Read aloud material written on the chalkboard or that is presented in handouts or transparencies.
- Provide the student with published book summaries, synopses, or digests of major reading assignments to review beforehand, and also downloads for Cliff notes are available for computer use (and for transformation to tape output).
- Although seemingly contradictory, it really means that some individuals find one or the other more helpful.

Research

- Review and discuss with the student the steps involved in

a research activity. Think about which step(s) may be difficult for the specific functional limitations of the student and with the student devise accommodations for that student.

— Consider alternative activities/exercises that can be utilized with less difficulty for the student, but has the same or similar learning objectives.

— Monitor the AD/HD students closely on field trips.

— Help the students feel comfortable with seeking assistance (most students with ADD will not ask for help).

— Give extra time for certain tasks. Students with AD/HD may work slowly.

— Use appropriate laboratory and field strategies.

Field Experiences

— Gradually reduce the amount of assistance, but keep in mind that these students will need more help for a longer period of time than the student without a disability.

— Repeat instructions in a calm, positive manner.

— Require a daily assignment notebook as necessary and make sure each student correctly writes down all assignments. If a student is not capable of this, the teacher should help the student.

— AD/HD students may need both verbal and visual directions. You can do this by providing the student with a visual model and a verbal description of what he/she should be doing.

— You can give an AD/HD student confidence by starting each lab assignment with a few questions or activities you know the student can successfully accomplish.

— To help with changes in assignments, provide clear and consistent transitions between activities and notify the student with AD/HD a few minutes before changing activities.

— Make sure all students comprehend the instructions before beginning their tasks (the AD/HD student will probably need assistance).

— Simplify complex directions. Avoid multiple commands.

— Repeat instructions in a calm, positive manner.

— Help the students feel comfortable with seeking assistance (most students with AD/HD will not ask for help).

— Assign only one task at a time.

— Keep in mind that students with AD/HD are easily frustrated and they need assurance of things that are common in science, e.g., when an experiment does not turn out as expected. Stress, pressure, and fatigue can help reduce their self-control and can lead to poor behavior.

— Monitor the AD/HD students closely on field trips.

Testing

— Make sure you are testing knowledge and not attention span.

— Give extra time and frequent breaks for certain of the examination tasks (e.g., math related). Students with AD/HD may work slowly.

— Keep in mind that students with AD/HD are easily frustrated. Stress, pressure, and fatigue an result in reduction of self-control and lead to poor behavior.

— Use especially some of the general strategies related to stress, i.e., management.

Testing accommodations such as: (1) Use of a highlighter; (2) computer with/without spell check/grammar/cut & paste features; and (3) suitable setting such as private room and preferential seating.

TEACHING STUDENTS WITH LEARNING DISABILITIES

Most people know, or are taught, at an early age, how to process information and develop an organized plan or strategy when confronted with a problem, whether that problem is social, academic, or job related. Others find such cognitive processes quite difficult. Learning disabilities have only recently been recognized as disabilities. This neurological disorder causes difficulty in organizing information received, remembering them, and expressing information and therefore affects a person's basic function such as reading, writing, comprehension, and reasoning. However, these students with learning disabilities can be taught effective learning strategies that will help them approach tasks more effectively.

GENERAL INFORMATION

Bring to the student's attention science role models with disabilities with a similar disability to that of the student. Point out that this individual got ahead by a combination of effort and by asking for help when needed. There are many types of learning disabilities as one person vary from another. Some of the situations commonly found are dyslexia (inability to read), dyscalcula (inability in math reasoning), dysgraphia (difficulty with syntax), visual, and audio difficulties. Generally, a person with learning disabilities experience difficulties in study skills, writing skills, oral skills, reading skills, math skills, and social skills.

In studying, students experience inability to organize time therefore unable to finish assignments on time, and they have trouble taking notes and following instructions. They often have difficulty spelling correctly and have frequent grammatical errors which results in poor sentence stucture and poor penmanship. If the lecturer speaks too fast, they will have difficulty understanding the lecture and recalling the words. They are usually slow readers and sometimes hae incorrect comprehension and poor retention. Confusion with math symbols are common, as well as difficulty with concepts of time and money. Realizing their inabilities result in low self-esteem which greatly affects their social skills. They might have impulsive behavior and disorientated in time. Dealing with students with learning disabilities takes patience. The following are some suggestions and guidelines for a teacher with students with learning disabilities.

General Courtesy

- Don't assume that the person is not listening just because you are getting no verbal or visual feedback.
- Don't assume that you have to explain everything to students with learning disabilities. They do not necessarily have a problem with general comprehension.
- onsult with the special education specialist to obtain help in understanding the specific nature of the learning disability for each student.
- Never assess a student's capabilities based solely on their IQ or other standardized test scores.
- Give student with learning disabilities priority in registration for classes.
- Allow course substitution for nonessential course requirements in their major studies.
- A student may have documented intelligence with test scores in the average to superior range with adequate sensory and motor systems and still have a learning disability. Learning disabilities often go undiagnosed, hence teacher observation can be a major source of identification.
- Bring to the student's attention science role models with disabilities with a similar disability to that of the student. Point out that this individual got ahead by a combination of effort and by asking for help when needed.

Teacher Presentation

Always ask questions in a clarifying manner, then have the students with learning disabilities describe his or her understanding of the questions.

— Use an overhead projector with an outline of the lesson or unit of the day.

— Reduce course load for student with learning disabilities.

— Provide clear photocopies of your notes and overhead transparencies, if the student benefits from such strategies.

— Provide students with chapter outlines or study guides that cue them to key points in their readings.

— Provide a detailed course syllabus before class begins. Ask questions in a way that helps the student gain confidence.

— Keep oral instructions logical and concise. Reinforce them with a brief cue words. Repeat or re-word complicated directions.

— Frequently verbalize what is being written on the chalkboard.

— Eliminate classroom distractions such as, excessive noise, flickering lights, etc.

— Outline class presentations on the chalkboard or on an overhead transparency. Outline material to be covered during each class period unit.

— Establish the clarity of understanding that the student has about class assignments.

— Give assignments both in written and oral form.

— Have more complex lessons recorded and available to the students with learning disabilities.

— Have practice exercises available for lessons, in case the student has problems.

— Have students with learning disabilities underline key words or directions on activity sheets (then review the sheets with them).

— Have complex homework assignments due in two or three days rather than on the next day.

— Pace instruction carefully to ensure clarity.

— Present new and or technical vocabulary on the chalkboard or overhead.

— Provide and teach memory associations (mnemonic strategies).

— Support one modality of presentation by following it with instruction and then use another modality.

— Talk distinctly and at a rate that the student with a learning disability can be follow.

— Technical content should be presented in small incremental steps.

— Use plenty of examples, oral or otherwise, in order to make topics more applied.

— Use straight forward instructions with step-by-step unambiguous terms. (Preferably, presented one at a time).

— Write legibly, use large type; do not clutter the blackboard with non-current / non-relevant information.

— Use props to make narrative situations more vivid and clear.

— Assist the student, if necessary, in borrowing classmates' notes. Consider cross-age or peer tutoring if the student appears unable to keep up with the class pace or with complex subject matter. The more capable reader can help in summarizing the essential points of the reading or in establishing the main idea of the reading.

Laboratory

- Clearly label equipment, tools, and materials. Color code them for enhanced visual recognition.
- Consider alternate activities/exercises that can be utilized with less difficulty for the student, but has the same or similar learning objectives.
- Provide clear photocopies of your notes and overhead transparencies.
- For students with learning disabilities, make available cue cards or labels designating the steps of a procedure to expedite the mastering.
- Use an overhead projector with an outline of the lesson or unit of the day.
- Allow extended time for responses and the preparation and delivery of reports.
- In dealing with abstract concepts, use visual tools such as charts and graphs. Also, paraphrase and present them in specific terms, and sequence and illustrate them with concrete examples, personal experiences, or hands-on exercises.
- To minimize student anxiety, provide an individual orientation to the laboratory and equipment and give extra practice with tasks and equipment.
- Find areas of strength in the student's lab experiences and emphasize those as much as possible.
- Allow the students with learning disabilities the use of computers and spell checking programs on assignments.

Reading

- Announce readings as well as assignments well in advance.
- Find materials paralleling the textbook, but written at a lower reading level. (Also, include activities that make the reading assignment more relevant.)

— Introduce simulations to make abstract content more concrete.

— Make lists of required readings available early and arrange to obtain texts on tape from Recording for the Blind or a Reading/Typing Service.

— Offer to read written material aloud, when necessary.

— Read aloud material that is written on the chalkboard and on the overhead transparencies.

— Review relevant material, preview the material to be presented, present the new material then summarize the material just presented.

— Suggest that the students use both visual and auditory senses when reading the text.

— Rely less on textbooks. Reading for students with learning disabilities may be slow and deliberate, and comprehension may be impaired for the student , particularly when dealing with large quantities of material. Comprehension and speed usually dramatically increase with the addition of auditory input.

— Spend more time on building background for the reading selections and creating a mental scheme for the organization of the text.

— Encourage students to practice using technical words in exchanges among peers.

— Choose books with a reduced number of difficult words, direct non convoluted syntax, and passages that deliver clear meaning. Also, select readings that are organized by subheads because this aids in the flow of ideas.

— When writing materials for reading by students with learning disabilities, some of the strategies referred to in the reading section of the hearing impaired presentation will be appropriate.

— Allow the student to use a tape recorder.

Group Interaction and Discussion

— Always ask questions in a clarifying manner, then have the students with learning disabilities describe his or her understanding of the questions.

— Assist the student, if necessary, in borrowing classmates discussion notes.

— Encourage questions during or after class to ensure that materials are understood by students with learning disabilities.

— Give individual conferences to guide students with learning disabilities to monitor progress and understanding of the assignment and of the course content.

— Give plenty of reinforcement when it is evident that the student with a learning disability is trying things that are made difficult by the disability.

— Have frequent question-and-answer sessions for students with learning disabilities.

Field Experiences

— Allow the students with learning disabilities the use of computers and spell checking programs on field notes and reports.

— Consider alternate activities/exercises that can be utilized with less difficulty for the student, but has the same or similar learning objectives.

Research

— Review and discuss with the student the steps involved in a research activity. Think about which step(s) may be difficult for the student's specific functional limitations and jointly devise accommodations for that student.

— Use appropriate laboratory and field strategies.

Testing

— Avoid overly complicated language in exam questions and clearly separate items when spacing them on the exam sheet.

— Consider other forms of testing (oral, hands-on demonstration, open-book etc.). Some students with learning disabilities find that large print helps their processing ability.

— Consider the use of illustrations by the students with learning disabilities as an acceptable form of response to questions in lieu of written responses.

— Eliminate distractions while students are taking exams.

— For students with perceptual problems, for whom transferring answers is especially difficult, avoid answer sheets, especially computer forms. Allow them to write answers (check or circle) on the test (or try to have them dictate their responses on a tape recorder.)

— For students who have reading difficulties, have a proctor read the test to the student.

— For students with writing difficulties, have someone scibe the answers for them or use a tape recorder to take down the answers.

— Gradually increase expectations as the students with learning disabilities gains confidence.

— Grant time extensions on exams and written assignments when there are significant demands on reading and writing skills.

— If distractions are excessive, permit the students with learning disabilities to take examinations in a separate quiet room with a proctor.

— Provide study questions for exams that demonstrate the format along with the content of the exam.

— Review with the student how to proofread assignments and tests.

— Do not test material just presented or outcomes just produced, since for the students with learning disabilities, additional time is generally required to assimilate new knowledge and concepts.

— Permit the students with learning disabilities the use of a dictionary, thesaurus, or a calculator during tests.

— Provide computer with spell check/grammar/ cut & paste features

COMMUNICATION DISORDERS

Communication Disorders involve a wide variety of problems in speech, language, and hearing. For example, speech and language disorders include stuttering, aphasia, dysfluency, voice disorders (hoarseness, breathiness, or sudden breaks in loudness or pitch), cleft lip and/or palate, articulation problems, delays in speech and language, autism, and phonological disorders. Speech and language impairments and disorders can be attributed to environmental factors, of which the most commonly known are High Risk Register problems, which include drugs taken during pregnancy, common STD's such as syphilis, and birthing trauma to name a few. Communication disorders can also stem from other conditions such as learning disabilities, dyslexia, cerebral palsy, and mental retardation.

Individuals with communication disorderto the student with a disability as you would any other student. Bring to the student's attention science role models with disabilities with a similar disability to that of the student. Point out that this individual got ahead by a combination of effort and by asking for help when needed.

— Students with communication disorders should be encouraged to discuss their functional difficulties and needs in private during the first week of classes and to talk about ways to compensate.

— When it appears that a student needs help, ask if you can help. Accept a "No Thank You" graciously.

— Encourage classmates to accept the student with communicative problems.

— Be a good speech model. This will indicate to all that good communication is desirable.

— An atmosphere conductive to easy and good interactive communication should be established and maintained in the classroom.

— Consult a Speech Language expert concerning each child with a communicative disorder in your class and work with him/her throughout the class.

— Keep up-to-date on the student's accomplishments in therapy.

— Give students with speech impairments opportunity to speak in class.

— Give them time to express themselves, do not interrupt or try to fill in gaps for them.

— Speak to them naturally.

Teacher Presentation

— Maintain contact with student.

— Allow students to tape lectures.

— Provide and interpreter (signed English or American Sign Language) to those who require another form of communication.

— Encourage and assist in facilitation of participation in activities and discussions.

— Be patient.

— Be a good listener.

Laboratory

— Allow more time for the student to complete activities.

— Place the student within reasonable distance from the instructor to meet their needs.

— Anticipate areas of difficulty in access and involve the student in doing the same. Together, work out alternate procedures while trying not to disengage the student from the activity.

— For students who cannot use the computer because of other physical limitations in their hands or arms, explore avenues for obtaining adaptive access software, (including Unicorn keyboards), special switches, Power Pads, eye controlled input systems, touch screens, footmice, and other special equipment.

— If appropriate, provide assistance, but also provide positive reinforcement when the student shows the ability to do something unaided.

— Use a peer-buddy system when appropriate.

— Lastly, consider alternate activities/exercises that can be utilized with less difficulty for the student, but has the same or similar learning objectives.

Group Interaction and Discussion

— Encourage classmates to accept the student with communicative problems.

— An atmosphere conductive to easy and good interactive communication should be established and maintained in the classroom.

— Encourage and assist in the facilitation of participation in activities and discussions.

— Allow more time for the student to complete activities.

Research

- Review and explain to the student the steps involved in a research activity. Think about which step(s) may be difficult for the specific functional limitations of the student and jointly devise accommodations for that student.
- Use appropriate lab and field strategies according to the nature of the research.
- Allow more time for the student to complete activities.
- With the student, work out alternate procedures which do not disengage the student from the activity.
- Anticipate areas of difficulty in access and involve the student with a communication disability in doing the same. Together, work out alternate procedures while trying to disengage the student from the activity.
- If appropriate, provide assistance, but also provide positive reinforcement when the student shows the ability to do something unaided.

Field Experiences

- Discuss with the student any needs, problems or alternatives he/she anticipates in the field learning environment.
- Consider alternate activities/exercises that can be utilized with less difficulty for the student, but has the same or similar learning objectives.
- Make special advance arrangements with curators during passive visiting field trips.
- When information gathering involves a physical action that the impaired student cannot perform, try a different experience yielding the same information.
- In the field, provide assistance, but also provide positive reinforcement when the student shows the ability to do something unaided.

Testing

— Allow more time for the student with communication impairments to complete tests in their optimal mode of communication.

— Design tests that are appropriate for the student's disorder (written, drawn, or oral.)

— Writers could be provided for test taking if the individual requires such assistance.

— Check to be sure that test instructions are completely understood by the child and provide any additional assistance that may be needed.

AUTISM SPECTRUM

Presently, autism is a condition still in the growing stages of research and treatment. We still have work ahead of us. When adults on the autism spectrum (like me) were young, autism was almost unknown; and therefore, not treated. Today, children on the spectrum are being diagnosed and treated. They have the advantage of receiving proper treatment and all the assistance they need as they mature. They have a very optimistic future. But, what about the older people? Presently, most services are geared towards children.

There are many adults and teenagers who have been recently diagnosed. They went through life the hard way, and are still experiencing challenges. They need assistance to make up for the lack of proper help in their growing years. Services for teenagers and adults on the spectrum are desperately needed! Problems that teenagers and adults on the autism spectrum experienced through their growing years include:

— Being considered neurotypical, and being expected to perform as such. Parents, family members, teachers, and friends did not understand why the individual was not matching one's capabilities; and became disappointed and expressed displeasure. The individual's self esteem became destroyed.

— Lack of proper guidance and counselling. Doctors, counsellors, teachers, and parents did not know much (if anything) about autism; therefore, had no idea how to help the individual. In extreme cases; parents and guidance providers became impatient and angry, lashing out at the individual and destroying one's self esteem.

— Peer pressure - a major issue. Children can be very cruel, finding anything different about any individual and ridiculing the person. Children with undiagnosed autism were prime candidates for receiving such abuse.

— Inability to perform successfully in school. Since the child on the spectrum was thought not to have any actual challenge, one was considered to have no excuse to struggle academically. It was thought that the individual simply chose not to put any effort into it. Obviously, proper counselling was never provided. Most individuals faced problems such as being wrongfully disciplined, being teased by peers, and failing classes.

— Difficulties in entering into employment. Many people with undiagnosed autism started their first job cold turkey, having no idea what to expect or how to perform. Many were unable to keep any job, and many were extremely intimidated by employment.

— Difficulty fitting in the social circle. In the past; one of the biggest problems with children on the spectrum was making friends. Because of their eccentric behaviour and so-called "shortcomings," other children did not want to socialize with them. As teenagers, most of them appeared totally unattractive to members of the opposite gender; therefore, had little or no chance in landing any dates. They became like "Ford Edsels," unwanted and forgotten.

As a result, most teenagers and adults on the autism spectrum face challenging situations including:

— Absence of social skills and experience. Many individuals on the spectrum cannot mesh smoothly into the social circle, and many have very few friends. Many of them have never been involved in a romantic relationship. They could end up leading a normally solitary life.

— Inappropriate (or lack of) employment and income. Many individuals on the spectrum were unable to maintain adequate education in the past, or had no idea as to what they wanted to do for a living. As well; many experienced problems with employment in the past, as mentioned. As a result; many of these individuals are either unemployed, maintaining inadequate employment, or in a job that they do not like.

— Problematic emotional wellbeing. Absence of friendship and romance causes the individual to feel rejected. Absence of accomplishment in life destroys one's self esteem. Low self esteem and demons from the past and present cause the individual to be normally frustrated. Anger, depression, shame, and moodiness are common in life.

Along with the many people out there who have been diagnosed with this condition, there are many more that are undiagnosed. If the condition is suspected, it *must* be diagnosed! Society has to be designed to better accommodate these individuals. These people are presently experiencing complications that they do not deserve to go through, and they are definitely entitled to a better life.

A move that would make this all possible is advertising. We must put out a word to encourage people who suspect being on the spectrum, or family members of such, to receive a proper diagnosis. This way; we can round up all the people on the spectrum and achieve a large human body, and action will be taken. We must also make the public well aware of this condition. One means is by creating and distributing pamphlets to medical centres and schools. Advertising can also be done via radio and TV. If advertising can be made possible ASAP, we can get the ball rolling quickly.

A major problem that presently persists is that there are few doctors and counsellors that specialize in autism. Obviously, we must expand medical/psychological education and provide more encouragement to create more doctors in this field. Again, this could only be made possible with a large body of people on the spectrum. Today, it appears as if there are not enough people with this condition for professionals to concentrate in this area — but the situation is not actually as it appears! There are many of those who need the assistance, and we require more professionals to accommodate them.

SERVICES FOR TEENAGERS

Counselling

Counselling is a major key in assisting teenagers; and of course, we need a large body of professionals. Adolescents and teenagers face many emotional challenges, and these problems are heavily magnified for teens on the spectrum. Many teenagers need to have a dependable person to come to for support, and this is especially true for those who are on the spectrum. One means that would be helpful is individual counselling, which is strictly one on one with counsellor and patient. This would be personal; and therefore, private and confidential. The counsellor can provide individual training in social skills, assertive skills, and organizational skills. The counsellor can maintain contact with the school which the patient attends, helping to monitor and assist in performance in school, and resolve ongoing problems.

The counsellor can provide vocational assistance, possibly through contacts, to assist in integrating the patient into the world of employment. The counsellor may also know contacts about programs and activities for the patient, such as support groups (which we desperately need!), leisure activities, and/or clubs (involvement groups). Another means would be family counselling. Immediate family members need to be thoroughly educated on autism, and how to deal with the individual properly. Any problems that occur within the family can be discussed and worked out in these sessions. If the family has little or no knowledge of autism (especially in the case of it being undiagnosed), it can be a very gloomy and messy situation for them.

Support groups are something desperately needed, but presently scarce. Again, it takes a large body of diagnosed teens to make this possible. Once there are enough of those diagnosed on the spectrum, it can be possible to create support groups of several categories based on level of challenge. This way; we would have several different groups of people who are similar to one another, and everybody would be receiving appropriate support. This kind of system can be made up of regular meetings, as well as frequent special events. Group meetings would enable teenagers to make friends who have much in common, as well as to learn social skills. In addition; frequent special events, including recreational activities, can make life more pleasureful for the teens.

School

School is a *major* problem for young people on the spectrum. As mentioned, these individuals can struggle in school. Peer pressure is another terrible experience that they have to endure in school. Oftentimes, teachers are of little or no help. To improve performance in school, intensified tutoring is needed. The individual needs a full-time personal tutor who can constantly monitor the student's performance. This tutor must always be available for assistance, and able to help the student out of any academic jam. If the teacher is not always available for extra help, at least the tutor will be. As well; the tutor can be someone that the individual can come to for help with any kind of problem in school, including peer pressure and conflicts with any teachers.

Ultimately, this tutor must be somebody that the student is totally comfortable with. Peer pressure is another major problem that must be alleviated. Each teacher should educate the class about the individual and one's condition, and discourage the peers from teasing. Whenever there is an ongoing problem with teasing (e.g. a certain group of people constantly harassing the individual), teachers should be informed and willing to take action to rectify the problem. Such a situation can be dealt with by meeting with the group of troublesome peers, and having a serious discussion about the situation. The peers must be convinced to stop the teasing, and be monitored on a regular basis as to prevent further problems.

One idea that may help in solving the problem of peer pressure would be a peer alliance system. This system would consist of a group made up of decent peers (who do not like to participate in teasing people), and victims of peer pressure. This group would act as a social circle at school, which peer pressure targeted teens can hang out with during spare times. These people would play the role as friends, providing support for socially-challenged teens. They can monitor how their friends are being treated by their peers, and stick up for them in a civilized manner whenever there is a problem. As well; the group can arrange social events outside of school time, giving socially-deprived teens a chance to have pleasureful times with decent people. People with many friends experience less teasing. As the saying goes, "United we stand, divided we fall!"

Vocational Assistance

Employment is another struggle for people on the spectrum. As mentioned; entering the work force without preparation can be a traumatic experience for a teenager on the spectrum, and employment can continue to be problematic in years ahead. A vocational integration plan can be a helpful solution, designed to gradually integrate teens on the spectrum into the work force. This plan can begin with theoretic preparation, similar to a classroom setting. The counsellor would discuss in depth about employment; describing what it is like, what is expected from employees, and different types of work. The next step would be practical preparation, in which the students can perform practice tasks, perhaps in a mock workplace. This would give them the feel of working.

Once the preparation sessions are completed, the student may be assigned to temporary placement. The vocational integration committee can meet with employers who are willing to participate, and educate them on autism. The individual may be gradually integrated from part-time to full-time employment, at one's own rate depending on the individual. The purpose of this is to gradually prepare the individual for employment. The program can assist in post-secondary education and career planning. This program would be able to match the young individual with a steady job for the time being. This can also lead to permanent employment if the individual desires, depending on one's career goal.

SERVICES FOR ADULTS

Counselling

Counselling is a major key in assisting adults; and of course, we need a large body of professionals. Adults on the spectrum sometimes need to have a dependable person to come to for support, and can use some counselling and guidance to account for what they have missed in their growing years. The system can be similar to what was explained for teenagers, but on an adult scale. Individual counselling, which is strictly one on one with counsellor and patient, would be quite helpful. This would be personal; and therefore, private and confidential. The counsellor can provide assistance in social skills, assertive skills, and organizational skills.

The counsellor can provide vocational assistance, possibly through contacts, if the individual is struggling in the world of employment. The counsellor may also know contacts about programs and activities for the patient, such as support groups, leisure activities, and/or clubs (involvement groups). There are presently support groups for adults on the spectrum, but they are general. With the present small body of diagnosed adults, we have very basic support groups that are mainstream. If more people on the spectrum come to surface, it can be possible to create support groups of several categories based on level of challenge.

This way; we would have several different groups of people who are similar to one another, and everybody would be receiving appropriate support. This kind of system can be made up of regular meetings, as well as frequent special events. Group meetings would enable adults to make friends who have much in common, find companions to date, and enhance social skills. In addition; frequent special events, including recreational activities, can make life more pleasureful and fulfilling.

Career Planning

Many adults on the spectrum would benefit greatly with assistance in career planning. Their condition should not deprive them of a career that is enjoyable and rewarding, nor restrict them to a mundane job. Upon completion of secondary education, a career-planning program would be very helpful for those individuals. This type of program would also come in handy for those who are on Employment Insurance, or Workplace Safety and Insurance Board. With this plan, the individual may be given approximately a year in this program to allow him/her to research various types of careers.

The individual may begin by providing a detailed portfolio of one's self, history, education, and past employment. The program may begin with a classroom-like setting, where the individuals may make inquiries and receive assistance in getting started. If necessary, the counsellor can discuss in depth about employment; describing what it is like, what is expected from employees, and different types of work. As well; lessons can be provided for job-searching skills, such as cover letters, resumes, phone inquiries, and interviews. The program can also provide practice tasks relating to certain careers considered, giving the individual an idea of what it is like. After that, the individual can take the time to decide what kind of occupation he/she would prefer. This program would be intensified, in order to find a suitable and enjoyable career for the individual.

Once the decision has been made, the program can provide assistance in proceeding in post-secondary education, if necessary. The counsellors in this program can assist in researching the educational requirements for the career, and finding a suitable institution (i.e. college, university, etc.). Upon graduation from school, the plan can provide assistance in placement. Job-searching skills can be reinforced, and any additional help required can be provided.

Dating

Finding a partner for a romantic relationship is another area where adults on the spectrum experience difficulties. Specialized dating services for people on the spectrum would be very helpful in assisting these individuals to experience the pleasure of being in love. Everybody needs a companion, and people with any kind of challenge should not be an exception. Many kinds of services may be provided, ranging from singles' gatherings to matchmaking services. Support groups may also be quite helpful.

Singles gatherings may be suitable for those who prefer to 'do it on their own.' This set-up may consist of regular meetings; either weekly, biweekly, or monthly. It can also provide special events, such as dinner, shows, games, and dances. This is ideal for making friends, finding dates, or simply having fun! These gatherings would be arranged in several categories, based on age and level of condition. Matchmaking services may be suitable for those who prefer full-scale assistance in finding the suitable companion. All individuals would be required to provide complete portfolios of themselves to enable adequate matching. This type of service would be, of course, totally personal and customized. Unlike some dating services, this service must be totally honest!

6

EDUCATION OF CHILDREN WITH ORTHOPAEDIC DISABILITIES

Motor impaired/orthopedic disabilities includes a heterogeneous grouping of conditions with a wide range of causes. Examples of some of the more common causes are: Nervous system disorders Traumatic spinal cord injury Stroke Muscular Dystrophy Cerebral Palsy Epilepsy Muscular-skeletal disorders Rheumatoid arthritis Cardiovascular disease Coronary heart disease Respiratory Disorders Emphysema Asthma Endocrine-metabolic Diabetes Amputation of all types.

One of the first considerations in the effective science education of individuals with motor/orthopedic impairments is a brief understanding of his/her impairment and the degree of educational limitation it causes. With such information, a set of mitigative strategies can be derived that are fully appropriate to that particular student, however, some of the strategies may not work for every student.

GENERAL COURTESY

— Accept the fact that a disability exists. Not acknowledging this fact is not acknowledging the person.

— Ask the student to tell you when he/she anticipates a need for assistance.

— Don't lean on a student's wheelchair. The chair is a part of the body space of the student who uses it.

— Don't patronize students who use wheelchairs by patting them on the head. This is a sign of affection that should be reserved only for small children, and most of them do not like it either.

— Encourage students who use crutches or canes to keep them within easy reach and make such a space available.

— Only push a wheelchair when asked.

— Have custodians use non-skid floor polish for students who use crutches and wheelchairs.

— If spills occur, keep floors clear of liquids.

— If writing is difficult, use a tape recorder.

— Speak directly to the student with a disability, confidentially, as you would other students.

— Students should be encouraged to talk confidentially with their instructors during the first week of classes to discuss their functional difficulties and needs, and to talk about ways to accommodate.

— Using a wheelchair when the person can walk with the aid of cane(s), brace(s), crutch(es), or a walker does not mean a student is "feigning" the degree of disability. It may be a means to conserve energy or move about more quickly.

— When it appears that a student needs help, ask if you can help. Accept a "no thank you" graciously.

— When talking to a student who uses a wheelchair for more than a few minutes, or so, sit down or kneel to place yourself at that student's eye level.

— Reserve parking space that is accessible and close to the building.

— Allow course waiver or course substitution for certain students.

— Always plan any field trip in advance to ensure accessibility.

— Words like "walking" or "running" are appropriate. Sensitivity to these words is not necessary. Students who use wheelchairs use the same words.

General Strategies

— Bring to the student's attention Science Role Models with Disabilities with a similar disability to that of the student. Point out that this individual got ahead by a combination of effort and by asking for help when needed.

— If the functional limitation involves the lack of arm use then the use of Dragon-Dictate may be extremely useful. It may be used for such things as computer aided drafting and design (CADD) and other computer applications.

— Arrange for library personnel to assist access to card catalouges, bookshelves, and microfiche and other equipments.

— Consider accessibility factor to classroom so that student is able to get to class on time.

— Be familiar with the building's emergency evacuation plan to assure that it is manageable for the students.

Teacher Presentation

— If breaks between classes are short (10 minutes or less), the student who has a mobility impairment may frequently be a few minutes late. Students and instructors may want to plan for these occasions, so students don't miss important material.

— Observe potential obstacles so you can be aware of what is accessible and what is not accessible to students in wheelchairs.

— Students may need to tape lectures (difficulty with writing or unable to write).

— Table-type desks, with adequate leg space, which have enough clearance for wheelchairs can be moved into classrooms.

Laboratory

— Adaptations such as: latching devices, keylocks, headmaster, and light talkers that simplify access to computers can greatly help the motor/orthopedic science student.

— Consider alternate activities/exercises that can be utilized with less difficulty for the student, but has the same or similar learning objectives.

— Allow more time for the student to complete the lab activities.

— Alter the height of tables to "fit" the students (e.g., a small ramp to a flat platform for high desks).

— Anticipate areas of difficulty in access and involve the student with disability in doing the same. Together, work out alternate procedures while trying not to disengage the student from the activity.

— Assign a lab partner who can help to reach or manipulate objects as needed.

— Be aware of, and prevent the possible overheating of students who have poor heat regulation.

— Have students in wheelchairs participate in activities as fully as possible.

— Built-in lab tables (or small ramp/platforms) may need to be modified to accommodate wheelchairs.

— For students who cannot fully use a computer because of physical limitations in their hands or arms, explore avenues for obtaining adaptive access software, altered keyboards (including Unicorn keyboards), special switches (latching devices, keylocks), and Power Pads, eye-controlled input systems, or touch-screens in conjunction with a light talker, trackballs, footmice, and other special equipment.

— If appropriate, provide assistance, but also provide positive reinforcement when the student shows the ability to do something unaided.

— If breaks between classes are short (10 minutes or less), the student who has a mobility impairment may frequently be a few minutes late. Students and instructors may want to plan for these occasions, so students don't miss important aspects of the activity.

— In the laboratory, place water, gas, and electric facilities in accessible locations.

— Increase size of wheels, dials, handles, and buttons on lab equipment.

— Lower supplies and equipment for easier access, or simply give them to the student as needed.

— Perhaps a change in aisles (by relocating desks and/or chairs) is needed for wheelchair access.

— For hoods in laboratories, have operating knobs and switches within easy access.

— Provide an accessible means for the recording of data, charts, or graphs.

— Select non-manual types of laboratory teaching techniques (e.g., electronic probes vs. pipette bulbs).

— Table-type desks, which are high enough for wheelchairs can be moved into labs.

— Use a peer-buddy system.

— Use electric hot plates instead of Bunsen burners as heat sources.

— Use laboratory sinks that are accessible from 3 sides for those with one side or those who are paralyzed.

— Use low-force electric micro switches for lights and equipment.

— Use modified lids on the tops of containers (wider and bigger).

— Use a portable eye wash.

— When information gathering involves a physical action that the student cannot perform, try using a different type of experience that will yield the same information.

Group Interaction and Discussion

— Include student in open discussions.

— Allow more time for the student to complete activities.

— Use ramps and raised platforms for student's access.

— Lower chalkboard and/or corkboard.

Reading

— Acknowledge understanding by blinking, nodding, or a pointer.

— Use a tape recorder.

— Use small sections of large text or readings.

— Use easels, portable reading racks, a standing table, and adjustable seats and desks.

— Allow more time for the student to complete the activities.

Field Experiences

— Anticipate areas of difficulty and involve the student with a disability in doing the same. Together, and in the planning stage, work out alternate procedures while trying not to disengage the student from the activity.

— Consider alternate activities/exercises that can be utilized with less difficulty for the student, but has the same or similar learning objectives.

— Be sure students in wheelchairs can fully participate in activities.

— When the activity involves field work or field trips, many of the students using a wheelchair will probably need other travel arrangements because they often need to rely on attendants, ramp adapted vans for transportation, or power lift vans for transportation to and from field activities.

— In the field, provide assistance, but also provide positive reinforcement when the student shows the ability to do something unaided.

— Increase size of wheels, dials, handles, and buttons on field equipment.

— Use a peer-buddy system.

— Use modified lids on the tops of containers (wide, bigger, and easier to open).

— When information gathering involves a physical action that the physically impaired student cannot perform, try a different experience yielding the same information.

— Make special advance arrangements with curators during passive visiting field trips.

— Make sure that field activity sites are accessible. Check the following:

  — Are there nearby parking spaces reserved for persons with disabilities?

  — Is there a ramp or a step-free entrance?

  — Are there accessible rest rooms?

— If the site is not on the ground floor, does the building have an elevator?

— Are water fountains and telephones low enough for a student in a wheelchair?

— Arrange with curators of museums, science centres, etc. for alternate activities if it is not possible to have the student in a wheelchair do the activities.

— Discuss any needs, problems, or alternatives with the student.

Research

— Review and discuss with the student the steps involved in a research activity. Think about which step(s) may be difficult for the specific functional limitations of the student and jointly devise accommodations for that student.

— Depending on the site of the research check the previous two sections.

— Use appropriate laboratory and field strategies.

Testing

— Allow more time for the student to complete the activities.

— Provide a seperate place for the test if necessary.

— Give completely oral tests or completely written tests, whichever is more appropriate to the students needs.

— Allow students to tape record answers to tests or type answers, as needed.

— Writers should be provided for test-taking if the student is unable to write (or give oral tests out of the earshot of other students).

— Students may write slowly and need extended time for tests.

— Develop a portfolio of the student's work, both singly and as part of a cooperating group. Orally quiz him/her to establish the extent to which the student contributed to the group-based accomplishments.

SPECIAL EDUCATIONAL NEEDS OF PHYSICALLY HANDICAPPED CHILDERN

A physically handicapped person is defined as a person who has a disability of locomotor and neurological origin which constitutes a disadvantage or restriction in one or more aspects of daily living activities, including work. However, from the educational point of view, not all pupils with physical disabilities require special school provisions. There may be variations in duration or severity among physical disabilities. In other words, the handicapping conditions may be temporary or permanent and mild or severe. Physically handicapped children may be multiply handicapped with mental handicap, visual or hearing impairment.

Based on the principles of provision of special education as stipulated in the White Paper on Rehabilitation 1995, for children with a disability who cannot benefit satisfactorily from education in a mainstream setting in an ordinary school, there are the provisions of special schools and special education classes in ordinary schools. Following this guiding principle, provisions listed below have been offered:

1. Special school provision for school age children with physical handicaps or their associated problems which result in their inability to withstand ordinary school routine and environment:

2. Ordinary school placement with supports like centre-based resource teaching, peripatetic teaching and advisory service from the Resource Help Service for Physically Handicapped Pupils Integrated in Ordinary Schools of the Services Division of the Education Department.

3. Hospital School teaching service for school age children staying in hospitals and home-based teaching service for home bound children who cannot attend school because of physical reasons.

EFFECTS OF PHYSICAL PROBLEMS ON EDUCATION

Mobility and Physical Fitness

Physical handicaps may cause various degrees of weaknesses and in co-ordination of the limbs which may affect mobility, posture and manual dexterity. Other physical problems such as heart diseases may cause poor exercise tolerance and low level of physical fitness. All these may directly result in pupils' difficulty to cope with ordinary school routine and limit their ability in exploring and understanding the environment.

Perception and Concentration

Besides the above mentioned motor problems, neurological impairment may also cause sensory deficiency or over stimulation which may disturb perception and concentration inducing specific learning difficulties for the pupils.

Intelligence

One associated disability among physically handicapped children, cerebral palsied children in particular, is mental handicap. As cited in the report of a survey conducted in the 95/96 school year by the Sub-committee on Special Education of the Board of Education, 56% of the pupil intake in schools for the physically handicapped are mentally handicapped.

Communication

Cerebral palsy, late stage of muscular dystrophy and facial burns may affect the pupils' ability in verbal communication. On top of this, their non-verbal communication may also be affected because these conditions may limit their facial expression and ability in signing.

Emotion

The disadvantageous position in which physically handicapped pupils are placed may cause them some of the emotional problems including low self-esteem, lack of self-confidence, fear of changes in environment, apathy, over dependence on others, low level of aspiration, anxiety and frustration. Some brain damaged children may also be hyperactive, aggressive or lack of emotional control. Based on the above possible effects of physical handicaps on children, their education programmes must be so designed as to help them overcome their physical handicaps and associated difficulties.

AIMS IN EDUCATING PHYSICALLY HANDICAPPED CHILDREN

It has been stated in the Information Sheet on Special Education issued by the Services Division, Education Department that the general aim of special education in Hong Kong is to provide children having special needs with education necessary to help them develop their potential to the full, achieve as much independence as they are capable of, and become well adjusted individuals in the community.

The general aim of education for physically handicapped pupils focused on the total development of pupils is similar to that for special education on the whole. Nevertheless, targeted at the specific needs of physically handicapped pupils, there are the following specific aims to consider when planning the curriculum :

1. To offer them a general education in ordinary, special day or special residential school setting according to their needs.

2. To prepare them for integration into ordinary schools or society, and to meet their psychological needs for security, love and affection, acceptance and success.
3. To teach them the basic daily living skills for independent living.
4. To help them realize their limitations and their potential and hence develop a realistic and positive outlook towards life.
5. To cultivate interests and hobbies for improving their quality of life.
6. To enhance their social development including their interpersonal relationship.
7. To provide them with medical and other auxiliary services such as physiotherapy, occupational therapy, speech therapy, career and vocational counselling.
8. To compensate for their loss of life experience due to mobility difficulties through organized excursions and outdoor activities.

A student is considered to have a physical disability or chronic health impairment based on the need for special educational services due to one or more of the following:

— nervous system impairment;

— musculoskeletal condition; and/or

— chronic health impairment.

Medical diagnosis, by itself, does not determine the special educational services required by students with physical disabilities or chronic health impairments. Students are only eligible for funding in this category if their education is adversely affected by their physical disabilities or chronic health impairments. To be eligible for supplemental funding for a student in this category, the following conditions must be met:

— the student must meet one or more of the above criteria; and

— a current IEP must be in place;.and

— direct, ongoing special education service(s) must be provided.

These services should be outlined in the IEP and directly related to the student's identified special need(s). The special education service(s) must be in addition to any services provided under formula funding based on total student enrolment (e.g., learning assistance, counselling). Reduction in class size is not by itself a sufficient service to meet the definition.

IDENTIFICATION AND ASSESSMENT

Assessments should integrate current, relevant information related to the student's intellectual, social/emotional, sensory, physical and communicative abilities as well as his or her ability to perform activities of daily living at school. Individual Education Plans should take into account specific health care and personal care needs, and outline specific strategies to address those needs. An extended school-based team would typically include medical professionals and consultation with parents in order to develop and implement an effective IEP.

Planning and Implementation

Medical diagnosis, by itself, does not determine the special educational services required by a student with physical disabilities or chronic health impairments. It is the extent and impact of the physical/medical condition, and the consequent need for services which enable the student to access an educational program and participate in a meaningful way, that are the determinants. Foı some students, increasing dependence is expected due to degenerative conditions or terminal illnesses. It is important that these students be encouraged to maintain normal routines as long as possible. At the same time, it is essential that the educational system affirm the rights of students and families to participate meaningfully in the individualization of the student's educational program.

Health care plans will need regular updating and will need to include emergency procedures to meet individual needs and circumstances. Students with physical disabilities or chronic health impairments should have opportunities to participate in school activities to the greatest extent possible. Adaptations to facilities or equipment to allow access to school areas and programs should be made as quickly as possible where physical barriers exist. In all situations where there is contact with body fluids, personnel are advised to follow the "Universal Precautions", and to contact the medical health officer as laid out in the School Act (section 9(4)) where there is a concern about safety of others.

Evaluation and Reporting

In most cases, students with physical disabilities or chronic health impairments will take part in the regular program with the necessary adaptations. Evaluation will be based on the regular standards (i.e., extent to which learning outcomes were achieved). The method of evaluation will be consistent with the IEP and with ministry reporting policies in respect to the use of comments and/or letter grades. Some students may require extensive modifications to parts of their program so that some of their learning outcomes will be substantially different from the regular curriculum. In these cases, evaluation will be based on the degree to which the individualized outcomes are achieved.

Evaluation would be referenced to individually set standards. Reports to parents should be provided on the same schedule used for all students. Progress should be reported with respect to all components of the program, and with reference to progress in relation to IEP goals. Reports should indicate the adaptations and modifications made to the student's educational program. All personnel directly involved in the ongoing educational program (e.g., classroom teacher, specialist teacher, speech- language pathologist) should report on student progress.

Teachers and other professionals

The Ministry of Education expects that with sufficient training and experience, classroom teachers will be capable of including most students with physical disabilities and chronic health impairments and providing a program in which they can be successful, provided that specialist support is available when needed. Inservice training opportunities and a collaborative team approach are recommended to support and encourage the development of the skills required. Teachers with responsibilities for supporting students with physical disabilities or chronic health impairments should fulfill the qualifications described for learning assistance. In addition, they should have advanced coursework in:

— the characteristics and needs of students with physical disabilities and chronic health impairments; and

— specialized instructional methodologies and technologies; and adaptation or modification of programs for students with physical disabilities or chronic health impairments.

There also may be a need for a qualified health professional to monitor the quality of the health services. Protocol agreements with the Ministry of Health identify the needs of these students as falling into three levels. Whenever there is any doubt as to who should provide health care in the school setting, the district staff and the school principal shall consult with the parents, the local health unit or the attending physician. Districts should ensure that staff who serve students with chronic and complex health needs are trained and qualified to perform the functions required. Recent and ongoing technological advances in adaptive devices related to computer access, environmental controls, and augmented communication have greatly enhanced learning opportunities for students with physical disabilities. Staff will need to stay informed of current developments and introduce new technology as appropriate. The service of SET-BC may be appropriate for some of these students.

Teacher assistants

Teacher assistants who work in classrooms with students with physical disabilities or chronic health impairments should have sufficient skills and training for the duties they are assigned, including:

— an understanding of the social, emotional, and educational implications of dependent needs;

— functional life skills and career development; and

— technological support.

It should be noted that teacher assistants work under the general supervision of a teacher or administrative officer. Inservice training should include opportunities to further develop expertise in these and related areas.

7

Administration and Organisation of Special Education in India

Throughout the world, Children With Special Needs (CWSN) were a neglected lot till the 18th century, when the ideas of fraternity, equality and liberty sweeping France and America inspired political reformers and leaders in medicine and education to turn their attention towards the educational needs of such individuals. France played a pioneering role in the area of special education. It was in Paris that Valentine Huay started a School for the Blind in 1785 and Father De L'epee developed an early version of finger spelling for the deaf. Jean Marc Gaspard Itard's case study of 'The Wild Boy of Aveyron' is a pioneering work in the field of education for the mentally retarded.

Along with other parts of the world, India too, witnessed the emergence of special schools for people with disabilities. The first school for the deaf was set up in Bombay in 1883, and the first school for the blind at Amritsar in 1887. There was rapid expansion in the number of such institutions. Today, there are more than 3200 special schools throughout India. However, these special schools have certain disadvantages which became evident as the number of these schools increased. These institutions reached out to a very limited number of children, largely urban and they were not cost effective. But most important of all, these special schools segregated CWSN from the mainstream, thus developing a specific disability culture.

INTEGRATED EDUCATION

The emergence of the concept of integrated education in India during the mid 1950s was seen as a solution to these problems. Small experiments in this area were begun by the Royal Commonwealth Society for the Blind. and the Christopher Blind Mission. The Ministry of Education, too, launched a comprehensive scholarship scheme in 1952 — a rudimentary beginning of the integrated education initiative by the Government.

Integrated Education for Disabled Children (IEDC)

Consequent on the success of international experiments in placing children with disabilities in regular schools, the Planning Commission, in 1971, included in its plan a programme for integrated education. The Government launched the IEDC scheme in December 1974. However, educational administrators have been slow in grasping the value of IE.

The aim of IEDC is

— to provide educational opportunities to CWSN in regular schools,

— to facilitate their retention in the school system, and

— to place children from special schools in common schools.

The scope of the scheme includes pre-school training, counselling for the parents, and special training in skills for all kinds of disabilities. The scheme provides facilities in the form of books, stationery, uniforms, and allowances for transport, reader, escort etc. Inspite of all these facilities, IEDC met with limited success — only a little more than one lakh CWSN have been covered. However, it was successful in creating awaren]ess on the importance of integrating CWSN in the mainstream of education, a fact noted in the National Policy on Education — 1986.

Project Integrated Education for the Disabled (PIED)

The next step was another experiment on IE in India. There was a shift in strategy, from a school based approach to a Composite Area Approach — and in 1987 the Ministry of Human Resources Development, along with UNICEF launched another experiment: Project Integrated Education for the Disabled (PIED). In this approach, a cluster, instead of the individual school approach is emphasised. A cluster, usually a block of population is taken as the project area. All the schools in the area are expected to enroll children with disabilities. Training programmes were also given to the teachers.

This project was implemented in one administrative block each in Madhya Pradesh, Maharashtra, Nagaland, Orissa, Rajasthan, Tamil Nadu, Haryana, Mizoram, Delhi Municipal Corporation, and Baroda Municipal Corporation. The approach is an improvement over the special schools in many ways and appears to be the only way towards universalising education of the disabled children. It is more cost effective and easier to organise, since existing school infrastructure is to be made use of.

Inclusion is:

— a philosophy built on the belief that all people are equal and should be respected and valued, as an issue of basic human rights.

— an "unending set of processes" in which children and adults with disabilities have the opportunity to participate fully in ALL community activities offered to people who do not have disabilities.

Under PIED, there has been a significant increase in the number of not only mildly disabled, but also severely disabled children, with the number of orthopaedically handicapped children far outstripping other disabled children. All these perform at par with non - disabled children; in fact their retention rate is higher than that of non - disabled children and absenteeism is low. PIED has also had a positive impact on the attitudes of the teachers, the heads of schools, as well as parents and the community in general. Also, the interaction between the disabled and the non - disabled children is good.

In India, the family is largely responsible for its members with disabilities. With the increase of women in the work force and with fewer joint family systems in the urban areas, many parents are concerned about their ability to take care of their children with disabilities. Also, parents have few opportunities to advocate for their children. Meetings are often difficult to organize and are poorly attended. In response to those needs, the National Institute for the Mentally Handicapped organized the first national meeting of the registered parent associations in 1990.

In India, few provisions have historically been made for students with disabilities. The responsibility of caring for children with moderate to severe and profound disabilities generally has been left to parents and the few institutions managed by voluntary organizations. These organizations often do not meet the demand. Only in the past decade has the Indian government enacted legislation that has empowered children with disabilities and their families. This legislation has also provided for training of personnel working with children with disabilities.

In 1992, India enacted its first piece of legislation related to special education: the Rehabilitation Council of India Act. The major purpose of the Rehabilitation Council of India Act was to mandate minimum standards of education for professionals working with individuals with disabilities. The Persons with Disabilities (Equal Opportunities, Protection of Rights and Full Participation) Act was initiated in 1995 and implemented in 1998. This comprehensive, breakthrough legislation provides for education and economic rehabilitation. This legislation stipulates that the government and local authorities ensure that every child under the age of 18 has a right to a free education. It further emphasizes the need for an environment and services that are conducive to learning.

The economic rehabilitation section under the act stipulates that certain posts in various government departments and in the public sector be identified, and a percentage of them be reserved for people with disabilities. In 1999, The National Trust for Welfare of Persons with Autism, Cerebral Palsy, Mental Retardation and Multiple Disabilities Act was passed. The focus of this act was to ensure the welfare of people with autism, cerebral palsy, mental retardation, and multiple disabilities on a national level. Readers might find it helpful to compare these three acts and their purposes with two pieces of U.S. legislation passed in the 1970s. Section 504 of the Rehabilitation Act (1973) was the first attempt at a national civil rights law for people with disabilities.

In 1975, The Education for All Handicapped Children's Act (Public Law 94-142) was passed. This law enabled all children, no matter how severe the disability, access to a public education that was free and appropriate.

Education Policy

After independence in 1947, India mandated its Universal Education for All policy, making education free and compulsory for all children age 6-14 years. In an effort to serve a mobile and vast population with limited resources, however, children with disabilities were not addressed. In the United States, children with disabilities are eligible to attend public school and receive free appropriate services.

Recent U.S. trends focus on various inclusive settings where children belong to the general classroom and spend the whole or part of their day there. In India, despite The Persons with Disabilities Act (1995), most of the services seem to be provided to children with disabilities through private or nongovernment organizations, where the family has to pay a fee or depend on charity. Only a small percentage of children are integrated into general education public schools that are governed by the Department of Education.

Private schools are often not an option because they provide an intense academic curriculum, which is not adapted to meet the needs of students with disabilities (Misra, 2000). The Ministry of Welfare, with assistance from the Department of Health, Labor and Employment, is responsible for special education schools. Approximately 681 of them serve children with mental retardation. Nongovernment organizations serving children with disabilities exceed the number of government schools and receive 90% of the funds earmarked for children with disabilities.

Personnel Training

Lack of appropriately trained personnel has been one of the many constraints in providing services for children with disabilities in India. Training programs were isolated with little or no collaboration. There were no standard syllabi and little uniformity in the teaching curriculum at various institutions.

The Rehabilitation Council of India was developed under the Ministry of Social Justice and Empowerment to promote the training of personnel/professionals working with people with disabilities. The following are included in its objectives:

The regulation of training policies and programs in the field of rehabilitation.

Standardization of courses to ensure that all programs, whether attached to a university or not, meet the minimum qualifications for working with people with disabilities. Research and collaboration with organizations providing direct service to people with disabilities.

The Rehabilitation Council maintains uniformity through continuous monitoring and evaluation of the various programs.

Family Issues and Involvement

Each country has its own religious, economic, and cultural differences that shape its attitude toward people with disabilities. In India, many parents believe that their children with disabilities are a gift-or a punishment from God. Because of the low literacy rate, inaccessibility to information, and poor medical care, the treatment of children with disabilities and their families is a concern that may be based on misinformation. In coping with children with disabilities, parents face many challenges: the child's behavior problems, lack of acceptance by extended family members and friends, and financial constraints. Families also report the lack of information, lack of empathy, and incorrect recommendations by their doctors and the medical profession.

In India, the family is largely responsible for its members with disabilities. With the increase of women in the work force and with fewer joint family systems in the urban areas, many parents are concerned about their ability to take care of their children with disabilities. Also, parents have few opportunities to advocate for their children.

Meetings are often difficult to organize and are poorly attended. In response to those needs, the National Institute for the Mentally Handicapped organized the first national meeting of the registered parent associations in 1990.

A MODEL PROGRAM

Most of the services for children with disabilities in India involve establishing special schools and providing grants to special schools run by nongovernment organizations. Though India has passed legislation to meet the needs of students with disabilities, these services have still not been provided to people with moderate to profound mental retardation. Public schools run by the government do not meet their needs. The few children that are integrated into the public schools primarily demonstrate sensory or physical disabilities. People with moderate to profound mental retardation are still largely served by private organizations.

The S.P.S. Sadhana School is one model private program that shows how initiative, dedication, and careful planning by professionals and parents can meet the needs of this population. There are currently 36 qualified staff members and 40 volunteers in the school serving 114 students with moderate to profound mental retardation. The program has involved parents and has become one of the few modei schools for providing services to children and young people with mental retardation.

According to Khanna, the S.P.J. Sadhana School for children with moderate to profound retardation is located at Sophia College, Bombay, India. As a private school, it cannot depend on the government for funds. Driven by the belief that the young adult with mental retardation can be a productive and contributing member of society, the main purpose of the S.P.J. Sadhana School is to educate and train young people with mental retardation for future integration into the mainstream economy.

The approach is a work-related curriculum where the main emphasis is integration into society and economic productivity to the maximum extent possible. The S.P.S. Sadhana School has made considerable efforts to contact organizations and seek community placements for their students. To ensure student success, staff members conduct follow-ups to monitor student progress. Because most families will be responsible for their children throughout their lifetime, staff make efforts to ensure that these children can contribute to the family at home by performing simple tasks and gaining a certain level of independence. This has resulted in the development of courses that are an extension of the prevocational and vocational training offered at the school level.

The school staff members believe that success begins with early intervention; thus, children begin school at 5 years of age. During their years in school, they progress through three major stages, as follows:

— *Basic stage*: Learning simple adaptive and social skills.

— *Prevocational stage*: Learning skills needed to facilitate learning at the vocational stage. Students learn functional academics, including concepts of time, money, functional reading, and daily living skills.

— *Vocational stage*: The school selects children for one of the three vocational courses: creative arts and crafts, fast food and catering, and office skills. These courses are offered after a careful analysis of the Indian market needs and the capabilities of the students in the school.

The S.P.S. Sadhana School has, through a lot of research and trial and error among teachers in the classroom, developed effective teaching strategies and educational technology technology to teach the complex skills needed at the vocational training stage. Appropriate use of computers and machines are included as an important part of the program. Additional services such as speech, physical, and occupational therapy are also provided.

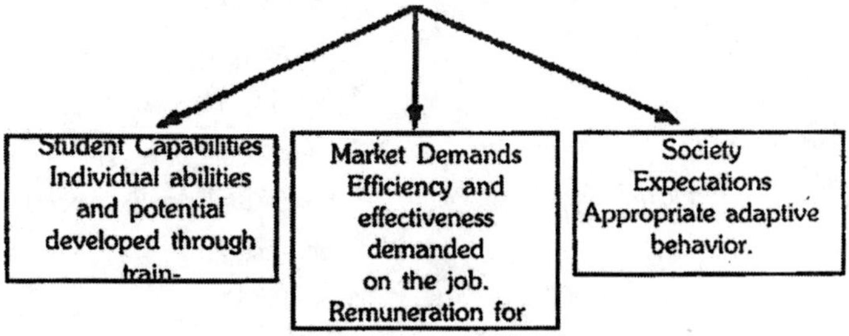

Figure 1. Factors Considered in Planning the Individualized Vocational Program

The school has created two cooperative business enterprises, or workshop employment opportunities, with donations and parent involvement. The purpose of these workshops is to include children who are unable to find employment in the community with an opportunity to be productive. Artistic goods created with the assistance of personnel are sold to the public.

Every student in the program has an integrated vocational training program, which is individualized and which seeks to empower the student (see Figure 1).

The combination of a functional approach with an emphasis on appropriate behavior allows teachers the freedom and flexibility to respond to the needs of the individual. Throughout the program, staff members include instruction in the competency skills essential for integration into society (see Table 1).

Table 1. Competency Skills Integrated into the Program

Basic Skills	* Listening
	* Speaking
	* Functional literacy
Thinking Skills	* Making decisions
	* Making choices
	* Generalizing
	* Thinking creatively
	* Solving problems
	* Reasoning
Personal Qualities	* Individual responsibility
	* Self-esteem
	* Sociability
	* Self-management
	* Integrity

BEHAVIOR INTERVENTION PLANS

Most students at the school demonstrate appropriate social behavior as a result of intensive behavior intervention programs. The counselor at the school provides a plan, which provides for rewards and consequences. For extreme inappropriate behaviors, children are removed from the classroom to consult with the counselor. This may result in the child being given a time out in a padded enclosure until the behavior subsides. To ensure consistency, behavior intervention plans are implemented by all personnel. Aware that generalization of skills to various one day, children have been taken on field trips that have been overnight or longer.

Facing Autism and Integrating Communication in the Environment (FACE).

By adapting some features of effective behavior interventions, the school has created an innovative program for students with autism. The purpose of FACE is to provide an integrated approach that allows for immediate intervention of problems. In this strategy, inappropriate behaviors are immediately replaced with appropriate behaviors and communication strategies that are effective. This approach has also been found to increase appropriate behaviors and communication skills in children with other severe disabilities.

INCLUSIVE EDUCATION

Another important paradigm shift in this area was initiated with the thinking that any difficulty that a child exhibited in learning was to be attributed not to a problem within the child, but to the school system. The organisation and management of schools, and the various programmes of teaching and interventions could also be one of the causes of children's learning difficulties. The new whole school policy is also referred to as the social or environmental model and rests on the theory that the child is a product of his/her experiences and the interventions the child has with various environments that impinge upon him/her. Thus to a great extent a child's growth and development depends upon this.

Inclusive Education in DPEP

This policy dictated the philosophy of inclusive education in DPEP. Moreover, DPEP also addressed core issues related to curriculum such as what factors limit the access of certain children to curriculum; what modifications are necessary to ensure fuller curriculum access. Thus, with its child - centered pedagogy, DPEP set a stage where children with special needs could be provided learning opportunities tailored to their needs. IED was formally added in DPEP in 1997. By 1998, many DPEP states had conducted surveys, assessment camps and evolved strategies to provide resource support to those children with special needs who were enrolled in DPEP schools.

The IED guidelines in DPEP clearly menton that , "DPEP will fund interventions for IED of primary school going children with integrable and mild to moderate disabilities". Towards this end DPEP supported:

— Community mobilisation and early detection

— In - service teacher training

— Provision of resource support

— Provision of educational aids and appliances

— Removal of architectural barriers

IED was initially introduced in the states in a small way by taking one block/cluster as a pilot project in each DPEP district. From a few hundred blocks in 1998, IED is currently being implemented in 2014 blocks of 18 DPEP states. Ten states of Gujarat, Haryana, Himachal Pradesh, Karnataka, Kerala, Madhya Pradesh, Maharashtra, Orissa, Tamil Nadu and Uttaranchal have upscaled the IED programme to all the blocks. DPEP estimates clearly showed that there were a large number of disabled children in the relevant age group. Gradually realisation dawned that UPE could not be achieved unless children with special needs were also brought under the ambit of primary education.

This led to more concrete planning and strategisation of providing resource support and remedial assistance to children with special needs. As the programme progressed many models of service delivery evolved with the sole aim of providing supportive learning environment to children with special needs. The thrust was on imparting quality education to all disabled children.

Constitutional and legal obligations and policies at the international and national levels

— UN Convention on the Rights of the Child, 1989

— UN Declaration on Education for All, 1990 (Jomtien Declaration)

— UN Standard Rules on Equalisation of Opportunities for Persons with Disabilities, 1993

— The Salamanca Declaration, 1994

— Article 45 and 93rd Amendment

— National Policy on Education, 1986

"...Future emphasis shall be on distance and open learning systems to provide opportunities and access to all the major target groups, especially the disadvantaged, viz., women, scheduled castes and scheduled tribes, the adult working class, and people serving in the far - flung remote areas."

Rehabilitation Council of India Act, 1992

Passed by Parliament in 1992, this act makes it mandatory for every special teacher to be registered by the council and lays down that every child with disability had the right to be taught by a qualified teacher. In fact it provided punishment for those teachers who engaged in teaching children with special needs without a license.

— Education Policy of Government of India, 1992 (Modified)

— Persons with Disabilities (Equal Opportunities, Protection of Rights & Full Participation) Act, 1995

A composite act covering all aspects, it mainly deals with education and employment.

— National Trust Act (National Trust for the Welfare of Persons with Autism, Cerebral Palsy, Mental Retardation and Multiple Disability), 1999

A landmark legislation, this trust seeks to protect and promote the rights of persons who within the disability sector, have been even more marginalised than others. The salient features are:

— First of its kind in the category of persons addressed

— Recognition of range of independence in Skills, Daily Living and Financial Management

— Protection - dominant, rather than autonomy - dominant

— Local Level Committee - District Level Coverage

— Decision making powers to Persons with Disabilities

— Legal Guardianship - even for parents

— Stake-holdership of Registered Organisations

— Legality/ Responsibility linked to Bequests

In her paper *Parental Perspective on IED* Ms. Shivagami, SPASTN, Chennai spoke about the expectation of parents of CWSN and how they were belied or fulfilled by the different approaches to the educational needs of these children. Special Schools which admitted special children were supported by welfare services and provided specialised services in the form of Consultants, Therapists, and Special Educators. They, however, promoted segregation, and the children enrolled in these schools could not escape from social stigma, nor could the lack of role models be overcome in these schools. In regular schools, however, a CWSN would face other problems such as access, attitudes, teacher's apprehension and peer acceptance, rigid curriculum and extra curricular activities. Inclusive education would be considered a success if mainstream schools developed a positive attitude towards the educational needs of disabled children and increase access through simple adaptations.

Apart from a general awareness in society, what needs to be done is teacher preparation and peer acceptance. Only thus can the diversity of the human condition be celebrated. Dr. Neelam Sinha, NIOS, New Delhi spoke on Inclusive Education Through Open Learning. The widening inequity in education is related to the problem of access. Deprivation of education is also due to the rigidity of the formal system of education in terms of fixed time, fixed curricula, evaluation system and learning pace. In order to meet the challenges, it is necessary to look for alternative strategies and approaches, particularly to ensure not only access, but also freedom relevance and quality. Innovative educational leaders are now talking about more flexible and learner friendly educational methods, which automatically respond to individual learner needs.

Open learning has emerged with a promise to make education a really effective tool for the process of democratisation and social justice. It is particularly characterised by removal of restrictions, exclusions, and privileges; by the accreditation of students' previous experiences, by the flexibility of the management of the time variable; and by substantial changes in the traditional relationship between teacher and students. It offers unique educational opportunities free from the constraints of time and space as well as rigidity of curricula. Inclusive education goes beyond physical presence of a child in the classroom situation; going through the same curricula as the non-disabled, appearing at the same examination with them and acquiring the same certificate.

National Institute of Open Schooling is promoting inclusive education by registering children with disabilities through Accredited Institutions (AI), Accredited Vocational Institutions (AVI), Special Accredited Institutions for the Education of the Disadvantaged (SAIED) and Open Basic Education (OBE). Some of the disabled learners may like to stay at home or study at their working places. Open schooling may reach any group of person at any given circumstance. Learning materials, audio-video cassettes, or working kit may reach at the doorsteps of disabled learners.

In spite of in-built flexibilities in the open learning system and concessions given in the tuition fee, it could not attract a large number of the children with disabilities. The reasons may be numerous. Perhaps, the existing curriculum is not relevant or the evaluation system or often procedures need revision. To enhance the access, retain them in the learning process and achieve development of the children with disabilities, NIOS has established a Cell for the Education of the Disabled (CED) in the year 2000. In the dynamic changing environment and rapid technological advancement, open learning has to play a significant role not only to provide access, but to retain persons with disabilities in the learning process and achieve success.

It is felt that the issues pertaining to relevant programmes, curricula and pedagogy are important and initiatives in these directions, specially for catering to the needs of learners with disabilities and the marginalised groups of children need to be addressed with seriousness. The formal, non-formal, adult education, vocational education, special education and open schooling systems all have to optimise their services and support to promote the full and equal participation of persons with disabilities. Ms. Ruma Banerjee, Director, Seva-in-Action, Bangalore, presented a paper on Teacher Training Strategies in IED. The success of IE depends on how responsive is the general school system to the challenges of children with disabilities. Seva-in-Action with DPEP developed an IE programme in 1998.

Through a study of the existing training programme, it was found that teachers had a positive approach towards IE, but lacked knowledge and practical skills for teaching special children. There was need for supportive materials for use by resource teachers and general teachers, and decentralisation of training at block level and cluster level with more practical input. The objective of the training is to develop Multi category Resource Persons (MRP) who can orient other teachers to promote the development of inclusive education in schools in rural society.

Inclusion means

— educating children with disabilities in the schools they would attend if they did not have disabilities

— providing services and support that parents and children with disabilities need in order to be in normal settings

— supporting regular education teachers and administrators

— having children with disabilities follow the same schedule as other children

— encouraging friendships between children with disabilities and their classmates/peers without disabilities

— teachers and administrators taking these concerns seriously

— teaching ALL children to understand and accept differences

Outline of training : 7 weeks:

— 1st phase — 15 days at Block Level

Philosophy, Awareness and Identification of Needs

— 2nd phase — 3 weeks at District Level

Overcoming Impairments

— 3rd phase — 15 days at Block Level

Adaptation of Teaching Methods and Classroom Management

Cluster Level Planning and General Teachers' Training

Methodology of training

— Brainstorming lecture and group discussion

— Viewing of video and discussion

— Training in use of special teaching aids for visual, hearing and physical impairment

— Training materials resource kit and training kit

— Getting an experience of the handicapping conditions & skills for overcoming disability.

Dr D.K.Palliwal presented a paper titled Integrated Education for the Disabled under Sarva Shiksha Abhiyan. The commitment of the Govt. of India to Universalisation of Elementary Education cannot be fully achieved without taking care of special educational needs of the physically and mentally challenged children. Sarva Shiksha Abhiyan (SSA), a project launched by the Department of Elementary Education and Literacy provides for IED to fulfil the objective of UEE. However, the provision of Rs.1200 per challenged child per year made under SSA is not sufficient, hence the possibility of convergence of the efforts of other departments / agencies of the Central Govt. is being explored.

The steps needed for implementation of IED under SSA are classified under three headings:

Direct Services to Children: The first step is identification of CWSN for micro-planning of IED in 'terms of Visual Impairment, Hearing Impairment, Locomotor Impairment, Mental Retardation, Learning Disabilities and Others. The next step involves formal and functional assessment of each identified child to determine the nature and extent of disability. This should be followed by preparation of individualised need based profile which delineates all the needs, special services required, duration of such services and evaluation procedures. After this the most suitable learning environment is to be identified for each child. All necessary required support, aids and appliances and learning material suitable to the special need of a challenged child should be provided. Finally, all schools must not only be barrier free and provide easy access to CWSN, but also be equipped with other facilities to take care of their special needs.

Support Services: There is need to generate awareness and appreciation of the potential and utility of the education of CWSN, and educate and sensitise parents, teachers, community leaders and the community as a whole. Parents of CWSN also need to be trained in coping with the disabilities of these children and helping them. Teacher training should form the backbone of inclusive education. Support services in the form of physiotherapy, occupational therapy, speech therapy, counselling etc. should be provided in the resource room. SSA missions may also plan for Vocational Education of disabled children at Upper Primary Level. The planning of IED may include extra curricular activities like drawing, painting, dance, music, sports, craft and indoor games. Use of technology is also advocated in the shape of special aids and appliances, computer assisted instruction and development of low cost/no cost Teaching and Learning Aids using indigenous material. While taking care of the special educational needs of CWSN, it is also necessary to consider adaptations in the evaluation system.

Monitoring and Evaluation: This is an important aspect for assessing progress and providing improvement in the process. Therefore, an adequate and efficient mechanism needs to be in place for this purpose.

SPECIAL CONSIDERATIONS FOR INDIVIDUAL PLANNING

A student with dependent needs is completely dependent on others for meeting all major daily living needs. She/he will require assistance at all times for feeding, dressing, toileting, mobility and personal hygiene. Without such assistance and personal care support, attendance at school would not be possible. Many students may also require health care as defined in the Inter-Ministerial Protocols. The estimated prevalence in British Columbia of school-age students requiring this very intense level of service is .07% of the student population.

These students must be receiving an additional special educational service on a regular and ongoing basis to be eligible for special education funding in this category, and a current IEP must be in place. Some students are born with conditions or disabilities that make them dependent, while others acquire conditions or disabilities. For some students, increasing independence as they learn and grow is a reasonable expectation. For other students, decreasing independence may occur due to degenerative conditions or terminal illness. To be eligible for supplemental funding in this category, the following conditions must be met:

— the student must meet the above eligibility criteria; and

— a current IEP must be in place; and

— the student must be receiving specific additional service directed at the identified special needs.

Direct, ongoing special education service(s) must be provided. These services should be outlined in the IEP and directly related to the student's identified special need(s). The special education service(s) must be in addition to any services provided under formula funding based on total student enrolment (e.g., learning assistance, counselling). Reduction in class size is not by itself a sufficient service to meet the definition.

A student who has been formally identified and assessed as having dependent needs is considered by the Ministry of Education for special education funding beyond that provided for low-incidence conditions. Assessments should integrate current, relevant information related to their intellectual, social/

emotional, sensory, physical and communicative abilities, as well as their ability to perform activities of daily living at school. There must be an Individual Education Plan that recognizes the broad range of intellectual abilities of the student, and that addresses the specific educational, health and personal care needs as well as the strategies to address those needs.

Developing an appropriate plan for a student with multiple needs frequently requires input from a number of specialists who are not typically part of a school-based team. These might include medical professionals, representatives of the Ministry of Social Services and the Ministry of Health, and individuals with expertise in augmentative/alternative communication. However, for ongoing management the team should include only key personnel. Careful documentation and clear procedures are required to address the health needs of these students while in school. Therefore, the following should be incorporated into the planning:

— available medical assessments;

— health care plans; and

— special emergency procedures.

Planning and Implementation

In providing services to a student with dependent needs, unique issues around seating, lifting, positioning, movement, feeding, medication, hygiene and safety will have to be addressed by the school-based team. Many of these can be carried out in a classroom environment, but others, for reasons of privacy and dignity, require a more secluded space. The student will also require adaptations to the learning environment to participate in aspects of school life and to maximize independence. The student should have access to as many parts of the school as possible, to increase opportunities for participation. Equipment accessibility in these areas will also have to be addressed. Adaptations to facilities or equipment to allow access to school areas and programs should be made as quickly as possible where physical barriers exist. The Provincial Integration Support program can provide information and strategies to maximize participation by students with multiple disabilities.

Recent and ongoing technological advances in adaptive devices related to computer access, environmental controls and augmented communication have greatly enhanced learning opportunities for students with dependent needs. It is expected that specialist staff will stay informed about current developments and introduce new technology as appropriate. The services of the SET-BC program may be appropriate for some of these students. A student with a degenerative and/or terminal condition who is or becomes dependent should have normal routines maintained as long as possible. Health care plans will need regular updating and will need to include emergency procedures to meet individual needs and circumstances.

Evaluation and Reporting

It is expected that districts and schools will include students with dependent needs in regular evaluation and reporting. Some students with dependent needs are of average or above average intellectual ability and can meet the learning outcomes identified in the prescribed curriculum if appropriate adaptations are made to instruction and assessment methods. The method of evaluation will be consistent with the IEP and with ministry reporting policies in respect to the use of comments and/or letter grades. Some students may require extensive modifications to parts or all of their program so that the learning outcomes will be substantially different from the regular curriculum. In these cases, evaluation will be based on the degree to which the goals and objectives in the IEP are achieved.

Evaluation would be referenced to individually set standards. Reports to parents should be provided on the same schedule used for all students. Progress should be reported with respect to all components of the program and with reference to progress in relation to the IEP goals. Reports should indicate the adaptations and modifications made to the student's educational program. All personnel directly involved in the ongoing educational program (e.g., classroom teacher, specialist teacher, speech- language pathologist) should report on student progress. Student Progress should be evaluated using a range of assessment techniques. These may include criterion-based measures, curriculum-based assessments, teacher observations, samples of student work, and the extent to which IEP goals have been achieved.

Teachers and other professionals

The Ministry of Education expects that with sufficient training and experience, classroom teachers will be competent in including students with dependent needs, provided that support is available. Inservice training opportunities and a collaborative team approach are recommended to support and encourage the development of the skills required. Teachers with responsibilities for supporting students with dependent needs should fulfill the qualifications described for learning assistance. In addition, they should have advanced coursework in:

— the characteristics and needs of students with dependent needs;

— specialized instructional methodologies and technologies; and

— adaptation and modification of programs for students with dependent needs.

There may also be a need for a qualified health professional to monitor the quality of health services on a regular basis. Protocol agreements with the Ministry of Health identify the health care of students with dependent needs. Districts should ensure that staff who serve students with chronic and complex health needs are trained and qualified to perform the functions required.

Teacher assistants

Teacher assistants who work in classrooms with students with dependent needs should have sufficient skills and training for the duties they are assigned, including:

— an understanding of the social, emotional, and educational implications of dependent needs;

— functional life skills and career development; and

— technological support.

It should be noted that teacher assistants work under the general supervision of a teacher or administrative officer. Inservice training should include opportunities to further develop expertise in these and related areas.

INDIVIDUALIZED EDUCATIONAL PROGRAMMES (IEP'S)

Parents, advocates, and school system personnel have all been concerned about the regulations with differing opinions about changes that should be made. Before the IDEA amendments of 1997, school personnel were only allowed to remove children to an interim alternative educational placement for up to 45 days if the child brought a gun to school or to a school function. According to 1997 amendments:

— Schools can remove a child for up to ten school days at a time for any violation of school rules as long as there is not a pattern of removals;

— A child with a disability cannot be long-term suspended or expelled from school of behaviour that is a manifestation of his or her disability; and

— Services must continue for children with disabilities who are suspended or expelled from school if the behaviour is a manifestation of a child's disability.

In addition, the 1997 amendments expand the authority of school personnel to remove a child who brings any dangerous weapon to school, or who knowingly possesses illegal drugs or who sells or solicits sale of any controlled substances. Schools can also request a hearing officer to remove a child for up to 45 days if keeping a child in his or her current placement is substantially likely to result in injury to that child or to others. Even though there are still disagreements over whether the regulations concerning the discipline of students with disabilities are helpful or harmful to these students, the final regulations do clarify some of the key issues. Unfortunately, many parents and advocates for children with behaviour disorders are concerned that the final regulations have weakened the rights of these students to a free appropriate education.

Removals of Up to Ten School Days at a Time - The regulations clarify that school personnel may remove a child with a disability for up to ten school days, and for additional removals of up to ten school days for separate acts of misconduct, as long as the removals do not constitute a pattern.

Services During Periods of Disciplinary Removal - Schools do not need to provide services during the first ten school days in a school year that the child is removed.

— After the first ten days, for any suspension that is for less than ten school days, schools must provide services to the extent determined necessary to enable the child to appropriately progress in the general curriculum and appropriately advance toward achieving the goals if the IEP. In cases involving removal for ten days or less, school personnel, in consultation with the child's special education teacher, decides what services are to be provided.

— During any long term removal for behaviour that is not a manifestation of a child's disability, schools must provide services to the extent determined necessary to enable the child to appropriately progress in the general curriculum and advance toward achieving the goals of the IEP. The child's IEP team decides what services are to be provided.

Conducting Behavioural Assessments and Developing Behavioural Interventions - Meetings of a child's IEP team to develop a behavioural assessment plan or, if the child has one, to review the child's behavioural intervention plan are only required when the child has first been removed from his or her current placement for more than ten school days in a school year, and when beginning a suspension that constitutes a change in placement. If additional suspensions occur, the IEP team members review the child's behavioural intervention plan and its implementation to determine if modifications to the plan are needed, and only meet if one or more team members believe that modifications are necessary.

Manifestation Determinations - Manifestation determines are only required if a school is implementing a removal that constitutes a change of placement.

Change of Placement - The regulations say that a change of placement occurs if a child is removed for more than ten consecutive school days or is subjected to a series of removals that constitute a pattern because they add up to more than ten school days in a school year, and because of factors such as the length of each removal, the total amount of time the child is removed, and the closeness of the removals to one another.

An Individualized Educational Program (IEP) describes the special education and related services specifically designed to meet the unique educational needs of a student with a disability. The program is developed at one or more IEP meetings, and its provisions are detailed in writing in the IEP.

The IEP is developed by a committee that includes at least a school administrator, the student's teacher, the parents, and the student when appropriate. It contains goals and objectives based upon the student's present level of educational performance. These goals and objectives are outlined by those involved in planning and providing services. In addition, the IEP specifies the educational placement or setting, and the related services necessary to reach these goals and objectives.

It also includes the date the services will begin, how long they will last, and the way in which student progress will be evaluated.

The IEP can be more than an outline and management tool of the student's special education program. It can be an opportunity for parents and educators to work together as equal participants to identify the student's needs, what will be provided to meet those needs, and what the anticipated outcomes may be. It is a document that is revised as the needs of the student change. The IEP is a commitment in writing of the resources the school agrees to provide. Also, the periodic review of the IEP serves as an evaluation of the student's progress toward meeting the educational goals and objectives. Finally, the IEP serves as the focal point for clarifying issues and cooperative decision making by parents, the student and school personnel in the best interest of the student. For all of these reasons, the IEP is the cornerstone of special education.

Thus an IEP is:

- *Comprehensive*: The IEP covers all deficit areas, including communication, behaviour, socialization, self-help, academics, perceptual-motor and gross-motor skills, vocational skills, and transition services, related services, and needed accommodations in both general (regular and vocational) and special education.
- *Specific*: The IEP goals and objectives are stated in measurable, observable behaviours.
- *Sequential*: The IEP is based on a developmental or functional sequence of skills.
- *Realistic and Appropriate*: The IEP goals and objectives should fit the student's current level of functioning and probable growth rate.
- *Understandable*: The IEP is written in language that is comprehensible to both parents and professionals. It communicates.

— *Mutuallu Developed*: The IEP represents a consensus among parents, the student, and school personnel.

Timelines for the Development of an IEP

The IEP must be developed for each student with a disability within thirty (30) calendar days after eligibility determination. The IEP must be developed before actual placement, and initiation of special education and related services. No special education and related services can be provided prior to the development of the IEP. Finally, all IEPs must be reviewed at least annually by the IEP committee. A parent or a teacher may request reviews of the IEP more frequently.

Composition of the IEP Committee

The IEP committee must be composed of at least the following:

— *School Administrator or Designee*. A representative of the school division, other than the student's teacher, who is qualified to provide or supervise the provision of special education;

— *Student's Teacher*. At the initial IEP meeting, this refers to the student's classroom teacher, or if the student does not have a teacher, a teacher qualified to teach a student of that age. At subsequent IEP meetings, this may be the student's special education teacher;

— *Parent/Legal Guardian or Surrogate Parent*. Parents must be given the opportunity to participate in the development of their child's IEP; however, they may choose not to attend the IEP meeting. If they so choose, then the other IEP committee members should meet and develop the IEP.

— *Student*. The student should participate when appropriate in developing the IEP. This is especially true at the secondary level when developing goals and objectives and transition services. Remember the IEP is to meet the unique educational needs of the student.

At an initial IEP meeting, the Committee must include a member of the evaluation team or someone knowledgeable about the evaluation procedures used with the student and the results of the evaluation. Transition services must be addressed on the IEPs of students who are 14 years old and older. They may also be addressed at a younger age when appropriate. Whenever transition services and planning are being considered at an IEP meeting, then the following people must also be invited to participate in the development of the IEP:

— *The Student.* If the student chooses not to attend the IEP meeting, it is required that the student be given alternative opportunities to have input into the transition plan and service decisions. The committee must document that the student's preferences and interests have been obtained and are considered when determining the needed transition services.

— *Adult Service Agencies.* If an agency is likely to be providing or paying for a transition service for the student, then a representative of that agency must be invited to attend the IEP meeting. If no representative can physically participate, then the committee must seek alternative ways of obtaining their input into the decisions. For example, individual communication or telephone conference calling can be used to meet this requirement.

At all IEP meetings the school division must ensure that the parents understand the proceedings. This includes the arrangements for an interpreter for parents who are deaf or parents whose native language is other than English.

IEP Meeting Notification

Parent /legal guardian or surrogate parent must receive prior notification of eat IEP meeting. This notice must contain the following information:

— the purpose of the meeting;

— the time, the date, and location of the meeting; and

— who will be in attendance.

Remember an IEP meeting must be scheduled at a mutuallv agreed time and place. If the parent(s) are unable to attend the IEP meeting, the school division must use other methods to ensure parent participation in the IEP development. This may include individual or conference phone calls. An IEP meeting may be conducted without the student's parents if the school division is unable to convince them that they should attend. However, there must be documentation of attempts to arrange a mutually agreed on time and place.

This documentation may include:

— detailed records of phone calls made or attempted and the results of those calls

— copies of correspondences sent to the parents and any responses, and

— detailed records of visits made to the parents' home or place of employment and the results of those visits.

Revising the IEP

Revisions in the IEP may be needed during the school year for which the IEP is written. These revisions may include changes in the special education and/or related services; changes or additions of goals and objectives; addition or termination of related services; changes or additions of accommodations; and changes in the participation in general (regular and vocational) education activities. To make these revisions an IEP committee must be convened which includes prior notice to the parent/legal guardian or surrogate parent. If the revised IEP results in the partial termination of special education and related services, then written parental consent is required before the partial termination occurs.

IEP Components

Present Level of Educational Performance

— The Present Level of Educational Performance is a written statement which describes the student's strengths, weaknesses and learning styles in:

- — academic,
- — vocational,
- — social,
- — behavioural,
- — perceptual,
- — physical,
- — communication, and/or
- — life skills, as appropriate.

This information should be recent, relevant data from both formal and informal assessments and observations. All data presented should be accompanied by an explanation that clearly indicates the student's current functioning level to all members of the IEP committee. Listing test scores, numerical attainment, age equivalent or simply naming the disability is insufficient. These descriptive statements must be as complete and accurate as possible, for they are the foundation upon which the goals and objectives are built and the needed supplementary aids and services are determined.

If formal tests have been administered, give the full name of the test, level(s) and form(s); and date administered. Do not abbreviate. List all subtests, and record percentiles and standard scores, record age and grade equivalent scores only if standard scores and percentiles are nat available. Also, when given a choice, standardized test scores should be computed according to age norms (best practice).

Annual Goal(s)

An annual goal(s) is a statement(s) of what a student with a disability can reasonably be expected to accomplish in a years time in a specific area(s). It is written to address an area of weakness identified in the Present Level of Educational Performance. THERE MUST BE A DIRECT CORRELATION BETWEEN THE ANNUAL GOAL(S) AND THE PRESENT LEVEL OF EDUCATIONAL PERFORMANCE.

Annual goals reflect answers to the question: What do we want the student to be able to do in a years time? The goals must reflect knowledge of the student's current functioning in each skill area, the next sequence of skills in that area and some estimate of the student's rate of learning. If the learning rate is underestimated and the student achieves the annual goal(s) earlier, then new goal(s) can be added. Priorities are established in choosing goals based upon the student's physical limitations, age, time left in school, and expectations for the future. Thus the annual goals in the IEP are:

— stated in terms of measurable, observable behaviours;

— inclusive of the major deficit areas identified in the present level of educational performance: communication, behaviour, academics, socialization, selfhelp, perceptualmotor, grossmotor, vocational, related services, and transition services;

— answers to the questions:

  — Who - will achieve?

  — What - skill or behaviour?

  — How - in what manner or at what level?

  — Where - in what setting or under what conditions?

— based on the student's present level of functioning;

— realistic in terms of the student's physical and cognitive abilities;

— prioritized on the basis of the student's age and amount of time left in school; and

— prioritized to meet the student's need and to help the student live independently.

Short-Term Objectives

Short-term objectives include a number of steps in the sequence of steps moving the student toward each annual goal. These objectives are not as specific as lesson plans, but rather the intermediate steps between the student's present level of educational performance and the related annual goal. The objectives must be stated in behavioural, measurable terms and state what the student will accomplish. Thus the shortterm objectives in an IEP:

— are based on annual goals relative to the present level of educational performance;

— are based on a sequence of skills;

— are stated in observable behavioural, measurable terms; and

— answer the questions:

  — Who - will achieve?

  — What - skill or behaviour?

  — How - in what manner or at what level?

  — Where - in what setting or under what conditions?

  — When - by what time an ending date?.

Evaluation Criterion

Evaluation criterion is the level of performance necessary for mastery of a given objective. This can be expressed in percentage of accuracy required, number of times a certain performance is required, etc.

Evaluation Frequency (Schedules)

Evaluation frequency is the schedule upon which a student is evaluated. It tells how often a student will be evaluated on a given objective. Objectives may be assessed daily, weekly, monthly, or on/by a specific date. The frequency of evaluation for each objective will vary based upon:

— the nature of the specific objective,

— the developmental level of the student, and/or

— the student's anticipated rate of growth.

Evaluation Procedure

Evaluation procedure is the manner in which the skill will be assessed. Procedures may include specific tests, teacher-made tests, curriculum materials, interviews, anecdotal records, observations, and student portfolios (academic and vocational).

Service Delivery

Service delivery includes special education and related services and participation in general (regular and vocational) education.

Special Education and Related Services

List all special education services required by the student and all related services required by the student to benefit from the student's special education program. The determination of the special education and related services is based upon the student's IEP goals and objectives that correlate to the student's present level of educational performance.

— *Direct Special Education Services*: Direct services are specialized instructional services provided directly to the student. Instruction may be provided in the general education classroom, the special education classroom, community or other appropriate settings.

— *Indirect Special Education Services*: Indirect services include consultation services, in which the special education educator is not responsible for direct instruction, but rather consults with the general education teacher(s) and other service providers (e.g., school psychologist, vocational counsellor, guidance counsellor) to assist them in developing programs appropriate for the student. The special educator may meet with the student for monitoring purposes. The general education teacher(s) of all mainstreamed students should be provided consultation services as needed.

— *Related Services*: Related services means transportation, and such developmental, corrective and other supportive services (including speech pathology and audiology, psychological services, physical and occupational therapy, recreation, including therapeutic recreation, social work services, counselling services, including rehabilitation counselling, and medical services, except that such medical services shall be for diagnostic and evaluation purposes only) as may be required to assist a child with a disability to benefit from special education.

— *Transition Services*: The IEP for students beginning no later than the age of sixteen (16) and annually thereafter (and at a younger age, if determined appropriate) must contain a statement of needed transitional services. This includes when appropriate, a statement of the interagency responsibilities or linkages (or both) before the student leaves the school setting.

Transition services are a coordinated set of activities for a student designed with an outcomeoriented process, which promotes movement from school to postschool activities, including:

— postsecondary education,

— vocational training,

— integrated employment (including supported employment),

— continuing and adult education,

— adult services,

— independent living, and

— community participation.

The coordinated set of activities shall be based on the individual student's needs, taking into account the student's preferences and interests, and shall include:

— development of employment and other postschool adult living objectives,

— instruction,

— community experiences, and, when appropriate,

— acquisition of daily living skills and functional vocational evaluation.

Time Frame and Personnel

For each of the services required by the student, one must include the following based upon the student's needs:

— Hours/Day: State the total number of minutes and/or hours per day for each service that is provided for the student

— Times/Week: State the total number of times per week that each service is provided for the student.

— Dates of Vitiation and Duration: Enter the month/day/year that you expect the service to begin and the expected month/day/year that you anticipate. the service will end.

Accommodations

Any accommodations including supplementary aids and services needed by the student to assist the student in both special and general (regular and vocational) education should be clearly listed and described in the IEP. This may include instructional modifications, assessment modifications, adaptive equipment, and/or assistive technology devices.

General Education Services and NonacademicActivites

Students with disabilities must be given the opportunity to participate with their nondisabled peers to the maximum extent appropriate in general (regular and vocational) education, nonacademic and extracurricular activities. The extent to which the student participates needs to be documented on the IEP. This may be done in the same manner as special education and related services.

Placement

Once a student's IEP has been developed, the next step is to determine where the student will receive the services outlined in the IEP. This decision is made only after the annual goals and short-term objectives have been agreed to. The student's placement must be based upon the student's goals and short-term objectives. The placement of the student must be in the least restrictive environment (LRE) appropriate for that student. When determining this, one must consider the following:

— that the student has the opportunity, to the maximum extent appropriate, to participate with nondisabled age appropriate students in academic, nonacademic, and extracurricular activities;

— that the student will be served in a setting as close as possible to which the student would be assigned if the student did not have a disability;

— that the amount of time and the distance the student must be transported from his/her home is considered

— that the student is removed from the regular educational environment only when the nature and severity of the disability is such that education in regular classes with the use of supplementary aids and services cannot be achieved;

— that consideration is given to any potential harmful effects the placement may have on the student;

— that the placement provides the quality of services the student requires; and

— that the program/services as specified in the student's IEP is appropriate to meet the student's needs.

To assist in determining the placement, the IEP committee should consider a continuum of services. Once chosen, a justification statement is needed to explain why the option was chosen. The continuum options include:

Option 1	Direct instruction and/or consultative services within regular/vocational education
Option 2	Direct instruction and/or consultative services within regulare/vocation education with content instruction in a resource room
Option 3	Direct instruction and/or consultative services within regular/vocationaleducation with content instruction in a more special education classes
Option 4	Self-contained in a special education classroom with integration as appropriate
Option 5	Self-contained in a special education classroom with no integration in regular public school
Option 6	Separate public day school for students with disabilities
Option 7	Separate private day school for students with disabilities
Option 8	Public and/or private residential facilities
Option 9	Homebound
Option 10	Hospital

Confidentially

Although student confidentially must be ensured, the contents of the student's IEP should be shared with all instructional staff serving the student. The individual managing the student's IEP should review the IEP's goals and objectives including accommodations with all of the student's general (regular and vocational) education teachers. One must remember that these individuals are considered to have a bona fide educational interest in the student and therefore, as such, have access to all confidential information.

GOVERNMENT INTERVENTIONS

The six National Institutes specialized in different areas of disabilities expanded their activities in the area of education, training, professional guidance, research and development of rehabilitation aids for improving the quality of services for the disabled. Also, 11 District Rehabilitation Centres functioning in 10 different States continued to provide comprehensive rehabilitation services to the disabled in rural and remote areas. Voluntary Organizations numbering about 403 offered a wide range of services benefiting about 1.26 lakhs disabled in the field of education, vocational guidance, counselling, rehabilitation, etc. For running these National Institutes, a total outlay of Rs. 10.61 crores was made available during 1998-99. For the year 1999-2000, an outlay of Rs. 16.41 crores was earmarked for these Institutes.

The scheme for Supply of Aids and Appliances continued to assist the needy disabled with simple, durable and modern aids and appliances. Till December, 1998, 589 implementing agencies located in different parts of the country were assisted to benefit 2.48 lakhs disabled persons. The scheme has been revised to make a provision for medical and surgical correction and intervention, prior to fitment of aids and appliances, whenever necessary. In order to provide cost effective aids and appliances with the application of modern technology – R&D

Projects were also funded for developing aids and appliances under the scheme of Science and Technology in Mission Mode Project for the Disabled. Also, steps were taken to start production of some of the selected aids and appliances developed under the scheme.

Of the total targeted outlay (1998-99) of Rs. 25.0 Crore for the scheme of Assistance to Disabled Persons for Purchase/ Fittings of Aids and Appliances, the revised expenditure was Rs. 22.0 crore. For 1999-2000, an outlay of Rs. 30.0 crores has been earmarked. The targetted outlay and the anticipated expenditure for the scheme of Science and Technology in Mission Mode Project during 1998-99 was Rs. 1.00 Crore and amount of Rs. 1.00 crore has been earmarked for the year 1999-2000 also.

To extend placement services to the disabled, 51 Special Employment Exchanges and 39 Special Cells for the disabled persons in normal Employment Exchanges continued to function during the year. Normal Employment Exchanges and Vocational Rehabilitation Centres also assisted the disabled persons in their placement. Efforts were made to implement the policy of 3% reservation of vacancies for the blind, deaf and orthopaedically disabled in group A, B, C, & D posts in Central services and in the Public Sector Undertakings. The outlay during 1998-99 was Rs 0.20 crore. For the year 1999-2000, an outlay of Rs. 1.45 crore was made available not only for continuation but also for expansion of the scheme.

With the commitment for improving the economic status of the disabled, the National Handicapped Finance and Development Corporation (NHFDC) extends loans to for promoting self-employment ventures. It also extends loans for pursuing general/ professional/ technical education besides upgradation of technical/ entrepreneurial skills. The NHFDC continued its activities as an Apex financial institution for routing funds through the channelising Agencies, authorised by the States/UTs. During the year 1998-99, the Corporation funded

268 Projects with an outlay of Rs. 28 crores,. For the Year 1999-2000, an outlay of Rs 20.0 crores was provided.

The Rehabilitation Council of India (RCI), which has a mandate to register rehabilitation professionals and issue Certificates, has so far, registered 1472 professionals/ personnel in the Central Rehabilitation Register and also issued Certificates to them. The Council also recognized 35 institutions during the year to conduct various training programmes and organized joint entrance examinations for admission to the National Institutes on all India basis for the courses in Physio-therapy, Occupational Therapy, Prosthetic and Orthetic Engineering. While an total outlay of Rs. 3.0 crores was made available during 1998-99, the outlay for 1999-2000 is Rs. 15.50 crores.

RIGHTS OF PERSONS WITH DISABILITIES

The 1995 Act of India, on rights of persons with disabilities, is a comprehensive piece of legislation. It spells out the state's responsibility towards prevention of impairments and protection of disabled persons' rights in health, education, vocational training, employment, and rehabilitation. In an effort to give people with disabilities a level playing field, it provides for non-discrimination against people with disabilities, reservation of jobs in all establishments, public or private, and free education until the age of 18. It also establishes a simple, inexpensive, and speedy mechanism for the redress of grievances.

Employment

The appropriate state government identifies posts in every establishment, public or private, that can be reserved for disabled persons and reviews them periodically, at least every three years, taking into consideration the development of technology. No less than three percent of posts must be provided to disabled persons in every establishment of which one percent each shall be reserved for individuals who are blind or who have low vision, individuals who are hearing impaired, and persons with motor disability or cerebral palsy. Each employer in an establishment is required to submit, in a prescribed form, to the Government certain information on vacancies that are available or will become available in the future for people with disabilities. Free education is guaranteed to every disabled person until he/she attains the age of 18 years.

Each state government and local authority is required to create schemes formulated to ensure the employment of disabled persons; such schemes may provide for the training, welfare, health, and safety of people with disabilities. They must also constitute an authority for administering the scheme. Every establishment, governmental or non-governmental, including corporations, must reserve at least three percent of their jobs for people with disabilities. Similarly, all educational institutions, too, must reserve at least three percent of their seats for the education of people with disabilities.

In establishing 47 Special Employment Exchanges and 41 Special Cells in the regular Employment Exchanges, the objective of the Governments is to assist disabled persons in obtaining gainful employment. The scheme has successfully led 49,000 disabled persons to obtain employment, of which 4,158 were visually impaired, 4,126 hearing impaired, and 40,589 orthopaedically disabled. The scheme is implemented through the State Governments.

Pre-employment training for disabled persons is provided under the Apprentices Act, 1961, by reserving three percent of the seats for training disabled persons. Since 76 percent of people with disabilities live in rural areas, in order to provide for their rehabilitation, a scheme to establish District Rehabilitation Centers (DRCs) in selected districts of the country was introduced by the Government of India. The objective is to devise a suitable delivery scheme for promoting the most cost effective technologies and restructure jobs of rehabilitation professionals so that a minimum number of specialists could be utilized for the delivery of services.

Vocational training for persons with disabilities is imparted in specialized institutions as well as in ordinary training institutions. The government of India has established 17 Vocational Rehabilitation Training Centres (VRCs) in the country in state capitals, two of which are exclusively for disabled persons. At seven of the above centers, skill training facilities have also been provided. Their main task is to assess training needs and to impart short-term training. Each year, the VRCs are able to rehabilitate about 7,000 disabled persons in various areas.

In addition, India has about 2,000 Industrial Training Institutes (ITIs), of which 852 are government undertakings and the remaining are privately owned. These give practical training in a variety of engineering and non-engineering occupations to about 332,700 trainees. Three percent of the seats in these institutes also have been reserved for people with disabilities.

A number of government-assisted, private, voluntary organizations, like Amar Jyoti Trust, Fellowship of the Physically Handicapped, National Society for Equal Opportunities for the Handicapped, the National Association for the Blind, and the All India Federation of the Deaf, etc. also impart vocational courses. Blind Men's Association runs a variety of vocational courses including technical trades, which are recognized by the Department of Technical Education, and stenography courses recognized by the Department of Education. Overall, there are 142 voluntary organizations that offer facilities for vocational training of people with disabilities.

By constituting Coordination Committees at the Central and State levels, the state has provided a mechanism for implementing the objectives of the Act. The committees, chaired by the Welfare Ministers and consisting of high officials and eminent personalities, including representatives of people with disabilities and other NGOs, discuss problems confronting disabled persons with the concerned authorities and the international organizations with a view to provide schemes and projects for them. They also review existing legislation and identify provisions and facilities that are discriminatory to people with disabilities. The law treats disability as a civil right rather than merely a health and welfare issue. Failure to adapt buildings and transportation vehicles to accessibility for facile entry of people with disabilities is deemed a violation of their civil right and is actionable as a ground for discrimination before the administering authority.

The Chief Commissioner for Disabled Persons and Commissioners in each state of India enforce the provisions of the Act for people with disabilities. State commissioners exercise powers of a civil court in matters of issuance of subpoena, production of documents, or recording of testimony when they adjudicate, after hearing the parties, and decide on issues affecting the rights of or discrimination against people with disabilities, non-implementation of laws, rules, bylaws, regulations, executive orders, guidelines, or instructions made or issued by the appropriate authorities. This procedure enables an aggrieved person to approach the above authority with a simple application to set the law in motion.

The commissioners, in ranks equal to the Secretary to Government, are empowered to investigate on their own and take necessary steps to safeguard the disabled persons' rights. They also monitor the utilization of funds dispersed by the Government. Any deprivation of a disabled person's rights or a violation of law, rules, and regulations is investigated. It is an expeditious forum for enforcement of the disabled persons' rights without cost to them and provides them relief against discrimination.

Whoever fraudulently avails, or attempts to avail, any benefit meant for a person with disabilities, shall be punishable with imprisonment for a term that may extend to two years or with a fine which may amount to 20,000 India rupees (US$420) or with both.

Public Services/Transportation

Special consideration is shown to people with disabilities in public services with respect to their transportation needs; they are granted specially discounted fares and concessions. In the case of railroads, disabled persons get discounts of up to 75 percent for travel in the first and second classes. The escorts accompanying the blind, orthopaedically and mentally disabled, are similarly entitled to a 75 percent discount in the basic fare. Airlines allow them 50 percent fare discounts. Transmission of "Blind Literature" packets, both domestic and foreign, by surface mail is exempt from payment of postage. All disabled employees of the Central Government are given an additional transportation allowance of up to 100 Indian rupees (US$2.05). The Ministry of Railways exempts people with disabilities from payment of baggage charge on wheelchairs.

There has been a growing awareness and concern for the issues of barrier-free environment and easy access for persons with disabilities. The 1995 Act provisions deal with non-discrimination against people with disabilities in matters of transportation and built environment. It requires all establishments in such businesses, within the limits of their economic capacity, to adapt compartments, buses, vessels, and aircrafts, including restrooms, in such a way as to permit easy access for disabled persons. They must also install auditory signals at red lights on roads, curb cuts and slopes on pavements and sidewalks, and engravings at the pedestrian crossings. In addition, they must install ramps in public buildings, adapt toilets for wheelchairs, and install Braille symbols and auditory signals in elevators.

No establishment or entity shall dispense with the services or reduce in rank a person who becomes disabled during the course of his/her employment. If the employee is no longer suitable for the job, which he/she held prior to his/her acquiring the disability, he/she may be moved to another job with the same pay scale and benefits. If it is not possible to fit the employee on any other post, he/she may be kept on a supernumerary post until the availability of a suitable position or until he/she attains the age of retirement, whichever is earlier. Also, a person cannot be denied a job based on his/her disability unless the Government, by notification, has declared exempt an establishment from compliance with the provisions of the Act.

Public Accommodation and Services by Private Entities

In affirming a disabled person's right to housing, the Act states that the appropriate Governments and local authorities shall create schemes in favor of such persons for the allotment of land at discounted rates for housing and setting up special recreation centers and businesses, etc. The banks offer people with disabilities loans at a lower rate of interest, thus, assisting them to buy homes and start business.

To further help their lives, private individuals have volunteered to provide their time and effort to assist disabled persons. According to a recent count, there are over 1,600 volunteer organizations in India engaged in the service of disabled people. These range from the very professional, well managed, high profile national and immensely successful to the well-meaning, small neighborhood groups.

The National Association for the Blind India (NAB) is a pioneering welfare institution for individuals who are blind in India, providing a wide range of services for the comprehensive rehabilitation of persons who are blind, including education, training, employment, and placement services. All India Federation of the Deaf (AIFD) was set up in 1955 with the aim of uniting people who are deaf all over the country, to strive for their welfare and total rehabilitation. Its activities include free distribution of hearing aids to the needy and the poor. It also counsels and guides other organizations of people who are deaf in cultural performances, painting, and other activities.

Telecommunications

The law also requires the appropriate state government to create schemes for making available aids and appliances to persons with disabilities. The Ali Yavar Jung National Institute for the Hearing Handicapped has developed a Loop Induction System, to facilitate communication of the hearing impaired at crowded places like railway stations, etc. Initially, 15 railway stations were proposed to be fitted with the system; Delhi Railway station has already been fitted with one. The Institute is an autonomous body and is under the administrative control of the Ministry of Welfare. Its main objectives are to:

— develop manpower by undertaking or sponsoring trainees and teachers, employment officers, psychologists, vocational counselors, and other personnel as deemed necessary by the institute for promoting the education, training, or rehabilitation of individuals who are hearing impaired.

— conduct, sponsor, coordinate, and subsidize research into all aspects of the education and rehabilitation of the hearing impaired.

— develop model services for rehabilitation of people with hearing impairments due to deficient hearing.

— serve as an apex information and documentation center in the area for individuals who are hearing deficient.

The Institute has its regional centers in main cities of the country and a State Collaborated Centre in Bhubaneshwar. It also runs the following training programs:

— Bachelor of Education (Deaf)

— Bachelor of Science (Audiology and Speech Pathology, Hearing, Language and Speech)

— Diploma in Education of the Deaf

— Diploma in Communication Disorders

For the visually impaired, the National Institute for the Visually Handicapped has developed a low cost Braille, which is under production by the Hindustan Tele Printer. The Government of India has also supported many Talking-Book projects for visually impaired persons. In order to provide suitable and cost-effective aids and appliances through the application of technology and also to improve the mobility, employment opportunities and integration of disabled persons in the mainstream, a scheme of Science and Technology (S&T) – Project in Mission Mode – was launched in 1988. The project represents a new approach aimed at ensuring that emerging inter-disciplinary efforts meet large-scale societal/national needs. It can fulfill their potential in a time-targeted manner.

The Government of India launched, for the first five years, a coordinated program for developing aids and appliances for persons with disability. So far, 45 projects have been identified for assistance and 37 of them are at various stages of completion, some of them have been put to commercial production. Some of the products developed for the use of people with disabilities are a speech synthesizer; interpointing Braille writing frame; closed-circuit TV with magnification facility; photo-voltaic charger; feeding aids for children with cerebral palsy; multifunctional wheelchair; telefilm for training of parents of children with mental disabilities; and microprocessor-based Braille embosser.

The PDA 1995 and supplemental state statutes apply to public and private employers and to all disabled persons. Most provisions set forth public policies and regulate public programs on specific benefits for people with disabilities. In particular the PDA1995 governs:

— Preventive health care;

— Public welfare and social security for people with disabilities;

— Access to education by reserving three percent of class seats for disabled children;

- Education free of cost until the age of 18 years and special educational institutions;
- Three percent quota of public employment and record keeping of employment;
- Job protection for incumbents but not applicants;
- Access to publicly funded recreation and other publicly funded accommodations;
- Tax and other financial incentives to establish businesses;
- Access to transportation and safety of disabled in public places;
- Implementation of the PDA 1995; and
- Legal enforcement and remedies.

Legislative Objective

Notwithstanding the act's terminology of protection against discrimination, the provisions of the PDA 1995 are predominantly service-oriented. The act encourages the Federal and state governments to work together with NGOs and private organizations to prevent disabilities and to provide basic living conditions for disabled persons to integrate them into society. This is mainly achieved through public and private programs, spanning the gamut from education of children free of cost to financial incentives for businesses creating jobs for people with disabilities. To this end the PDA 1995 defines "disability" as:

- no less than 40% impairment of vision and hearing
- leprosy-cured
- mobility disability
- mental disability and mental illness

The PDA 1995:

- Provides for a wide range of public or publicly funded programs;

— Provides for interdepartmental coordination; and

— Provides for affirmative actions by the government.

RIGHTS OF THE DISABLED: TOWARDS A NEW UN CONVENTION

In June 2003, the United Nations (UN) Ad Hoc Working Committee on the Rights of People with Disabilities will hold its second meeting to discuss reports from member states, UN bodies, National Human Rights Institutions (NHRIs) and NGOs to consider proposals for a new and comprehensive convention to promote and protect the rights and dignities of persons with disabilities. The proposed convention would be similar to existing human rights instruments on the rights of women, children, and refugees.

The movement towards creating an international convention is the next step in a struggle that has already lasted 20 years. Its goal has been to integrate the human rights approach into discussions of disability rights on the international level. Although the process has been a gradual one, the shift in approach has been quite radical—from treating disabled persons as objects of charity to mandating changes in society that will allow disabled persons to participate on an equal level with non-disabled persons.

The first changes came in 1982 when the World Program of Action Concerning Disabled Persons was accepted by the General Assembly of the UN. The United Nations Standard Rules on the Equalization of Opportunities for Persons with Disabilities (UNSR), formulated by the UN at the end of their Decade of Disabled Persons in 1992, followed the World Program as the next treaty to address the issue of disability. Both of these defined handicap as "the encounter between the person with a disability and the environment," effectively shifting the focus of disability legislation all over the world from aiding the disabled person to adapting their surroundings to permit equal participation in society. This change reflects the lessons learned from the human rights movement, but there is still considerable scope for integration of the rights based approach with discussions of disability.

The Standard Rules have been criticized for having many gaps. Neither the gender dimension nor the needs of children with disabilities are treated sufficiently. The document also fails to address the issue of housing. It is notable that these gaps occur at areas where significant human rights instruments already exist—the Convention for the Elimination of All Forms of Discrimination Against Women (CEDAW) and the Declaration of the Rights of the Child—or where rights legislation has been proposed—such as in this year's draft resolution on the right to adequate housing. Indeed, both the Special Rapporteur on Disability for the Committee on Social Development and a recent UN Report on human rights and disability suggest that the existing human rights mechanisms at the UN have been underused in protecting the rights of persons with disabilities and call for more integration between the two.

Considering the existence of powerful human rights institutions that protect all people, including the disabled, and treaties that protect solely disabled persons—the World Program of Action, Standard Rules, Beijing Declaration on the Rights of People with Disabilities, Declaration of the Rights of Disabled Persons, Declaration on the Rights of Mentally Retarded Persons, and Principles for the Protection of Persons with Mental Illness—one might wonder why there is need for a new convention. Firstly, none of the treaties that deal specifically with disabilities are legally binding.

Secondly, the very existence of human rights conventions for refugees, women, and children indicates that there are specific groups that are especially vulnerable and require a single set of binding norms and a separate body to monitor respect for their rights. Arguably, disabled persons fall into this category as well. Lastly, a convention will allow for clarity—it will encourage more robust human rights expertise on disability as well as creating a focused body to which NGOs can direct their claims.

The Ad Hoc Committee is only inviting proposals for a convention, so each group that participates in this conference should emphasize the need for such a convention. Discussion about the convention should consider the breadth of coverage of the Standard Rules as a model, while keeping in mind its deficiencies. The drafting of a new convention can take many years. In the meantime, the Standard Rules should be revised and upheld. Additionally, the Committee should consider appointing a Special Rapporteur for Disabilities who can act as a suitable focal point for disability in the human rights system during the long drafting process. The last Ad Hoc Committee meeting in New York was exceptional in its exclusivity; NGOs and even NHRIs were not invited to attend. It is important that these two groups are included in the drafting process because, in the absence of political will, the burden of implementation and monitoring largely falls on these bodies. Fortunately, the second meeting of the Ad Hoc Committee will have NGOs and NHRIs as participants. Hopefully, their contributions to the committee will be emphasized.

The international change in attitudes towards the rights of persons with disabilities is especially important for the Asia Pacific Region since approximately 400 million of the world's 600 million disabled people live in the region. Nearly one third of disabled persons live below the poverty line, and less than ten percent of youth with disabilities attend school. Governments of developing nations, of which there are many in Asia and the Pacific, have been reluctant to champion the rights of disabled persons because of the enormous cost involved in implementing suitable policies. However, the scale of the problem alone should assure governments that protecting these rights are not a matter of choice.

The United Nations declared 1981 the International Year of Disabled Persons, and the adoption of the World Program of Action concerning Disabled Persons (1982) and the declaration of the Decade of Disabled Persons (1983-1992) followed soon thereafter. These events provided the catalyst for major revisions in the way disabled persons were regarded by governmental and non-governmental institutions. The Asia Pacific Region was the first to follow up with a regional Decade of Disabled Persons in 1993.

Inter-country meetings to discuss possible methods of intersectoral collaboration and to assess the success of the Asian Pacific Decade of Disabled Persons were held in India, Malaysia, Singapore and South Korea. Partly in response to the increased international and regional attention, a significant amount of legislation has been passed in the region regarding disabled persons. However, the laws are uneven in scope, implementation and monitoring processes. A closer examination of the legislation of the different nations will reveal areas where these laws are weak and give rise to general recommendations.

Australia and Japan have both passed comprehensive disability laws. In Japan the process of getting these bills passed involved the initiative of many NGOs and the input of disabled individuals in high political positions. However, most other countries have piecemeal legislation that only covers one aspect of disability rights such as the Rehabilitation Council of India Bill that only covers education. On the surface, much progress has been made regionally for the incorporation of the rights perspective into disability legislation. Examples include the India's Persons with Disabilities (Equal Opportunities, Protection of Rights and Full Participation) Act in 1995 and the Philippines' Magna Carta for Disabled Persons in 1991. However, appearances can be deceptive.

The Indian Persons with Disabilities Act suffers from vague terminology and lacks adequate monitoring mechanisms. The caveat that reforms should only be undertaken within the limits of a state's economic capacity all but nullifies the Act's potential for change. In the Philippines, the Magna Carta relies on the courts for enforcement of the regulations, but the first talk of a court case came a full decade after the bill was passed, and the case has yet to actually be heard.

The example of the Philippines is by no means exceptional. Most disability legislation in the Asia Pacific region relies on the courts as mechanisms of observance and enforcement. Yet, most disabled people, and disability advocacy groups in the region for that matter, do not have the time, money, or expertise to fight long court battles. For example, courts in India are notorious for backlog, which can delay cases for years. The importance of incorporating NHRIs that conform to the Paris Principles and NGOs into the legislation and legislation making process is especially acute here. These are the agencies that have the mandate to monitor and enforce the laws created by legislatures that do not have the political will, financial support and efficient bureaucracy to implement them successfully.

NHRIs and NGOs are also important means of spreading information about any legislation, and can create strong advocacy groups that can in turn demand more from the government. The success of the Asia Pacific Decade of Disabled Persons depends not just on creating appropriate legislation regarding disabled persons but putting into place mechanisms for accurately monitoring such legislation.

ROLE OF NON-GOVERNMENTAL ORGANIZATIONS

1. Association for the Welfare of the Handicapped

This organization works for the advancement of the disabled and works in collaboration with the Alzheimer's Related Disorders Society and the Hemophilia Society. They serve PWDs that have the following types of disabilities; Cerebral palsy/spastic, hearing impaired, mentally handicapped, orthopedically impaired, slow learner and the visually impaired.

2. *Blind Peoples Association*

The BPA was formed by a group of blind people in 1954 as a recreation club. Today, it serves not only the blind but people with all categories of disability - hearing impaired, mentally challenged, locomotor disabled, multiply disabled including deaf-blind, and the elderly. The organization has received the National Award and FICCI Award. They are recognized by the Rehabilitation Council of India, the Ministry of Social Justice and Empowerment, CAPART, as a nodal agency.

3. *Devnar Foundation for the Blind*

The Foundation was established in 1991 and currently operates a school with over 220 students housed in buildings owned by the Foundation and provides CBR programs, parental and genetic counseling and operates Braille printing presses. The Foundation also manages the Ramananda Centre for Advance Learning and Research for the visually impaired vocational training.

4. *Indian Institute of Cerebral Palsy*

The West Bengal Spastics Society was formed in May 1974 and became the Spastics Society of Eastern India in 1981 and is currently the Indian Institute of Cerebral Palsy. The Institute is a nationally recognized professional institute for training and research.

5. *Jan Madhyam*

Jan Madhyam provides disability awareness and holistic development through creative work and training programs, while integrating the disabled into their existing programs.

6. Karnataka Parents'Association for Mentally Retarded Citizens

The Association was formed in 1978 and began providing teacher training programs in the field of intellectual disabilities and specific learning disabilities and autism. Since its formation, the Association has trained over 1,000 special educators and provides three diploma courses. The Association also organizes workshops, seminars and awareness programs.

7. Manovikas Kendra Rehabilitation and Research Institute for the Handicapped (MRIH)

The Institute has been in operation for over 28 years providing special education and vocational training while conducting early intervention and parental counseling. The Institute also operates a research and diagnostic unit and conducts CBR and prevention and public awareness campaigns

8. National Centre for Promotion of Employment for Disabled People

The NCPEDP is a non-profit organization working as an interface between government, industry, international agencies and the voluntary sectors towards increased employment opportunities for disabled people.

9. National Federation of Parents' Associations for Persons with mental Handicap/Retardation, Autism, Cerebral Palsy and Multiple Disabilities (PARIVAAR)

PARIVAAR was formed in 1995 and is recognized by the Government as an APEX organization representing over 100 parents' associations across India. The Federation is a member of Inclusion International, the world body of Parents' Associations of PWDs.

10. Spastics Society of Northern India (SSNI)

SSNI provides technical rehabilitation inputs, such as special education therapy, assessment, vocational training, rural and urban community based rehabilitation, awareness, advocacy. It receives some form of financial assistance or grants from the Ministry of Social Justice and Empowerment.

11. Spastics Society of Tamil Nadu

The Spastics Society of Tamil Nadu was founded in 1981 as a welfare provision organization. The Society is dedicated to the empowerment of people with disabilities through human resource development, community inclusion and participation. They aim to provide people with disabilities the best possible opportunity to participate in community life through education, employment and rehabilitation services. They operate three special education centers, which provide education at all levels to meet the needs of children with disabilities and are recognized as a State-level Training Center on disability for governmental personnel, ECCD and educational sectors.

12. SWEEKAAR Rehabilitation Institute for Handicapped

Sweekaar is a non-profit organization with over 26 years of service to the mentally handicapped, physically disabled, and others. The Institute services over 1,900 people per day in providing service delivery, training, awareness and community participation programs.

13. Thakur Hari Prasad Institute of Research and Rehabilitation for the Mentally Handicapped (THPI)

THPI was established in 1968 as a rehabilitation center for children. Today it is an institute employing more than 250 professional and paraprofessionals in paediatrics, clinical psychology, special education, speech pathology, psychiatry, occupational, hydro, art and music therapies. In 1992, the THPI Community-Based Rural Project was established and serves approximately 36 villages.

INTERNATIONAL ORGANIZATIONS

1. *ActionAid India*

ActionAid India has been a development funding agency since 1972, and works with organizations to reach out to the marginalized and socially deprived sections in the country. ActionAid India works with a professional team located in 14 regional offices and the country head office in New Delhi. ActionAid supports approximately 300 voluntary organizations across India.

2. *Disabled People's International*

Disabled Peoples' International is a network of national organizations or assemblies of disabled people, established to promote human rights of disabled people through full participation, equalization of opportunity and development. The goals of DPI are to promote the human rights of disabled persons, promote economic and social integration of disabled persons and develop and support organizations of disabled persons worldwide.

3. *Helen Keller Service Society for the Disabled*

The Helen Keller Service Society is a voluntary organization established in 1979. The organization implements service projects for the welfare of the disabled in Tamil Nadu, founded by Dr G Thiruvasagam for the service of people in the field of welfare of the disabled in rural areas.

4. *Hope Worldwide*

Hope Worldwide began operations in India in 1991 and currently has over 80 programs across 17 cities that meet the needs of the urban poor including PWDs.

5. *Rehabilitation International*

Rehabilitation International is a worldwide network of people with disabilities, service providers and government agencies working together to improve the quality of life for disabled people and their families. Founded in 1922, it now has more than 200 member organizations in 90 nations.

8

Towards Inclusive Education

Owing to lack of knowledge, educational access and technology, disabled children were initially treated as unwanted and segregated from other children. Later their education was carried out in special schools. In recent times there has been a shift towards having children with disabilities attend the same schools as non-disabled children. The educationists now feel that each child should be allowed to learn in his own way. The concept of inclusive education has been spelt out in the Salamanca statement and the framework for action on special needs education 1994. It states that all governments have been urged to "adopt as a matter of law or policy, the principle of inclusive education, enrolling all children in regular schools unless there are compelling reasons for doing otherwise".

The basic premise is that the school should meet the educational needs of all children irrespective of their disabilities or limitations. It is the implementation of the 'policy and process' that allows all children to participate in all programmes. 'Policy' means that disabled children should be accepted without any restrictions in all the educational programmes meant for other children. It denotes equality, and accepts every child with his own unique capabilities. This principle must be accepted by all the international, national and local programmes. The 'process' of inclusion denotes the ways in which the system makes itself welcoming to all.

In terms of inclusion of disabled children, it means the shift in services from 'care of the disabled child' to his 'education and personal development'. Inclusive education goes one step further by defining these children as 'children with special needs' who need special attention, rather than children who are 'impaired' or 'handicapped'. Inclusive education is nothing but 'Making the programme for disabled children as an integral part of the general educational system rather than a system within general education'.

OBJECTIVES OF POLICIES

— The governments have to give the highest policy and budgetary priority to improve their education systems to enable them to include all children regardless of individual differences or difficulties.

— The governments have to adopt as a matter of law or policy the principle of inclusive education, enrolling all children in regular schools unless there are compelling reasons for doing otherwise.

— The training programmes for the teachers have to include the education of disabled children.

— All children have access to general education system, to expand the coverage to reach the unreached population.

MOVEMENT OF INCLUSIVE EDUCATION

— UNESCO (1994) states that 'All children learn together, whatever possible, regardless of any difficulties or differences they may have. Inclusive schools must recognise and respond to the diverse needs of their students, accommodating both different styles and rates of learning and ensuing quality education to all through appropriate curricula, organisational arrangements, teaching strategies, resource use and partnerships with their communities'. Inclusive education promotes child-to-child learning and participation of parents and community in planning and execution of services for children in general and disabled children in particular.

Inclusive education is the most feasible plan of getting across education to each child. When a country talks about education, it is education for all, without leaving out people. At present, mainstream education leaves out large categories of people, not just the challenged. For instance, certain communities cannot enter schools in Tamil Nadu. Special institutions came into being to fill the vacuum. But these only perpetuated the gap between children with disability and the others.

Special schools do not enable those with disability to compete on an equal footing. Their standards are lax, reinforcing the view that those with disability need a charitable approach. The fact of the matter is that normal kids stand as much of a chance of learning from those with disability as vice versa. If all children were to study under a more uniform system, it would enrich their experience, improve their exposure and raise social sensitivity levels. It also makes economic sense to have one type of school for all students. Therefore, the time has come to give children with disability a choice between mainstream and special institutions, for which the former would have become more accommodative. Inclusive education does not mean doing away with special institutions.

In India special schools have demonstrated ability in rehabilitation, but they are driven by an impulse of charity. As a result, the level of accountability in these institutions is not the same as in mainstream schools. The latter are bound to a certain level of deliverability, whereas special schools focus on disability rather than performance. Teachers in special schools are not under challenge to perform as a result of which the potential of the challenged children is not realised. The curriculum is watered down in these schools. Mainstream schools also have the advantage of reach.

Government infrastructure has wide access. Inclusive education should be implemented through government schools. India is a signatory to the international covenant on Education for All by 2015. This ideal cannot be achieved without government infrastructure playing a key role. Inclusive education is gaining ground. Throughout the world, teachers and others involved in education are working to develop positive educational experiences that all children and young people can enjoy and benefit from, together. For disabled children and those experiencing difficulties in learning, this means inclusion in mainstream schools and classrooms alongside their non-disabled peers. For all children - and adults - it means a more enriching and rewarding educational experience.

Internationally, the drive towards inclusion is fuelled by a number of initiatives and treaties, including the UN Convention on the Rights of the Child , the UN Standard Rules on the Equalisation of Opportunities for Persons with Disabilities and the UNESCO Salamanca Statement. Together, these documents recognise the human right of all children to education which is inclusive. 193 countries have signed the Convention on the Rights of the Child, with Somalia being the most recent in May 2002. All but two countries (Somalia and the United States) have also agreed to be bound by the Convention by ratifying it. Some countries have made significant advances towards promoting inclusive education in their national legislation. Examples include Canada, Cyprus, Denmark, Iceland, India, Luxembourg, Malta, the Netherlands, Norway, South Africa, Spain, Sweden, Uganda, the United Kingdom and the United States. Italian law has supported inclusive education since the 1970s.

As the 1999 report by the Organisation for Economic Co-operation and Development (OECD), Inclusive Education at Work: Students with Disabilities in Mainstream Schools, states: 'The rights of students with disabilities to be educated in their local mainstream school is becoming more and more accepted in most countries, and many reforms are being put in place to achieve this goal. Further, there is no reason to segregate disabled students in public education systems. Instead, education systems need to be reconsidered to meet the needs of all students.'

From Rhetoric to Reality

This drive towards inclusion is not only rhetoric. Rather, the reality of inclusive education is transforming the lives of millions of children - and teachers - in countries across the world. According to the OECD report, there is a decline in the proportion of students in 'special' schools in most countries. CSIE's Index for Inclusion, which helps ordinary schools break down barriers to learning and participation, is being taken up in a range of countries around the world. Diversity in the mainstream is increasing in many countries. The vast majority of disabled children and young people in Iceland attend their local schools.

In Italy, more than 99.9% of all children in the state sector are educated in ordinary schools. In the province of New Brunswick, in Canada, there are no 'special' schools - all children are educated in local mainstream schools. A national study on inclusion in the United States in 1995, carried out by the National Centre on Educational Restructuring and Inclusion, reported a huge growth in inclusive education for students with all levels of disability. A report from the Ontario School District in Oregon stated: 'The only criteria for a student to attend any of our six elementary schools, our middle school or our high school is they must be breathing.'

In Uganda, the human rights of disabled people are enshrined in the Constitution and sign language is recognised as an official language. Deaf children now attend their local schools, with appropriate support to enable them to learn. One observer noted: 'Instead of sitting silently and unnoticed in their classrooms, they now have sign language interpreters provided.' In the district of Douentza, in Mali, West Africa - one of the 'poorest' areas of the world - villagers worked together with outside agencies to set up a much needed local school, which disabled boys and girls attend together with every other child. One of the teachers said: 'To begin with we had the commitment to include disabled children, but we did not really believe that they could be in school. Now we have seen for ourselves, and we have moved from commitment to conviction.'

No room for complacency

Despite these significant advances, however, large numbers of disabled children and young people throughout the world - including in the United Kingdom - continue to be subjected to negative, deficit-based language and exclusion from good quality mainstream education. Some countries - such as Italy, Uganda and Norway - clearly see inclusion as meaning all children and young people learning together in mainstream provision. But all retain a dual system of 'special' and ordinary education. The existence of legislation supporting inclusive education does not necessarily mean that inclusion is happening in the everyday lives of children and young people. For example, there is a strong Government commitment to the philosophy and goals of inclusion in India, but this is not yet fully reflected in practice.

German national policy and legislation support inclusive education but high proportions of students are placed in 'special' schools. The Norwegian policy of not providing 'special' schools is undermined by the practice of parents sending their children to 'alternative centres'. In Denmark, a pioneering country in terms of inclusive education, the number of children placed in 'special' classes has been markedly rising.

Not about money

It is not simply a question of funding. It is a common assertion that 'full' inclusion - all children and young people learning together, including all disabled children - would be too expensive. Yet the example from Mali demonstrates that inclusion can happen whatever resources are available. International work by both the World Bank and OECD has shown that it is far more expensive to operate dual systems of ordinary and 'special' education than it is to operate a single inclusive system. In Reykjavik, Iceland, local authority staff calculated that the cost of educating a child requiring the most intensive support in a mainstream school was no greater than the average cost of sending students to 'special' schools.

The real problem lies with the historical investment in separate, segregated systems of 'special' schools, the lack of political will to make inclusive education available to all, and the uncertainties of some parents that inclusion will benefit their children. But throughout the world, people are seeing the benefits of inclusion for themselves. Everywhere, those who have experienced inclusive education - including providers and disabled and non-disabled students - are convinced that inclusion is the way forward.

From strength to strength

These experiences must be built on. The urgent task is to change hearts and minds, encouraging openness to the values and aims of inclusive education and a commitment to the human rights of all children and young people. Non-government organisations and individuals must also continue to lobby Governments, and raise awareness among teachers and parents of the advantages of inclusion. People directly involved in inclusive education need to share their knowledge and experiences with those just starting out. Progress needs to happen on all fronts, from Governments passing legislation and formulating policy to people in schools working inclusively with real students.

As one school director in Swaziland said: 'I had thought the problem of integration of children with difficulties was difficult to solve, and a problem of the state. But all my conversations have now confirmed my opinion that someone had to start, to break the mould, and fight against the isolation of children with special needs.' Exchanging information about examples of good practice in the restructuring of mainstream schools in the UK and overseas is an essential step towards ending discrimination in education. In persisting with these efforts to secure a worldwide move from ordinary and 'special' education to inclusive education, we can press on towards the goal of making inclusion an everyday reality for all children and young people.

In several parts of India, the Project Integrated Education for the Disabled (PIED) has been functioning since 1987. A Composite Area Approach (CAA) is followed where regular classroom teachers, specialist teachers, parents and community members jointly work in the programme. The regular teachers are given training in handling disabled children.

STRATEGIES TO IMPORVE THE QULATIY OF INCLUSIVE EDUCATION

Organising self help groups

A self help group is a voluntary association of people, which functions democratically and accountably, to attain the collective goals of the group.

Feature of Sustainable self help groups

— SHGs may be formed for any purpose. Some examples are: savings and credit groups, empowerment groups, rights groups, learning groups, mutual support groups and so on.

— The size of the SHG can vary from group to group depending on the context, though homogenous, democratic and accountable groups are better sustained.

— An external facilitator may facilitate the formation of the group. But the group is controlled by its members.

— The goals of the SHG need to be clear, to arise out of the aspirations of its members and should be known to all members.

— The SHG is better sustained if all its members have contributed to its formation in some way.

— SHGs are dynamic. Hence their composition may change, and their life span is as long as the members' 'felt needs' persist.

— Intra-group conflicts may reduce the cohesion of the group, resulting in its dissolution.

Orgánising disable People

In the past 2 decades, CBR has evolved to include new ways to assist people with disabilities to live a little more independently, to live with their families and in their communities. The assistance includes mobility aids, assistive devices, inclusion in regular schools and other training institutions, self employment, income generation activities and so on. Many CBR programmes have successfully helped people with disabilities to live and work in the community. A lot of this has also depended on the disabled persons' motivation to improve themselves.

For persons with disabilities and many others too, it is not enough to be merely independent, but it is also necessary to have a group that supports and provides an empathetic relationship. Such a group acts as a forum to meet, to discuss and to represent their interests and needs to the outside world. Now that the state administration has begun to recognise the special needs of disabled people, such a group can also work collectively to seek the support services from those in authority, more as a right than a benefit, to improve on their existing situation.

Organising people in self help groups serves different purposes, depending on the situation and the need. Such a forum can help people to be visible members in the larger community. Members can support one another through sharing information on referral services and other available resources, help make decisions on family and individual matters etc. Self help groups with the support of other such groups, can advocate jointly to obtain services, aids and equipment, and for integration in the larger community.

Condition necessary to organise disable people are:

— To bring them together in regular meetings with an agenda for discussion

— To meet in places that are convenient to reach, bearing in mind the need for accessibility

— To discuss matters that concern and affect them directly

— To let the group choose a leader and an assistant leader, but to ensure that these leaders do not dominate and discuss only matters of their own interest

— To introduce and talk about issues of common interest and on disability issues, such as conditions of disability, the causes, the needs of disabled people, the lack of opportunities, etc.

— To set up and agree on tasks to be done by group members before the next meeting

— To educate the group members on the services available from the government and other institutions

— To help the group members to take the initiative to meet their needs

— To orient them on savings and credit management activities

— To discuss issues related to raising of resources for income generation activities

Risk Factors in fromation of self help groups

— The group may focus too much on the benefits that they can get from the government and other schemes.

— The group may pay too much attention to savings and credit programmes.

Though these two issues are important, groups that have a wider perspective on disability issues are needed, and they can perform better.

INTEGRATION OF GENETIC COUNSELLING

Genetics is the science of heredity. It deals with the transfer of biological information from cell to cell, from parents to offspring and thus from generation to generation. Genetics has a major impact on all the areas of medicine. Genetic diseases make up a large proportion of the total disease burden in the population. Each human cell has approximately 50,000 to 100,000 different genes responsible for the human development and functions. Alterations in these genes or a combination of these can produce genetic disorders. Over 9,000 human genetic disease are known to date and the number increases day by day.

In fact each one of us carry nearly 20 silent mutant genes. The overall incidence of single gene disorders is 1 in 100 live births and that of chromosomal abnormalities is 1 in 150 at birth. Genetic counselling represents one of the central foci of medical genetics, which helps people to identify and understand what particular traits that may pass on to their children and also to determine particular risks that may influence pregnancy outcome. Genetic counselling is the process by which patients or relatives at risk of a disorder that may be hereditary, are advised of the consequences of the disorder, the probability of developing or transmitting it, and of the ways in which this may be prevented, avoided or ameliorated. Genetic counselling will help in making the best possible adjustment to the disorder in an affected family member.

Since there is no therapy or treatment for various genetic disorders (except for the biochemical/ inborn errors of metabolism) prevention of the occurrence of genetic disorder is the key to management. Prevention can be done through correct diagnosis/ identification of at risk family members, and prenatal diagnosis whenever possible, or by adopting other reproductive options. The at risk population includes anyone who has a disability due to genetic disorder or has a family member with a genetic disability. These disabilities are different from those caused by environmental factors such as infection e.g. poliomyelitis, encephalitis, TORCH group of infections, or birth trauma. These non-genetic disabilities do not recur in the next offspring provided the environmental factors are taken care of.

The genetic factors responsible for genetic disorders with disabilities are

— Chromosomal abnormalities e.g. Down Syndrome, trisomy of other chromosome or structural abnormalities of chromosome

— Single gene disorders e.g. Biochemical disorders of Inborn errors of metabolism e.g. PKU, organic acidemias, galactosemias etc. or other genetic syndromes e.g. Cystic fibrosis, hemophilia, thalasenimia.

— Multifactorial disorders which are due to a combination of multiple genes as well as environmental factors are many. Birth defects such as cleft lip and / or palate, neural tube defects, heart disease, diabetes and cancer belong to this category.

Other developmental and learning disability e.g. Autism, attention deficit disorder and emotional behaviour disorders also have a genetic component.

Prevention of Recurrence in Multi-factorial Disorders

Periconception Vitamin therapy

Cleft lip and/or palate and neural tube defects are caused by a deficiency in folic acid and its receptors in the mother. The neural tube closes by 23rd day in embryo. Any defect in this closure gives rise to the neural tube defect. These defects can be prevented by periconceptional vitamin therapy. In Periconceptional vitamin therapy the prospective mother should take 4mg of folic acid 4 weeks prior to her conception and continue for 12 weeks after she conceives during the organogenesis period. This will prevent the recurrence of these defects in the offspring. Similarly this therapy also prevents recurrence of cleft lip and palate, so much so that in the US the flour and bread is fortified with 0.4 mg of folic acid. This prevents the occurrence these birth defects in the population and has reduced the incidence.

Early detection and treatment of inborn errors of metabolism of single gene disorders

New-born screening methods for inborn errors of metabolism can be incorporated in the rural and district community health care. A drop of blood that is collected from 3 or 4 day old babies onto a filter paper, can be mailed to the reference laboratories, and thus the metabolic disorders can be detected early. This is very important as early detection and dietary management will prevent the occurrence of the mental deficiency and other problems. Counselling can be a helpful intervention for many life issues like adjustment or acceptance of given disability, management in terms of training, adaptive or vocational guidance and can help in finding employment and living independently.

The most important aspect of training of these counsellors is to identify genetic disorders in a given population. This can be done by simply taking a detailed family history and recognising some of the genetic disorders. They can then advise the families about further tests to be done to screen them or organise courier services and liaison with reference labs/hospital to do these tests. The advice can then be given accordingly. If the couple have a child with a genetic disorder the counsellor can be of great help by providing a complete and accurate view of the situation, the nature of the birth defect and what its recurrence would mean in practical terms for all involved.

The counsellor can also provide emotional support and understanding during what can be a very difficult time. If there are decisions to be made about the pregnancy, care of a child, having more children, or about the ability of the family to cope with ongoing problems, the parents can make informed choices with the facts in hand. The concept of genetic defects can be frightening and confusing. A genetic counsellor is trained to help translate the information clearly and to be an emotional resource to help affected individuals deal with the situations they face.

Vocational rehabilitation

Vocational rehabilitation provides an opportunity for an individual to become self sustaining and so gain self respect and independence. In a rural situation, sometimes people with minor disabilities are rehabilitated in various rural occupations, without any serious attempt. But persons with severe disabilities from an early age tend to be neglected and often meet with premature death. Generally, vocational rehabilitation involves vocational training, although it is not absolutely essential. Vocational training can be 'non-formal' or 'formal'.

As to whether vocational training is essential for rehabilitation or not, the situation may vary. Very often, for vocational rehabilitation, vocational training becomes necessary and for appropriate vocational training, basic education can be very useful. For many non-disabled people, the occupations they are involved in are not based on the vocational training that they had received. There are also cases where high levels of training has not led to employment in the area of training. If this is the case for non-disabled people, for persons with disabilities, the situation can be the same except that usually a lot more is demanded of persons with disabilities, than in the case of some one who is not disabled.

Many companies employ persons who are not disabled and they go through on-the-job training and grow up with the organisation, sometimes reaching up to the management levels. However, the very same organisation would demand prior training and make the disabled persons go through a screening process including the administration of psychological and dexterity tests. Vocational rehabilitation means that a person has been well rehabilitated and merged into the community to become an independent income generator. 'Occupational' therapy may in some cases lead to employment, but vocational training should lead a person to economic self sufficiency.

Community based rehabilitation (CBR)

Over the last two decades, there has been a major growth in the number of community based rehabilitation (CBR) projects around the world, providing the minimum services required for disabled people in countries that had scanty resources and poorly developed services. Alongside, there have been many changes in the understanding and implementation of community based rehabilitation interventions. The focus has now begun to shift from the issue of a minimum level of service delivery, to other management issues that influence effectiveness of services, such as planning and management, monitoring and evaluation, research, information generation and dissemination, and so on.

Programme Planning

A close look at many CBR programmes in India and other South Asian countries shows that they originated as a set of activities without clear goals. Some programmes were started because of the availability of funds for that particular activity. With shifts in donor priorities, the activities of some of these organisations also changed accordingly. These programmes often did not have monitoring and evaluation systems, nor did they define their outcomes or attempt to measure them. Instead, they repeated a set of activities year after year, with some illustrations and anecdotes from their clients, to justify why they had to continue their activities. Such activities tended to be donor dependent, cost-intensive, seldom successful, and rarely sustained once the donor withdrew support.

Consumer satisfaction was also limited, as client needs were rarely taken into account for these activities. The major lacuna in these programmes had been the absence of a sustained, long term and systematic planning process, which is a crucial factor influencing outcome of development activity. Often, programme planning is mistaken to mean merely a project proposal to donors for funding purposes, or it is seen as a rigid process, usually according to donor formats, that curtails individual programme creativity. However, programme planning is a process to be carried out within the implementing organisation for itself, out of which various proposals may arise for fenders. Similarly, while the principles of planning may be common, there is tremendous scope for creativity in the way the principles are operationalised, from programme to programme. Planning thus actually enhances creativity within a programme instead of curtailing it.

Pre-policy stage :Many programmes are started merely because of availability of funds for that activity, without doing a feasibility exercise, checking if there is a need at all for that activity, whether other services are available, what the major needs are in that community, and so on. A very good plan of action, which does not address these issues, can fail because there really was no demand for the programme, or because it is different from what the community perceives as its major need, or because there are too many agencies providing the same service in that area.

In the context of a CBR programme, the pre-policy stage needs to determine if disability is perceived as a 'problem' that needs intervention on a priority basis in the target community. This is followed by a situation analysis, which helps to confirm whether there is a need for intervention, what priority the consumers assign to the proposed problem in relation to other problems, whether the consumers view the proposed intervention as beneficial to them in addressing their problem, and so on. Since CBR interventions influence the lives of disabled persons, their families and their non-disabled peers in the project area, the needs of the different groups have to be identified before undertaking strategic planning for the programme. The different groups in the same community can have differing needs that conflict with each other. For example, the needs of disabled persons may not necessarily be related to the priorities identified by other groups. They may also differ widely from the priorities of other groups in the same community, which usually are short term poverty alleviation and curative health interventions.

In situations where the needs of the different constituent groups differ from the priorities of the CBR programme, the first strategy should be to reduce this attitudinal gap by changing the attitudes of people favourably towards the rehabilitation interventions. For this purpose the existing beliefs and attitudes of the different constituent groups need to be studied, and strategic plans designed to introduce changes in the attitudes of the groups. The community's attitudes may also be influenced by its experiences of services that existed in the past in the project area. Needs analysis helps to assess the opinions of different groups within the local community, as well as of interested groups outside the community, such as the government, donor organisations, catalyst NGOs and so on. In the pre-policy stage there is also a need to identify the different material, financial and personnel resources available locally for later use, their accessibility, and the modifications required for utilising them. The resource analysis gives an idea in advance about what new resources will have to be generated for the programme

Policy development :Successful completion of the pre-policy stage usually progresses to policy development, which includes defining the vision, mission and objectives of a programme. Very few organisations actually have policy statements containing these elements. In some instances where such documents exist, they have been put together by a few people, without the participation of all stakeholders. In some organisations one finds that while the organisational members are able to articulate the organisation's vision and mission well, they have difficulties in clearly stating their objectives and activities. They often describe numerous objectives that are over-inclusive, without considering whether it is feasible for the organisation to fulfil them at all, in the available time. Sometimes activities are confused with objectives and vice versa, which results in poor strategic plans.

The 'vision' is the ultimate goal of the programme as long as the programme lasts, while the 'mission' is the sum of all activities to achieve the vision. The vision and mission are timeless and concise statements of what the programme stands for. Objectives are the medium term directions to achieve the vision, that may be changed sometimes if deemed necessary after an evaluation. These components of the policy are best evolved in a participatory and democratic manner involving all stakeholders of a programme, rather than by any particular group. A participatory process of policy development will help to avoid future conflicts and enhance collective action. Once a policy is formulated, it requires to be widely disseminated amongst all stakeholders and other associates of the project.

Activity planning : Selection of activities and formulation of a strategic plan are usually the responsibility of the executives of the programme, and are executed with the approval of the governance. Many organisations repeat the same set of activities year after year, without targets or defined outcomes. As a result, their annual reports also contain repetitious descriptions of activities, without any indication of how effective these activities were. Some other organisations usually enumerate their activities with quantitative measures of coverage, in the belief that they can represent outcomes and impact. Most organisations continue to face difficulties in defining outcomes and indicators of impact. However, without these measures, it is impossible to know if a programme has been genuinely successful.

Individual activities of a strategic plan are short term components of a programme, usually planned for a calendar year or a financial year. In order to monitor a programme easily, the activities need to be defined precisely, with well defined, quantitative targets for achievement for each activity in a unit time. The expected outcomes, the indicators to measure the outcomes and the resultant impact are also required to be defined clearly. Although some effort is required to develop a detailed strategic plan with well defined activities, targets, expected outcomes and their indicators, such a process can be of great benefit to the programme in many ways. It helps the organisation to monitor and control the progress of their efforts easily, to clearly define the individual responsibilities to the programme personnel, and to make the programmes transparent and accountable to the stakeholders.

Budgeting: Most organisations tend to repeat their budget heads and figures every year, with a correction sometimes for escalation of costs. Often the budget and the programme plan are unrelated, and the budget may only relate to how much money is available in the coming year from the donor. Very few organisations carry out the exercise of activity costing, from which a realistic budget can be made. Similarly, cost effectiveness and cost benefit studies are rarely carried out by organisations involved in CBR. Because of this, large amounts of money tend to be wasted by both implementing and donor organisations on repetitious activities.

In a good plan, each activity that is to be carried out needs to be costed. The sum total of all the activity costs makes up the budget. An exercise of resource matching for the different activities will also need to be carried out to see what kinds of resources are available. In case of a shortfall in resources, the planners may decide to defer or drop some activities. A realistic activity costing and budgeting will also help the programme personnel to carry out cost effectiveness and cost benefit analyses, and thus reduce wastage of resources.

Monitoring and evaluation: Monitoring and evaluation are important because they help the implementers to know if the programme works, if it is of benefit to the clients, and to plan for the future. Some organisations carry out some form of monitoring of their activities, particularly quantitative monitoring. However, most of them do not systematically analyse, interpret or draw inferences from the data generated, or they tend to interpret the data randomly. Many organisations are also resistant to the concept of evaluation for various reasons. It is important for programme implementers to understand that monitoring and evaluation primarily address their own need for better and more cost effective service delivery methods. Even with simple methodologies, a great deal of valuable information can be elicited, which needs to be systematically analysed and interpreted, and which can be of value in planning and improving the programme.

Enhancing Community Participation

Community participation was considered as an essential part of CBR ever since it was promoted as a suitable approach for rehabilitation in developing countries. In practice, however, most programmes have found it difficult to achieve community participation for several reasons. Many developing countries had a period of colonial rule before they became independent, followed by socialist governance in which the state is viewed as solely responsible for all welfare and development work. Concepts of decentralisation and bottom up approaches are relatively new in many of these countries even today. Besides, the majority groups in the community are not altruistic enough to address the needs of the minorities such as disabled persons, until their own needs are met. Another issue is that small, but powerful groups in the community often corner the benefits from development programmes, ignoring the needs of marginalised groups.

Community participation of the highest degree, where the community members take on the responsibility for planning, implementing, sharing the risks of and monitoring a CBR programme which benefits disabled people, is desirable, but difficult to achieve. Depending on the cultural context, the ideal level of community participation is viewed in different ways by different people. On the one extreme, a community may be viewed as passively participating by being a recipient of services, while on the other extreme, participation may be viewed as complete ownership of the programme. Developing countries are still unfamiliar with Western notions of consumer ownership of programmes. Hence to begin a programme with the concept of full ownership by the consumers sometimes results in failures. In these countries, it is often necessary to enhance community participation from the inception of the project, in a planned manner, keeping in mind the difficulties that can be encountered as the concept of full community responsibility is introduced.

In the context of CBR programmes, ways have to be found to motivate the marginalised groups of disabled persons, their families, and communities to achieve a participatory mode of development, in which the community will assume some of the responsibilities to begin with, and move on at a later stage to take on most of the responsibilities of the rehabilitation programme. As in any other strategic plan, enhancing community participation requires clear understanding of the attitudes of people in the community, their current level of participation in the programme and the expected level of participation to be achieved in the future. Though it is difficult to speedily enhance community participation in programmes from developing countries, having a strategic plan to enhance participation and monitoring its success periodically can result in better sustainability in the long run. It will also influence more realistic goal setting practices during the planning stage.

Planning for Sustainability

Concerns about sustainability of CBR programmes surfaced with the threat of diminishing funds for welfare work, and the increasing emphasis on accountability and cost effectiveness.

However, the term 'sustainability' tends to be commonly associated even now with 'finding funds' for a CBR programme. Such an interpretation of the term ignores the other important aspects that contribute to the meaning of sustainability. Financial sustainability also often refers mistakenly, to the ability of the organisation to access enough funds to maintain its structure and personnel. When funds become scarce, the organisation may change the goals of the programme, sacrificing the programme in the interest of maintaining itself. This is counterproductive and detrimental to the interests of the programme and its clients.

Sustainability of the programme, in more accurate terms, refers to sustaining the vision and mission of the programme, and to keep the programme going till the vision is realised. In planning for sustainability, it is important for planners to first identify the different factors that influence sustainability of a programme in its given social and cultural milieu, and then to develop strategies to improve sustainability in relation to the different factors identified through this exercise.

POLICIES OF NGOS

— Multiple sources of funding for the programmes (activity designated funds) rather than a single source to ensure long-term financial continuity.

— Establishment of information sharing network of allies working in the same field.

— Starting the programme in a small way and developing it incrementally (Learning through actions).

— within the limits of vision and mission, allow flexibility to introduce new ideas and close redundant operations.

— Expand operations in the related areas after gaining sufficient experience rather than expanding too fast to unrelated areas.

— Introduce 'bottom-up' management by encouraging generation of ideas from the grass-root level (Encourage grass-root workers, consumers and others close to the grass-root end of the channel to express their ideas and make decisions in a consensual manner).

— Clarify the level of participation expected from the community right from the beginning of the programme, and develop a strategy to achieve it based on the capacity of different community groups. (A. Participation to the extent of 'contribution' of material, manpower, or finances to the programme, and no 'decision making' power. B. Participation to the extent of establishing an 'organisation' to follow the pre-determined strategies, with no 'decision making' power over the strategies. C. 'Empowerment' of the community to establish its organisation and develop its strategies, entirely by itself.)

— Introduce strategies to carefully fulfil the short-term needs of the community with regard to rehabilitation, while emphasising the long-term needs simultaneously (in order to avoid rejection of the programme by the community).

ROLE OF PARENTS

The itinerant plan of teaching method that is adopted by many voluntary organisations implementing integrated education for visually impaired children, envisages clear cut roles for the significant others, namely, sighted children, parents, regular teachers, head masters and community volunteers. Organising periodic meetings of these different groups have the following major objectives :

— To bring them together to exchange views and ideas regarding the programme

— To help them realise their respective roles in promoting integrated education

— To train them in the techniques and methodologies involved in teaching visually impaired children

— To share success stories of visually impaired persons in their own fields of work

— To seek their co-operation and involvement in the integrated education programme

These meetings have to be organised separately for parents, regular teachers and head masters because their respective roles and the nature of their work vary quite widely. Apart from meetings with parents, teachers and head masters, it is very important to organise meetings of selected sighted children from each class where the visually impaired children are enrolled, to promote child-to-child learning. The involvement of sighted children in educating visually impaired children has a tremendous impact on the learning ability of the latter in terms of academic and co-curricular activities. Hence periodic workshops, maybe on an annual basis, involving sighted and visually impaired children to promote learning, caring and sharing would contribute towards better integration of visually impaired children. Similarly, the contributions of other family members, neighbours and community volunteers is equally important.

The success of an itinerant plan of teaching method in an integrated education programme depends on how best the integrated education units can make use of community support and seek their involvement in the programme.

Planning A Campaign to Improve Awareness

Steps to consider during planning

— What is the message that is required to be communicated?

— What budget is available for the plan ?

— To which group should you communicate it ? (Primary audience : Those who make decisions, Secondary audience : Those who influence the decision makers)

— How should you communicate it ?

- How many times the message should be communicated ?
- Are there special occasions when the communication is more effective than the usual ?
- How long should it go on for effective communication ?
- Which media has the most effectiveness ?
- At which place should the communication take place ?
- What time of the year should the message be communicated ?
- Are the strategies planned realistic in nature ?
- Would you like to test it on a representative sample for adequate duration before it is implemented ?

Comparison of different media for their strengths and weaknesses

- Television
  - *Strengths*: Fast awareness, high impact, availability of sponsorship, can be scheduled when needed.
  - *Weaknesses* : High costs, up-front commitments, uneven delivery, unable to select the audience.
- Radio
  - Strengths : Low cost, schedule when needed.
  - Weaknesses : Low profile medium, Lack of impact available with visual field, audience per
  - spot is extremely small, unable to select the audience.
- Magazines
  - Strength : Audience selectivity, long life of the message, large audience per insertion.
  - Weaknesses : Long lead time for commitment, readership accúmulated slowly, uneven delivery of message.

News paper

- Strength : Large audience, immediate reach, short lead time.
- Weaknesses : Difficult to target specific groups.

Evaluation ad Training of Courses

Key questions to be evaluated

- Whether participants have achieved course objectives.
- Whether participants have learned what they are supposed to learn.
- What unexpected positive outcomes have occurred that can be incorporated in the future courses.
- What are the courses strengths and weaknesses.
- Whether the job performance has improved after training.

Types of evaluations

During the course:

1. Reaction of the participants. (Do they like the course, what do they like about it, what do they dislike.)
   - Learning objectives are met.
   - Learning objectives are relevant.
   - Course content is realistic.
   - Training methods are suitable.
   - Facilitators are effective.
   - Training environment is adequate.

(Oral feed-back/written feed-back Open ended questions/ close ended questions.)

2. Learning. (What have they learned, have they learned what they are expected to learn.)
   — What do they know before training.
   — What do they know after training.
   — Is the knowledge what they are expected to know.
3. performance. (Have the new skills being applied, what attitudinal changes have occurred to them.)
4. Impact. (Has the training and application of the new skills improved the results of application.)

CHALLENGES TO THE EDUCATION OF DISABLED CHILDREN

Callous school managements and over-anxious parents of abled children are barring 90% of India's 40 million disabled children from entering the nation's classrooms says Gaver Chatterjee. In an uncaring society which has earned a notorious global reputation for hypocritical piety and institutionalised neglect of the poor and disadvantaged, it's the ultimate cruelty. Across the subcontinent 90 percent of India's estimated 40 million children aged four-16 years with physical and mental disabilities are out of school. And the overwhelming majority of them are vagabonds not out of volition but because callous school managements and over-anxious parents of abled children in a travesty of humanity and social justice have consistently discouraged them from entering the nation's classrooms. Social justice and equity which are dominant sentiments of the Constitution of India demand that India's 35 million physically disabled, if not the 5 million mentally challenged, children should be given preferential access into primary and secondary schools. Instead nine-tenths of them are systematically excluded.

The cover of this conspiracy of exclusion of challenged children from the education system was dramatically blown in mid March when Star TV and several newspapers reported the refusal of every school — government and private — in Kerala (officially India's most literate state) to admit seven-year-old Benson and his five-year-old sister Bensy, whose parents died of AIDS. Though it's well-known that the HIV-AIDS virus is not communicable, both children were dismissed from the Kaithakuzhi Government Lower Primary School after the school's parent-teachers association backed by villagers launched a stir for their expulsion. Opinions voiced by doctors and social workers to the effect that there was no risk of other students in the class contracting AIDS were ignored. And following the example of this government school every other school has refused to admit Benson and Bensy.

It's against this backdrop of continuous neglect to develop the potential of this large minority of challenged children that over 150 delegates from 30 countries converged upon Kochi, Kerala, in late January to discuss ways and means to right this manifest wrong, not only in India but around the world. The four-day conference titled 'North-South Dialogue II on Inclusive Education: From Rhetoric to Reality', culminated in the Kochi Declaration which calls upon governments around the world to recognise and enforce the right of disabled children to be included in mainstream education institutions. An intervention in community development, teacher training and public awareness programmes has resulted in a dramatic change in attitudes in and around primary schools in Dharavi, Mumbai, reportedly the largest slum settlement in Asia.

"It's a cruel scandal that over 90 million physically challenged children worldwide, of whom 36 million are in India, are being systemically excluded from mainstream education. The aim of the North South Dialogue II was to initiate focused discussion on this subject and to suggest ways and means by which children with disabilities can be integrated into mainstream education in India and worldwide. Many countries have made policy changes to that effect, but few — including India — have put these policies into practice. The Kochi Declaration adopted at the end of the North South Dialogue II offers a clear road map to third world countries and especially the government of India, to initiate policy changes to urgently integrate physically and mentally challenged children," says Sathi Alur, a Mumbai-based economist and financial advisor to the Spastics Society of India (SSI) and National Resource Centre for Inclusion (NRCI).

The Kochi conference was a sequel to the successful North South Dialogue I, held in Mumbai in February-March 2001. While the objective of the North South Dialogue I was to examine models of inclusive education in countries in the industrialised northern hemisphere (UK, Canada, Norway etc) and in developing countries in the southern hemisphere (Sri Lanka, Bangladesh, South Africa), the objective of the second dialogue was to focus on how the ideology and philosophy of inclusive education can be actualised through changes in classroom, school, community values and by influencing local, state and national governments. Both the North South dialogues on inclusive education have been orchestrated by the Mumbai-based NRCI, which was promoted in 1999 by Dr. Mithu Alur with moral and material help from the Canada-based Roeher Institute and the Canadian International Development Agency (CIDA). A celebrated activist and champion of the disabled, Mithu Alur founded the pioneer Spastics Society of India (SSI) in Mumbai way back in 1972. Over the years SSI has helped develop a network of 18 associated schools spread over 16 states which together have brightened the lives of over 10,000 children with multiple disabilities.

The main objective of the North South Dialogue II was to measure the progress of inclusive education in India and in other countries and to learn from each other's experiences. For example in India NRCI has successfully developed a model of desegregation which enables able-bodied children to study happily with the physically and mentally challenged. Following the development of this model, the SSI centres across the country are considering throwing open their doors to able-bodied children as well. In NRCI and several SSI centres all children learn together side by side. I wholly subscribe to the national objective of Education For All. But, 'all' should include disabled children as well. Therefore we have begun networking with other NGOs across the country and have formed an All India Regional Alliance for Inclusive Education to attain the EFA goal," says Mithu Alur, who became involved with the cause of challenged children following the birth of her daughter Malini in 1966.

According to Alur, the inclusion of disabled children into main-stream schools will inevitably result in their acceptance into society and also within their own families many of whom still hide away children with disabilities. "If all children grow up together there is less likelihood of resistance towards and ostracism of the disabled. The character of children, the nation's classrooms, and of society itself will become more compassionate and caring. With 36 million challenged children out of the education system and an additional 40 million people suffering from some kind of disability, can we afford to waste this resource by ignoring their education? It's important to understand that physically challenged people can be highly productive, contributing citizens.

The world would have been poorer if Cambridge had spurned (the well-known and utterly disabled scientist) Stephen Hawking," says Alur. Even though it's a relatively unknown concept in India, inclusive education has been tried and tested here, and it works. A focused intervention by NRCI activists in community development, teacher training and public awareness programmes has resulted in a dramatic change in attitudes of peers, parents and teachers in primary schools in Dharavi, Mumbai, reportedly the largest slum settlement in Asia. An experiment in mainstreaming disabled children, which began in 1992 in Dharavi's Noorani Memorial Karuna Sadan School, has spread to 12 anganwadis (play schools). Able-bodied as well as disabled children from 5,000 households are living proof of the efficiency of inclusive education prompting the transformation of four Spastics Society of India centres into inclusive schools in which able-bodied children study happily with their challenged classmates.

Persuading parents of 'normal' children to accept disabled children as classmates certainly wasn't a cakewalk, given deeply entrenched social prejudices. "We had to work hard to persuade parents that inclusive education was possible. Most parents in this slum who were barely literate themselves believed that disabilities were contagious. Some of them expressed the opinion that their children would be scared or upset if they witnessed a disabled child getting a seizure or a fit or behaving unusually. But after we counselled them to give it a try and they experienced inclusive education, they are quite at peace with the whole idea," recalls Varsha Hooja, an NRCI researcher and activist.

The Dharavi story of successful inclusive education is undoubtedly an exception. Most parents, including educated middle class citizens, display little sympathy and sensitivity towards children with visual, auditory, motor or intellectual limitations. There is no shortage of instances where educated middle class parents have fought proposals to include disabled children in their children's classes and even to promote special schools in their neighbourhoods. In the national capital, the Tamana School for the Handicapped founded by former Delhi Public School principal Shyama Chona in 1984 ran into unexpected illogical resistance. "It's shocking but true that residents of Delhi's up-market Vasant Vihar where the Tamana School is located objected on the grounds that it would despoil the neighbourhood.

It's sad that in north India, even educated people tend to turn their minds and faces away from people with disabilities rather than attempt to mainstream them. If every school in Delhi admitted even 20 handicapped children, the problem of educating challenged children would be solved. But schools don't accept them, and even if they do, the poor child may have to be withdrawn 'because other parents object'," laments Purnima Jain, the principal of Tamana, who has been associated with the school since 1986. However the times and attitudes are changing, albeit slowly. The enlightened managements of some mainstream schools across the country are waking up to the need — and advantages — of inclusive education. But even where there is a will, the way forward is difficult.

The lack of disability-friendly transport services, buildings and sensitive teachers who can handle the learning needs of special children are greater problems than social prejudice and parental attitudes. Meanwhile following the celebrated visit of almost wholly disabled physicist-mathematician Dr. Stephen Hawking to India in January 2001, the awareness that the mentally and physically challenged can become valuable, contributing members of society has slowly impacted academia, even taken root. Sustained media reportage on the outstanding achieve-ments of Hawking, Sir Richard Branson (chairman of Virgin Atlantic, a dyslexic), Christopher Reeve (Hollywood movie star crippled neck downwards) and Sudha Chandran (renowned dancer and television star who lost both legs in an accident) has created widespread awareness that with a little help India's 36 million children with physical disabilities can be transformed into national resources.

Back home a high-profile, high-achiever, physically challenged intellectual who has emerged as a champion of the disabled is Malini Chib. A graduate of St. Xavier's College, Mumbai, Chib pressed on to read for a Masters at London University's Institute of Education. Currently she is trustee of SSI and NRCI and is in the forefront of the growing national movement for inclusive education. In 2001, she launched ADAPT (Able Disabled All People Together), an NGO whose objective is to "break down architectural, attitudinal and social barriers so that disabled people can lead normal lives".

"Most public buildings in India are neither friendly nor accessible to disabled people and serve to exclude them from participating in the public discourse. The objective of ADAPT is to pressurise people and institutions to make buildings disabled-friendly and create a barrier-free environment. People in all societies are interdependent socially, emotionally, physically and intellectually. Ignoring the reality of co-dependency will result in the creation of selfish and self-focussed societies. In ADAPT we believe that by projecting personal experiences into the public domain, we can persuade people to change their attitudes towards the physically challenged and create a disability-friendly society," says Chib.

Certainly within the small but influential five million-strong community of teachers and academics across the country, consistent advocacy of the cause of mainstreaming physically challenged students into institutions of education by SSI and NRCI has transformed societal attitudes. Says Roda Billimoria, the Mumbai-based managing trustee of the Sir Shapurji Billimoria Foundation, which also advocates the cause of integrated education; "Classrooms should be representative of the society in which we live. Can you show me any society without people with disabilities? Therefore why shouldn't this country's classrooms include disabled students to mirror society?"

Though the statistic that 90 percent of physically challenged children in India are out of school is shocking, the condition of their counterparts in other developing countries isn't any better. According to Diane Richler the Toronto-based chairperson of Inclusion International and Inclusion Inter-Americana, across Latin America only one-third of the disabled children receive any type of education at all and in some countries such as El Salvador and Nicaragua the percentage of special needs children in school is as low as 1-3 percent. Focussed upon forcing governments and international funding institutions such as the World Bank and IMF to accept the logic of inclusive education, Inclusion International has notched up some notable successes. It has persuaded the Organisation of American States (OAS) to amend the Declaration of Managua. 1991 which guarantees universal primary education to all children in member nations of the OAS, to mandate mainstream education of challenged children as a fundamental human right.

Moreover it has persuaded the G8 nations' education task force which is working towards universal education for all (EFA) globally by the year 2015, to include special needs children within the EFA perspective. "Even in the industrial developed nations of the North there is considerable resistance to the logic of mainstreaming special needs children. For example in the Canadian province of Ontario though all challenged children are in school, only 50 percent of them have been mainstreamed. In Inclusion International our objective is not only to wrest policy commitments from national governments, but also to create awareness of the socio-economic advantages of inclusive education among international funding agencies and donor organisations," says Richler.

Resistance to the idea of inclusive education within parental communities — even if not within governments — is rooted in a lack of awareness that the subject has been deeply researched around the world to the extent that the know-how and methodologies to introduce the concept in classrooms have been developed, though inclusive educationists insist that such know-how has to conform to culturally appropriate practices and precepts (CAPP). According to Dr. Seamus Hegarty, director of the National Foundation for Educational Research, London, the basic know-how for implementing inclusive education is freely available and it is possible for all children regardless of mental or physical disabilities to receive quality education.

"The critical prerequisites of realising the inclusive education ideal are parental education and expansion of national teacher pools. NGOs and voluntary organisations can play a major role in creating awareness that mainstreaming challenged children is an investment in people and that educating disabled children can transform them into net contributors to the economy. If parents are educated about the advantages of inclusive education which develops the virtues of empathy and compassion in children, they become a strong pressure group of the cause. However it's also true that inclusive education requires manageable classrooms so that challenged children receive teacher attention. Therefore it is imperative that in developing countries such as India where classroom pupil-teacher ratios tend to be high, more qualified and trained teachers — not para teachers —are recruited to effectively implement inclusive education precepts and practices." says Hegarty.

Most people, especially the aware and educated in developing nations including India, concede the point that economic arguments apart, the imperatives of social justice and equity mandate the education of physically and mentally challenged children. However the traditional response has been to promote special schools for special needs children, the presumption being that special needs children slow down the rest of the class. But proponents of inclusive education believe it is this exclusivist mindset which requires radical alteration.

"Special schools are dead-ends for special needs children. They promote isolation, alienation and social exclusion. It is this dominant attitude of exclusion which needs to be changed to build harmonious and compassionate societies. Having been tested and proven efficacious, inclusive education has transformed into a human rights issue. Special schools are a medical intervention. What the large number of people with disabilities in all societies need is a social development model which respects the right to self-esteem of this large minority. Children won't learn unless they are happy and included. Therefore teachers must be taught to practise inclusion and respect disabilities. That's what the growing inclusive education movement is all about," explains Richard Rieser director of Disabilities in Education, a London-based NGO.

Contemporary India is one of the few countries worldwide where the education of disabled children doesn't fall within the purview of the education ministry. It is the burden of the omnibus ministry of social justice and empowerment. Inevitably, back home in India politically correct enabling legislation has been enacted. But the Persons with Disabilities Act, 1995 which stipulates that "appropriate govern-ments and the local authorities shall endeavour to promote the integration of students with disabilities in the normal schools", is practiced more in the breach than observance. Likewise the Union government's newly unfolded Sarva Shiksha Abhiyan (Education for All) campaign to deliver "useful and quality elementary education" to all children in the six-14 age group by year 2010, makes politically correct noises about the education of girls and special needs children emphasising a "zero rejection policy for children with special needs".

Moreover the 93rd Amendment to the Constitution of India (now renumbered as the 86th), passed by the Lok Sabha on November 28, 2001, makes it mandatory for the government to provide free and compulsory education to "all children of the age of six-14 years", with its preamble clarifying that "all" includes children with disabilities as well. Yet inevitably again, vital loose ends of such enabling policies and legislation are not tied up. Contemporary India is one of the few countries worldwide where the education of disabled children doesn't fall within the purview of the human resource development (a.k.a. education) ministry. It is the burden of the omnibus ministry of social justice and empowerment.

"The prime focus of the Union ministry of social justice and empowerment is rehabilitation, not education. In fact, till today it does not have education as part of its agenda and the issue of education of children with disabilities remains invisible, hidden from the public domain, a private problem for families and NGOs to deal with. It's time that government agencies, as well as mainstream institutions woke up to the reality that segregation of children is morally unjustifiable and a violation of human rights. Indeed there is no other way to provide education to 36 million disabled children. Seventy-eight percent of our population lives in rural areas. Where is the money for special schools there? Therefore inclusive schools have to address the needs of all children in every community and the central and state governments have to train their teachers to manage inclusive classrooms," says Mithu Alur.

Quite clearly the seeds of the rapidly growing global movement for inclusive education have germinated in India where a massive population of 80 million citizens including 40 million children have been callously excluded from the education system, and consequently from the national development process. One of the beneficial fallouts of the communications revolution has been the free flow of ideas, concepts and development models across national borders.

Research studies around the world and NRCI's pilot project in Mumbai have clearly demonstrated that inclusive education is not only imperative on the grounds of morality, social justice and equity but also makes economic sense. With the Kochi Declaration of Jan 31 having drawn up a clear road map for implementing the much-delayed Education For All agenda, an opportunity for translating politically correct EFA rhetoric into classroom reality has devolved upon the central and state governments — and citizens — across the country. The national interest as much as the realisation of the fundamental right to education of India's 40 million challenged children demands that this opportunity to right a continuous wrong is not muffed.

Index